Spanish Dollars and Sister Republics

Spanish Dollars and Sister Republics

The Money That Made Mexico and the United States

Tatiana Seijas and Jake Frederick

ROWMAN & LITTLEFIELD
Lanham • Boulder • New York • London

Published by Rowman & Littlefield
A wholly owned subsidiary of The Rowman & Littlefield Publishing Group, Inc.
4501 Forbes Boulevard, Suite 200, Lanham, Maryland 20706
www.rowman.com

Unit A, Whitacre Mews, 26-34 Stannary Street, London SE11 4AB, United Kingdom

Copyright © 2017 by Rowman & Littlefield

Cover images, clockwise from top left:
1: "20 pesos" (Mexico, 1866). Courtesy of the National Numismatic Collection, National Museum of American History. Public Domain.
2: "8 reales" (Zacatecas, 1859). Museo Zacatecano. Photography by T. Seijas. Reproduction authorized by the Secretaría de Hacienda y Crédito Público, México.
3: "Continental currency" (1776). Photo by Yale University Art Gallery. Public Domain.
4: "Half Dollar" (1836). Photo by Yale University Art Gallery. Public Domain.

All rights reserved. No part of this book may be reproduced in any form or by any electronic or mechanical means, including information storage and retrieval systems, without written permission from the publisher, except by a reviewer who may quote passages in a review.

British Library Cataloguing in Publication Information Available

Library of Congress Cataloging-in-Publication Data Available

ISBN 978-1-4422-6520-2 (cloth : alk. paper)
ISBN 978-1-5381-0046-2 (pbk. : alk. paper)
ISBN 978-1-4422-6521-9 (electronic)

∞™ The paper used in this publication meets the minimum requirements of American National Standard for Information Sciences—Permanence of Paper for Printed Library Materials, ANSI/NISO Z39.48-1992.

Printed in the United States of America

For Our Students

Contents

	Timeline	ix
	Introduction	1
Chapter 1	Emblems of Liberty	9
Chapter 2	The Ghost of a Dollar	27
Chapter 3	Minting Mexico's Independence	47
Chapter 4	North America's Third Republic	63
Chapter 5	Buying Mexico	81
Chapter 6	Border Coppers	103
Chapter 7	Gold Recklessness	123
Chapter 8	Defending the Republics	135
	Conclusion	151
	Acknowledgments	159
	Glossary	161
	Bibliography	165
	Index	175

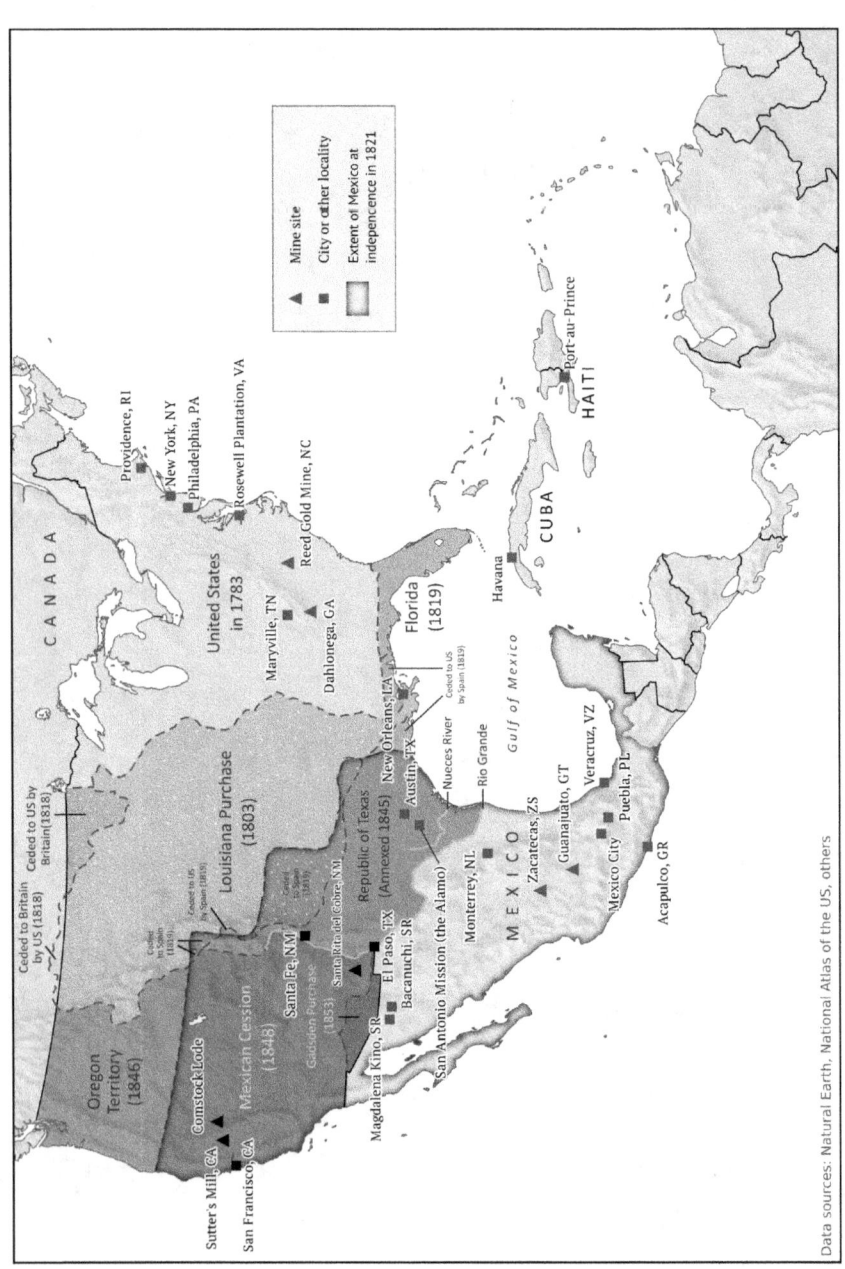

This map of Mexico and the United States illustrates the evolving relationship between the sister republics and notes places mentioned in the book. The shaded areas show the progressive westward expansion of the United States and the diminution of Mexican territory.

Source: Map by Evan Centanni, Political Geography Now (www.PolGeoNow.com).

Timeline

1535   Spanish Crown establishes Royal Mint in Mexico City (first in the Americas).

1775   May, Continental Congress issues first paper notes, known as Continentals.

April, War of Independence (1775–1783) begins in the United States.

1779   U.S. Continentals are discontinued.

1785   U.S. Congress adopts Thomas Jefferson's decimal model for currency.

1787   U.S. Continental cent (fugio cent) is first minted.

1788   U.S. Constitution is ratified.

1789   John Page is elected to the First U.S. Congress.

1790   U.S. Congress votes to redeem all outstanding Continental notes at one-hundredth of face value.

U.S. government national debt is estimated at more than $54 million.

1791   First Bank of the United States is chartered (1791–1811).

1792   January, U.S. Congress passes An Act Establishing a Mint and Regulating the Coin of the United States.

First U.S. National Mint is established in Philadelphia.

1794   U.S. silver dollar is first minted.

1799   Reed Gold Mine is discovered (near Charlotte, North Carolina), setting off the first U.S. gold rush.

1801	More than 20 million Spanish pesos are minted annually in Mexico (1801–1810).
1803	Louisiana Purchase takes place.
	Napoleonic Wars begin (1803–1815).
	United States suspends production of silver dollar coins (1803–1836).
1807	U.S. embargo of French and English trade begins (1807–1809).
1810	War of Independence begins in Mexico (1810–1821).
1811	Stephen Girard purchases the recently closed Bank of the United States to create the Bank of Stephen Girard.
	Royal Mint in Mexico City loses its monopoly on coin production; new mints are set to open near silver mines.
1812	War of 1812 begins (1812–1814).
1815	Manila Galleon trade ends after 350 years.
1816	Second Bank of the United States is chartered (1816–1836).
1819	Panic of 1819 sets off first U.S.-wide economic depression (1819–1821).
1821	First Mexican Empire is established under Emperor Agustín I (1821–1823).
	Stephen Austin leads U.S. expatriates to settle in Texas as legal immigrants.
	Great Britain goes on the gold standard (switches from silver).
1822	Mexican dollar coin, based on the piece-of-eight, is first minted.
	Emperor Agustín I authorizes paper notes.
	Mexican Treasury acknowledges a debt of MX$45 million.
1823	Mexican Congress passes new immigration laws to increase the population on the country's northern frontier (1823–1824).
	Mexican government issues paper money for the first time.
	Monroe Doctrine is pronounced in the United States.
	After a successful rebellion against the Mexican emperor, power devolves to an interim triumvirate.
1824	Mexican Constitution is proclaimed (slavery is officially abolished).
	First Federal Republic of Mexico begins (1824–1835); Guadalupe Victoria becomes the first president of Mexico.
	José Ignacio Esteva begins his term as minister of finance (serving intermittently between 1824 and 1829).
	Mexican republican dollar coin is first issued.
	Mexican Treasury stops production of paper money.
	Mexico accepts two loans from London banks totaling MX$32 million.

1825	Mexican military removes Spanish troops from the fort in Veracruz.
	Green DeWitt issues handwritten paper notes for his Texas colony in U.S. dollars rather than Mexican pesos.
1827	Mexican Treasury is unable to service foreign debt, leading to Mexico's first loan default.
1828	April 25, the United States and Mexico sign the Treaty of Amity, Commerce, and Navigation.
	Gold is discovered in Dahlonega, Georgia, setting off the second U.S. gold rush.
1829	President Vicente Guerrero decrees the prohibition of slavery in Mexico (in effect since independence) due to persistent violations in Texas.
	Spain makes a final attempt to reconquer Mexico.
1830	Mexican Congress bans further immigration from the United States.
1832	October, First Texas Convention includes discussion of response to Mexican immigration bans.
	December, Sam Houston arrives in Texas.
1833	Antonio López de Santa Anna is elected president of Mexico for the first time.
1834	Santa Anna proposes Cuernavaca Plan to centralize the Mexican state and rescinds the 1824 Constitution.
	U.S. Congress declares the dollars of Mexico, Peru, Colombia, and Chile to be legal tender.
1835	The Consultation (representative body of the resistance) meets.
	Texas War of Independence begins (1835–1836).
	First Centralist Republic of Mexico begins (1835–1846).
	Dr. Robert Maskell Patterson begins tenure as director of the U.S. Mint (1835–1851).
	U.S. Congress approves new branches of the U.S. Mint in Charlotte, North Carolina (opened in 1837), Dahlonega, Georgia (1838), and New Orleans, Louisiana (1838).
1836	March, Consultation declares Texan independence.
	Sam Houston begins his first term as president of Texas (1836–1838).
	U.S. executive order Specie Circular says U.S. General Land Office will only accept gold and silver for the purchase of federal land.
	U.S. silver dollar production resumes.

1837	United States recognizes Republic of Texas.
	Texas government issues "Star Notes."
	Panic of 1837 sets off U.S. economic depression (1837–1843).
	U.S. Congress passes new mint regulations (drawn up by Patterson).
1839	Texas issues "redbacks."
1841	Sam Houston is elected for a second time, becoming the third president of the Republic of Texas.
1842	Santa Anna orders the restoration of national mint building.
1845	United States annexes Texas, which becomes the twenty-eighth state.
1846	Second Federal Republic of Mexico begins (1846–1863).
	Mexican-American War (U.S. Intervention) begins (1846–1848).
1847	September, U.S. forces capture Mexico City.
1848	February 12, United States and Mexico sign Treaty of Guadalupe Hidalgo, creating the Mexican Cession, which transfers more than five hundred thousand square miles of Mexican territory to the United States.
	U.S. Congress passes the Independent Treasury Act (placing the United States on a strict hard-money standard).
	Gold is discovered at Sutter's Mill, setting off the California Gold Rush (1848–1855).
1849	March, U.S. Congress approves new gold coins.
1850	John R. Bartlett is named chief commissioner of the U.S.-Mexican Boundary Survey.
1852	U.S. Congress approves a new branch of the U.S. Mint in San Francisco, California (opens 1854).
1854	Gadsden Purchase is finalized.
	Mexican Congress begins to issue a series of liberal laws called the Reform (*la Reforma*) (1854–1857).
1857	February 21, Congress makes U.S. coins the sole national currency (Mexican silver dollars are no longer legal tender).
	September 11, steamship *Central America* sinks off the coast of South Carolina with thirty thousand pounds of gold.
	The Panic of 1857 involves the United States in an international economic crisis for the first time (1857–1859).
	September 16, Mexican Congress proclaims new Constitution of Mexico.
	War of the Reform (*Guerra de Reforma*) begins (1857–1861).

U.S.-Mexican Boundary Survey representatives agree on maps that define the new international border.

Mexican Congress agrees to adopt the decimal model for currency, but the plan stalls.

1858 Benito Juárez begins his first term as president of Mexico.

1859 The Comstock Lode (silver) is discovered in Utah Territory (later Nevada).

1860 November, Abraham Lincoln is elected president of the United States.

December, South Carolina votes to secede from the United States.

1861 President Lincoln's administration lends support to Juárez's government by signing two loan treaties.

Ten additional states succeed from the Union and establish the Confederate States of America.

U.S. Civil War begins (1861–1865).

U.S. Congress passes Legal Tender Act, allowing the printing of paper money not redeemable in specie (known as "greenbacks").

Confederacy issues "greybacks."

In response to President Juárez's two-year suspension of Mexican loan payments, France, Spain, and Britain sign the Convention of London, authorizing military intervention.

December, Spanish naval vessels arrive in the port of Veracruz, followed by British and French forces, beginning the French Intervention in Mexico (1861–1867).

1862 April, Spain and Britain negotiate a settlement with the Juárez government and leave Mexico, while six thousand French soldiers march inland from the gulf coast.

May 5, Mexican forces defeat the French at the Battle of Puebla.

1863 January 1, U.S. executive order and the "Emancipation Proclamation" end slavery in states controlled by the Confederacy.

Second Mexican Empire is established; Austrian Ferdinand Maximilian Joseph accepts the title of emperor (1863–1867).

1864 May, Maximilian and Carlota arrive in Veracruz, Mexico.

London Bank of Mexico and South America opens a branch in Mexico City.

1865 U.S. Civil War ends in Union victory.

U.S. President Andrew Johnson sends fifty thousand U.S. troops to the Texas border in response to the French occupation of Mexico.

	France loans 534 million francs to Mexico as part of the French Empire.
1866	Maximilian decimalizes the Mexican currency and issues the first Mexican coin to include the word "peso."
	French troops withdraw from Mexico.
1867	June 19, Emperor Maximilian I of Mexico is executed.
	Restoration of the Republic of Mexico (1867–1876).
1872	Mexican silver peso is issued with a new design.
1873	U.S. Coinage Act ends the use of silver to back U.S. currency; silver is demonetized (only fractional currency will be made with silver, not dollars).
1877	Global collapse in silver prices begins as most of the world moves to a gold standard.
1879	Unites States goes on the gold standard.
1905	Mexico goes on the gold standard.

Introduction

Imagine holding a Spanish "piece-of-eight" (*real de a ocho*) coin from the late eighteenth century. It is heavy and perfectly circular, and you can feel the embossed lettering with your fingertips; it reads ULTRAQUE UNUM (both are one). This silver object was the currency of the Spanish Empire and one of the most famous coins in world history.[1] The Latin words made reference to Spain's sovereign power on both sides of the Atlantic—in Europe and the Americas, where the Crown turned silver mined in Mexico and Peru into coins that circulated around the world. From the late sixteenth through the nineteenth centuries, the Spanish piece-of-eight served as the first global currency. During this time, you would have been able to take your silver coin to a store in Boston, Mexico City, London, or Beijing and use it to pay for any manner of goods. Merchants in these diverse places would gladly have exchanged their merchandise for your piece-of-eight. Its high silver content and craftsmanship, along with the backing of the Spanish Crown, guaranteed its value from Madrid to Canton. People have valued silver for millennia, but never more consistently than as pieces-of-eight.

Today, money is a medium of exchange that includes coins and bills backed by a sovereign state. These objects have little inherent value in and of themselves—a government, not their composition, guarantees their worth. Until relatively recently, however, coins had an intrinsic value derived from the precious metals used to make them, principally silver and gold. The nations that produced those coins assured their value by guaranteeing that they contained the claimed amount of silver or gold. States make their money trustworthy.

The people who built the United States and Mexico in the late eighteenth and early nineteenth centuries understood this reality: to have money meant to own silver (or gold). The founding fathers of both countries certainly held pieces-of-eight in their own hands and admired this form of money. After independence, these statesmen chose the piece-of-eight as the standard for their countries' new currencies. The money of the United States and Mexico, they hoped, would one day be as valuable and easily recognized as that of Spain. In the meantime, the coins of each country would have to be created and these new national monies minted to support their countries' economies.

The piece-of-eight is the natural beginning for the story of money in the early histories of the United States and Mexico, narrated in parallel in the following chapters. Coins had to be designed, mints built, Treasury Departments organized, and banks established, along with the fulfillment of myriad other responsibilities before Mexico and the United States had their own money. This foundational work took place between the 1770s and 1860s during times of war and peace. By the end of this period, both countries had survived existential threats, including civil wars and foreign invasions, and both emerged as functioning republics with national currencies that confirmed their national identities.

The Spanish piece-of-eight was a uniquely American coin—made from Mexican and Peruvian silver and minted in the Americas in astronomical numbers. The Royal Mint (*casa de moneda*) in Mexico City, founded in 1535, coined more than 1.5 billion silver pesos between 1690 and 1821.[2] The piece-of-eight derived its name from the fact that it was worth eight *reales*. The early piece-of-eight was a hand-hammered, often irregular coin, little more than a slab, with a cross on one side and the coat of arms of Spain on the other (see figure I.1). By the 1700s, it was a much more refined, perfectly circular coin, with a grooved or milled edge, which served as an antitampering device to prevent anyone from shaving silver from the edge of the coin. Colonists in British America appreciated this feature, referring to the coins as "Spanish milled dollars." The richest merchants in colonial New York and Veracruz kept them in their safes, but never, to their minds, in sufficient numbers.

U.S. and Mexican statesmen looked to the piece-of-eight when creating their own money in part because, as colonists, they had suffered from a widespread shortage of coin money. The British colonies did not have a royal mint, and Britain disallowed the export of silver coins (pounds sterling) to the Americas. Colonists, thus, had to use the coins of other countries, like Spain or Holland. While these other European coins were far more common than British pounds, they too were in short supply. Most often colonists had to rely on credit and local tokens for everyday exchanges. The Viceroyalty of

Introduction   3

Figure I.1. This hand-cut piece of eight "cob" is hardly coin shaped at all. It was minted in Mexico City in the 1640s. The Spanish coat of arms on one side and the cross on the other served as testament that the slug contained the proper weight of silver. The hand-hammered impressions on the coins testified to their value. The two "chop marks" likely date from its circulation in Asia.
Source: "Mexican Silver Cob" (1640s). Photography by Kris Lane, from his personal collection. Reproduced with permission.

New Spain, on the other hand, made plenty of coins, but a minority of those remained in the colony; instead, shiploads of pieces-of-eight sailed away each year to Asia and Europe to pay for all manner of goods, from Chinese silks to German weapons. This shortage of coin was an obstacle to commerce and precisely the problem that the U.S. and Mexican founding fathers sought to fix by minting their own coins.

The United States and Mexico both use the "$" sign to indicate their currencies, a symbol that recalls the piece-of-eight. Imagine again holding such a coin. On its back is the image you see in figure I.2. If you look at it closely, you can make out the Pillars of Hercules, a heraldic symbol of the Spanish Empire (representing the Strait of Gibraltar at the opening from the Mediterranean Sea to the Atlantic Ocean). Banners wrap around each of the two pillars, like an S, each showing one word of the motto PLUS ULTRA, meaning "further beyond." It has been said that this picture is the origin of the $ sign. The choice of the piece-of-eight as the original standard for the money of the United States and Mexico provides some support for this interpretation.

Another, more sinister story for the same symbol has to do with slavery, and it too references the joined history of Mexico and the United States. The word for slave in Spanish is *esclavo*, which contains the sounds for the letter S and the word *clavo*, meaning "nail." In a number of places, slave traders who branded their human chattel used an abbreviation of this word, with the letter S superimposed on the representation of a nail (a vertical line). The brand thus looked like our $ sign. Slaves were capital, so the association with

Figure I.2. On this 1818 Spanish piece-of-eight minted in Zacatecas, it is easy to see why some people attribute the origin of the $ sign to the *S*-shaped banner wrapped around the right-hand Pillar of Hercules.
Source: "Moneda de 8 reales, plata" (Zacatecas, 1818). Museo Zacatecano. Photography by T. Seijas. Reproduction authorized by the Secretaría de Hacienda y Crédito Público, México.

money is pretty clear. The English and Spanish colonies had economic sectors based on slavery, as did the United States (Mexico abolished slavery at independence). This alternative story for the origin of the $ sign is especially noteworthy in light of the countries' founding ideals of liberty and justice.

There are additional explanations for the origin of the symbol, such as the claim that "P^s," the abbreviation for "peso" (a common term for a piece-of-eight), formed the basis for the sign. Superimposing the *S* over the *P* also creates a character reminiscent of the $ sign. The specific origin will likely remain a matter of historical debate. Regardless, the currency symbol used in Mexico and the United States clearly has a Spanish heritage. To clarify usage in the context of this book, amounts of money in U.S. dollars are marked US$, while amounts in Mexican dollars/pesos are marked MX$.

The stories of eight men serve to highlight moments in this lengthy and somewhat complicated economic history. Each of the following chapters features a protagonist who thought deeply about the role of money in building a nation and examines a historical question connected to the book's larger topic. Chapter 1 sees John Page arguing to his fellow congressmen that the design of the new U.S. dollar should reflect republican ideals rather than, like the pound of Great Britain, monarchical values. What does this insistence on symbolic imagery tell us about money in the context of U.S. independence? Chapter 2 shifts to the businessmen who benefited from freedom of trade after independence. The experience of financier Stephen Girard exemplifies how U.S. merchants entered the international market and how republican government facilitated their efforts. To what extent did wealthy men's ties to government shape early financial policy? Chapter 3 moves the narrative to Mexico, which transitioned from colony to empire to republic in just three years, between 1821 and 1824. Statesman José Ignacio Esteva helped to organize the Mexican Treasury soon after independence. What does Esteva's commitment to fiscal policy reveal about managing a nation's finances in a postcolonial context?

The next three chapters focus on the territory claimed by the United States after the Mexican-American War (the Mexican Cession) in order to highlight the nations' shared geography. Chapter 4 examines Sam Houston to chronicle the anglicization of Texas, its secession from Mexico, and its failure to create a currency. In what ways did Texas's lack of money for commercial transactions determine its political path? Chapter 5 looks at Antonio López de Santa Anna, who presided over the loss of more than five hundred thousand square miles of Mexico's national territory at the end of the Mexican-American War. What was this vast territory worth to the nations that fought over it? In chapter 6, we follow the work of John R. Bartlett, chief commissioner of the U.S.-Mexican Boundary Survey, as he made his way from Texas to California. How did the value of money change in the Mexican Cession?

Chapter 7 concentrates on the work of Robert Maskell Patterson as director of the U.S. Mint from 1835 to 1851 and also looks forward in time to consider the consequences of the California Gold Rush. Why did increased gold circulation lead to economic crises? The book's last chapter focuses mainly on Emperor Maximilian I of Mexico, who issued the first Mexican coins based on the decimal system and inscribed with the word "peso." Mexico's modern national currency was born in the middle of the French Intervention (1861–1867) and the U.S. Civil War. What does this timing tell us about the two nations' responses to internal and external threats to republican governance?

Eight stories bring to life the history of money in Mexico and the United States. The protagonists illustrate how the two countries instituted their own currencies, designed their coins to represent their national ideals, and then spent decades trying to establish the legitimacy of their money domestically and abroad. This overarching story, in turn, provides a framework for examining the links between the two countries, which are joined, most obviously, because Mexican territory became part of the United States, but also because they share certain historical circumstances. The visionary historian Herbert Eugene Bolton once called on students to think beyond present-day borders and to imagine instead the "Epic of Greater America."[3] For him, writing continental history (which would also include Canada) promised to counterbalance national narratives that have tended to overemphasize uniqueness in the service of state formation. This book takes up Bolton's challenge by investigating Mexico and the United States' common financial ancestor, the piece-of-eight.

In the twenty-first century, Mexico and the United States might appear at times to share very little beyond a very long and problematic border. This book invites the reader to historicize this relationship by learning about the two countries' formative periods, when they confronted similar challenges. Their responses sometimes differed but were often premised on similar ideals. For better, and at times for worse, Mexico and the United States have shared a currency, a history, and even a geography. The two nations were called sister republics in the nineteenth century; this North American bond might yet help overcome today's geopolitical divides.

Notes

1. The Spanish empire recognized a number of coins that changed value over time (vis-à-vis their weight in silver or gold). A royal decree (the *Pragmática de Medina de Campo*) of 1497 first set standards for Castile, where 1 *real* made of *vellón* or billon (a metal alloy with some silver)—also called *real de Castilla*—equaled 34 *maravedís* (a medieval coinage), and 8 *reales de vellón* equaled 1 peso; 1 *escudo* (made of twenty-two-karat gold) equaled 350 *maravedís* of silver. The most common coins minted in the American colonies were silver pesos (called *reales de a ocho*) and silver *reales*. One *real* (equal to 34 silver *maravedís*) was conceived as having sixteen parts, so *real* coins were minted in denominations of 0.5, 1, 2, and 4. A gold coin called *doblón de ocho*, which equaled 16 silver pesos, was sometimes used for larger quantities. T. A. D. Marien y Arróspide, *Tratado general de monedas*,

pesas, medidas y cambios de todas las naciones reducidas a las que se usan en España (Madrid: D. Benito Cano, 1789).

2. The exact amount is 1,578,718,264 silver pesos. There is no reliable data prior to 1690. J. J. Tepaske and K. W. Brown, *A New World of Gold and Silver* (Leiden: Brill, 2010).

3. Historians have long debated the extent to which the United States and Mexico have a shared history. For a thoughtful overview of this debate, see L. Hanke, ed., *Do the Americas Have a Common History? A Critique of the Bolton Theory* (New York: Alfred A. Knopf, 1964).

CHAPTER ONE

Emblems of Liberty

It was late March 1792. Inside the Federal Building in New York City, Congress was engaged in an acrimonious debate over the Senate's Act Establishing a Mint and Regulating the Coins of the United States. According to the act's original language, U.S. coins were to depict an eagle on one side and a bust of President George Washington on the other. But for Virginia congressman John Page, putting the face of the nation's leader on coins smacked of royalism. The United States of America was a republic and beholden to the will of no single man. If the coins were to represent the source of the country's power, they should bear an image emblematic of liberty. To New Hampshire's Samuel Livermore, such nitpicking was absurd; the imagery on coins had no bearing on the liberty of the citizenry. Page disagreed. In a new nation, with a constitution just four years old, all government decisions were important as they would set precedents—even those regarding images and coins. Cautioning his fellow U.S. congressmen, Page railed against "imitating the flattery and almost idolatrous practice of Monarchies with respect to the honor paid to their Kings, by impressing their images and names on their coins."[1] No U.S. leader, not even George Washington, deserved higher recognition than the principle of liberty, which underlay the creation of the new country. In the end, Page won the day.

The protagonist in this chapter, and our entry into the themes of nation building and currency, is John Page, congressman and later governor of Virginia, who resolutely insisted that the coinage of the United States represent revolutionary ideals rather than mirror the monarchical traditions of the

Figure 1.1. Pictured here as a young man, John Page went on to become one of the first representatives to the U.S. Congress and also governor of Virginia. He argued that the faces of national leaders had no place on the coins of the new United States. Instead, U.S. coins should bear symbols "emblematic of liberty."
Source: "Portrait of John Page of Rosewell (1744–1808)" by John Wollaston (circa 1758). Oil on canvas. Muscarelle Museum of Art at the College of William and Mary. Gift of Dr. R. C. M. Page. Reproduced with permission.

past (see figure 1.1). The first coins of the Early Republic bore an allegorical likeness of Lady Liberty. The selection of Lady Liberty to represent the new nation's identity was in large part Page's doing. When U.S. citizens held their nation's coins, it was important to prompt them to remember the country's democratic principles ("liberty under the law"). What does this insistence on symbolic imagery tell us about money in the context of U.S. independence?

This chapter offers a brief history of how statesmen like Page and others established a national currency and made the first coins of the United States. The reader will see how they determined the value of U.S. coins, how they enacted a new system to count U.S. money, and how they set up a mint to produce the coins. Taken as a whole, this story about moneymaking serves as a reminder that it is much easier to imagine and design a new currency than to produce one.

John Page, born in 1743, spent his life in service to Virginia and later in support of the new United States. Like his friend and fellow Virginian Thomas Jefferson, Page was raised in privilege on an enormous estate, and he too attended the College of William & Mary. During the Seven Years War (known in British North America as the French and Indian War), Page served under the command of another Virginian, Colonel George Washington. Years later, when the war for independence broke out in 1775, Page served the patriot cause by supporting the boycott of British commerce through the Virginia Committees of Safety, while his younger brother, Mann Page, attended the Continental Congress. Page also served for a few months as a state militia officer. His revolutionary experience shaped his subsequent views regarding the importance of trade and personal liberty and also confirmed him as a man foremost devoted to serving his government. After a stint in Virginia's House of Delegates, Page was elected to the First U.S. Congress in 1789, serving as a representative for eight years before returning home to lead Virginia as governor. His life story played out in the most formative years of the new nation, which, as he wisely predicted, needed a foundational symbol: Lady Liberty. Page's stand on the floor of Congress in 1792 demonstrates early leaders' commitment to a core political principle: liberty would be exalted in the most ordinary of objects.

Wartime Money

Money was at the forefront of revolutionary concerns during the fight for independence, both materially and symbolically. The revolutionary army was consistently desperate for funds, so much so that militia commanders themselves often bore the cost of fighting British troops. Page, for example,

12 ~ Chapter One

paid for many of his regiment's supplies out of his own pocket. The Continental Congress tried to alleviate such financial strains by securing foreign loans, but the voracious fiscal demands of war also forced them to create new money.

The "Continental dollar" or "fugio dollar" coin marked American rebels' concern with symbolism. The word FUGIO (meaning "I fly" in Latin), inscribed in a circle around a sundial, conveyed the idea that time flies, perhaps to hasten the war's end (see figure 1.2). The reverse of the coin displayed thirteen links, each inscribed with the name of a rebellious colony, united into a circle of chain. In the center appeared the words WE ARE ONE, a proclamation that the colonies' strength derived from their unity in the fight against Great Britain. The fugio dollar represented both a declaration of the power of the union and also a public plea to stay the course. The circle of links surrounded the motto MIND YOUR BUSINESS, which in contemporary speech reminded Americans to tend to their responsibilities. Although the fugio dollar coin never actually entered into circulation, it nonetheless foreshadowed how the nation would use its currency to help forge a sense of identity. Later, the first official one-cent coins used the initial design for the fugio dollar.

Figure 1.2. The 1787 copper fugio cent coin pictured here was based on the original wartime fugio dollar. Its imagery was used earlier on continental currency. The sundial and Latin inscription FUGIO convey that time flies. These images and the motto MIND YOUR BUSINESS come from Benjamin Franklin and were meant to encourage a strong work ethic. The linked rings and phrase WE ARE ONE on the reverse of the coin symbolize the union of the thirteen colonies (now states). During the fight for independence, these messages sought to unify the colonies in war; by 1787, these messages aimed to maintain that unity in order to build a functioning independent government.
Source: "Pointed Ray Fugio Cent" (1787). Photographic image courtesy of Yale University Art Gallery. Public Domain.

The Continental Congress had intended for the fugio dollar to be equivalent to a Spanish silver milled dollar, or piece-of-eight, but it lacked the necessary bullion to produce coins. So instead Congress relied on paper notes. First printed in May 1775 (with a face value based on the Spanish dollar), they nonetheless conveyed similar revolutionary messages. The one-third dollar note incorporated the same chain-of-states device used on fugio dollars, while the forty-dollar note depicted a ring of thirteen stars. The paper money notes printed by the individual colonies also reflected the concern for symbolic imagery. The notes of Massachusetts, for example, showed a patriot holding a sword in one hand and the Magna Carta in the other. The message declared a defense of English freedoms that George III had so wrongfully breached. Virginia asserted the rebel sentiment more boldly. Its notes bore the likeness of the goddess Virtue holding a sword above a banner reading SIC SEMPER TYRANNIS (Thus always to tyrants). By implication, the tyrannical king of Great Britain would soon be defeated. The Continental Congress's concern with money and symbols, matched in colonies like Massachusetts and Virginia, prefigured the more generalized anxiety about national imagery that concerned the republic after independence.

Figure 1.3. The one-sixth-dollar note, like other wartime paper currencies, served as a substitute for the coins that the rebellious colonies could not produce. The imagery on the note symbolically linked the thirteen colonies together with links of chain. Each link represented one of the thirteen colonies. Inside the circle of links, AMERICAN CONGRESS described the system by which the colonies came together in a single cause. In the center, the phrase WE ARE ONE stressed the unity that was essential to winning the war for independence.
Source: "One-Sixth of a Dollar" (Philadelphia: Printed by Hall & Sellers, 1776). Print from woodcut. Original in Prints and Photographs Division, Library of Congress, LC-USZ6-861. Public Domain.

Imagery aside, precious little backed up the notes printed by the Continental Congress—a fact that could potentially devalue the currency. The revolutionary government promised people that they would be able to cash in the paper money at war's end (or in four years' time) and receive Spanish silver dollars in their place, but there was little certainty of that future. The escalating costs of war, moreover, meant that Congress continued to issue paper money without any reserves. Approximately US$6 million in notes were in circulation by December 1775, and they began to lose their value as soon as they were printed. What if Great Britain were to defeat the rebels and no continental government survived to redeem the notes? This concern made people want to get rid of the notes as soon as possible (rather than waiting for the four years to pass), even if that meant exchanging them at less than their printed value.

Members of Congress were at pains to stop the Continental's downward trend, but their only recourse was to issue increasingly threatening proclamations about the penalties for not accepting the bills at face value. At the same time, Congress continued to print more and more paper money in order to pay for goods and services incurred by the war effort, which ultimately hastened the devaluation. By the time Congress discontinued the Continental dollar in 1779, its value had collapsed to just pennies on the dollar. Ultimately, in 1790, Congress passed a funding bill to redeem all outstanding Continental notes at one-hundredth of their face value. More than US$2 million in government currency had been ruinously diminished.

To the new U.S. government, one lesson was clear. The only money with reliable value was metal coins, and those had to be minted by an internationally recognized government. The Continental Congress, though legitimate in the eyes of many, did not have the power to infuse paper with value.

A New Counting System for New Money

The money used in the British and Spanish empires mainly consisted of silver and gold coins whose value rested on their weight and purity. The United States aspired to implement a similar system but possessed almost no gold or silver resources of its own. As noted, the Continental Congress had earlier adopted the Spanish milled dollar as the standard unit of currency because Spanish coins (most of them minted in Mexico) were the most trusted currency in the world. The U.S. Congress followed this precedent and pegged the U.S. dollar to the Spanish piece-of-eight, while also pushing for considerable innovation.

All facets of government were open to reinterpretation in the first decade of independence, including the nation's system of weights and measures. What counting system would the United States employ to measure its money? Thomas Jefferson advocated eliminating the imperial system altogether (based on the pound) and moving instead to a measuring system based on units of ten. European mathematicians had used decimal fractions since the sixteenth century because dividing numbers through decimals (separated from whole numbers by a period) was far less cumbersome than doing so by halves, quarters, eighths, and so on. Decimal arithmetic, however, remained limited to academic circles. At the time of American independence, no nation had yet embraced this new system, preferring instead to maintain their leagues, miles, yards, pounds, and ounces. Jefferson, scientifically minded, wanted to rationalize all these various units, which derived from an agglomeration of medieval and classical traditions. Miles divided into 320 rods, 1,760 yards, or 5,280 feet and pounds comprising sixteen ounces were all artifacts of a pre-enlightenment age. According to Jefferson, a modern nation required a new, rational system to measure its growth, and this extended to currency.

Thomas Jefferson's call for a new measuring system stemmed from practicality as much as philosophy, especially in the realm of currency. Prior to independence, colonists used coins from Britain, France, Holland, Spain, and elsewhere, denominated in pounds, *reales*, *livres*, and more, with each subdivided according to its home country's rules. All were treated as foreign currency, including the English pound, and were thus subject to varying rates of exchange set independently by each colony. After the war, British coins made up just a fraction of the currency circulating in the new United States, but most citizens continued to reckon pricing according to the British system, counting in terms of pounds, shillings, and pence (one pound equaled twenty shillings; one shilling equaled twelve pence). The Spanish system presented the same problem; one Spanish dollar equaled eight *reales*, and one *real* equaled thirty-two *maravedís*. Spanish dollars, in fact, were often cut into separate wedges, or "bits," to be used as fractional currency. The term "two bits," which was common slang for a U.S. quarter well into the twentieth century, is a holdover from this system. The sheer variety of foreign coins in circulation (all divided into uneven units and subject to varying exchange rates) was simply antiquated and posed a potential obstacle to the growth of U.S. trade abroad.

The new nation needed a common currency that was also rationally divided into equal units to facilitate accounting and foreign exchange. As a solution, Jefferson pushed Congress to adopt the arithmetic-friendly decimal system for the U.S. dollar, but his plan met with some resistance. In 1782, Superintendent of Finance Richard Morris reported to Congress on the various currencies circulating in the United States and their exchange rates. He argued that the United States needed a unit of currency that could reconcile all of these complex rates and suggested that the dollar be divided into 1,440 subunits. These subunits would be easy to reconcile with foreign currencies: an English shilling would equal x subunits, and one Spanish *real* would equal y subunits. Jefferson, on the other hand, maintained that instead of trying to accommodate all the other national currencies floating around in the United States, the nation would be better served by the establishment of an entirely new system.

According to Jefferson, the new American currency would have to meet three basic needs. One, it would have to be based as closely as possible on a currency that people already used (a requirement easily met by the Spanish dollar). Two, it would need to be conveniently sized, with small denominations for day-to-day use. Three, it had to be easy for the average citizen to understand and calculate its units. To meet this last challenge, Jefferson proposed to Congress in 1784 that the U.S. dollar be divided not into eighths, like Spanish dollars, but according to the decimal system, with one dollar equal to one hundred subunits, or cents. Jefferson urged congressmen to remember their school years, when they "used to be puzzled with adding the farthings, taking out the fours and carrying them on; adding the pence taking out the twelves and carrying them on."[2] Congressional leaders apparently did indeed recall scratching their heads in frustration as they scribbled arithmetic on their classroom slates, for they responded favorably to Jefferson's proposal.

A congressional act in May 1785 adopted Jefferson's model, making the United States the first nation in the world to employ the decimal system for its new currency. Additionally, Congress authorized the creation of a national mint to produce it. The more pressing challenge of establishing a functional constitution, however, shifted statesmen's attention away from the issue. The United States ostensibly had a decimal model of currency between 1785 and 1792, but it had no coins of its own. As such, U.S. citizens continued to use British, Spanish, and French coins as before.

Minting Coins in the Constitutional United States

U.S. leaders returned to the matter of creating a national currency and opening the federal mint after the adoption of the Constitution, with Secretary of the Treasury Alexander Hamilton leading the effort. His requirements were simple; the currency had to consist of coins made from specie and could not include paper bills. Hamilton laid out his formulation for how to achieve a viable currency in the Mint and Coinage Act of 1792, which dictated that the legal unit of money in the United States was the dollar, divided into one hundred cents, and that the standard of value for one U.S. dollar was equal to one Spanish milled dollar.[3] Hamilton, like his colleagues, remembered the disastrous devaluation of the Continental dollar during the war and felt that only metal coins could be trusted to keep their value.

The establishment of these coins required several steps, including determining how much the U.S. dollar coin would actually weigh. Congress had already decided that the coin would be based on the Spanish silver dollar, but the Treasury still needed to ascertain the exact amount of silver to use. To this end, Hamilton ordered a survey of Spanish dollars in circulation. Officially, new Spanish silver dollars came out of the mint in Mexico City and elsewhere containing 377 grains of silver. Hamilton's study, however, found that coins became worn as they passed from hand to hand or jangled in purses and pockets, losing a minute quantity of silver with each new owner. Consequently, the average Spanish dollar in circulation in the United States only contained 371.25 grains of pure silver. This slightly worn average became the standard value of one U.S. dollar. A new Spanish dollar, in other words, would weigh more than a U.S. dollar, but the difference was considered negligible and deemed justified as it saved the Treasury a few grains of silver per coin.

As for the subunits, Hamilton simply followed Jefferson's recommendations from 1785. The U.S. dollar was to be divided into cents according to the decimal system. Coins of one cent and one-half cent were to be minted in copper. All other coins were to be made of silver, including those denominated as five cents (half *disme*), ten cents (*disme*), twenty-five cents, and one, two and one-half, and five dollars. The weights and denominations were set, but Hamilton still had symbolism to consider.

What would the coins look like? Coins are among the most ubiquitous standardized objects in any nation, and each conveys a message about the government that issues them. In the United States, citizens weighed in with numerous suggestions about what constituted an image of the American ethos. Some wanted the coins to show the nation as a place of plenty and a home to people committed to hard work. So one contributor urged the government to include images of sheep, wheat, and a man carrying a shovel. Others wanted to foreground the United States as a land that favored peace, illustrated with a dove or olive branch.[4] The imagery of coins had to communicate national ideals, convey power, and inspire trust: a tall order for such a small object.

Imagery also related to the matter of trust. The U.S. government declared that silver dollars would have the inherent value of silver, but that declaration did not suffice to make them trustworthy. Silver coins are never made of pure silver. They have to be alloyed with some other base metal, often copper, to harden them so that they can stand up to the wear incurred by circulation. One cannot see exactly how much pure silver is in any given coin in everyday exchanges, and historically governments have debased their coins by including more base metals and less specie without changing their stated value. Given this reality, people who accepted a U.S. silver coin would have to take a leap of faith that it contained the requisite amount of silver. The problem at the time, however, was that U.S. citizens found it easier to believe the Spanish government than their own.

Spanish dollars were the model of reliable coinage in the late eighteenth century. The public trusted Spanish coins at first glance, in part as a product of the coin's design, which helped to convey and protect that reliability. Eighteenth-century Spanish dollars were well made and perfectly circular, with milled edges to thwart "sweating" or "clipping," making it difficult to shave a little silver off the edge of the coin without it showing (see figure 1.4). This design built trust that the coins contained enough silver to equal their face value. The imagery on the coins also expressed the power of the Spanish state. Their faces showed a bust of the sitting monarch; their backs bore symbols of empire: the crest of the Kingdoms of Castile and Leon, the Pillars of Hercules, and a banner with the motto PLUS ULTRA (further beyond). The Latin phrase HISPANIE ET INDIARUM (Spain and the Indies) surrounded these symbols. Anyone holding a Spanish dollar knew that the Spanish king, who ruled a vast empire, attested to its value. U.S. coins, if they were to gain people's trust, would also need to portray their strength and reliability.

American citizens at the turn of the eighteenth century traded in a variety of coins from across the Atlantic, all of which shared similar imagery. They showed the faces of kings and queens who ruled "by the grace of God." As noted at the top of this chapter, a Senate committee in 1792 proposed employing the same kind of symbols in U.S. coins. "Upon one side of each of the said coins there shall be an impression or representation of the head of the President of the United States for the time being, with an inscription which shall express the initial or the first letter of his Christian or first name, and his surname at length, the succession of the Presidency numerically, and the year of the coinage."[5] President George Washington was to stand

Figure 1.4. This piece-of-eight, or Spanish dollar, employs strong messages of both national and imperial authority. On the face of the coin, the shield of the Kingdoms of Castile and Leon is surrounded by the Latin phrase KING CHARLES III, BY THE GRACE OF GOD, OF SPAIN AND THE INDIES. On the reverse of the coin the two hemispheres of the globe are depicted between the Pillars of Hercules. The motto ULTRAQUE UNUM (both are one) describes the connection between the Spanish Empire and the home country. Banners wrap around each pillar, reading PLUS ULTRA (further beyond). Some scholars have claimed that the S-shaped banner around the right-hand pillar is the origin of the $ sign in use today.
Source: "Mexico Carlos III Pillar Dollar of 8 Reales" (1771). Wikipedia Commons. Photograph courtesy of Heritage Auctions.

in as the requisite representative of the state and to embody the same kind of authority as backed the coins of other nations. Having so far struggled to maintain the value of U.S. currency, it was only logical for lawmakers to suggest that the new coins follow tradition and display a supreme ruler as a way to establish faith in their value. The idea was that people holding a U.S. dollar coin would look at the face of President Washington and make the association that he, like the Spanish king, testified to the government's ability and intention to produce coins with a set amount of silver (i.e., containing their value in bullion).

Virginia congressman John Page argued the contrary. In his view, the very normality of placing the image of a ruler on the coin of the realm made such a practice wrong for the United States. In support of this motion, Page said, "It had been a practice in monarchies to exhibit the figures of heads of their Kings upon their coins, either to hand down, in the ignorant ages in which this practice was introduced, a kind of chronological account of their kings, or to show to whom the coin belonged." He continued, "We have all read, that the Jews paid tribute to the Romans, by means of a coin on which was the head of their Caesar. Now as we have no occasion for this aid to history, nor any pretense to call the money of the United States the money of our Presidents, there can be no sort of necessity for adopting the idea of the Senate."[6]

Ultimately, Page's argument that the nation's currency belonged to the citizenry prevailed. Congresses endorsed his amendment to use an image "emblematic of Liberty." Debate, however, continued regarding what image would most effectively convey that idea. Representative Livermore had mockingly suggested they might consider a bear who "broke loose from his chain" to be "a fit emblem of liberty," complaining that this abstract idea had no accepted universal image. But this was not altogether true.

Picturing Liberty

There was no single representation of liberty in the eighteenth century, but designers did have well-accepted icons to draw on, especially from classical Greek and Roman history and mythology. In the years leading up to the Revolutionary War, the patriot movement had deployed classical imagery for its cause in the context of virtue and military victory. The Roman goddess of Liberty simultaneously represented freedom and the struggle against tyranny, so she often appeared as a knight. Near the war's end, however, popular classical imagery moved away from celebrations of conquest and triumph and toward representations of loyalty, devotion, and restraint. On retiring to civilian life, for example, George Washington was compared to Cincinnatus, a Roman statesman who famously abdicated all authority once he had fulfilled his responsibilities to the republic. After independence, the goddess Liberty put down her weapons and took on a more peaceful visage as the embodiment of what the war had secured: the creation of a peaceful republican society.

Back in 1782, Benjamin Franklin had commissioned French artist Augustin Dupré to design a medal to commemorate the U.S. victory over Great Britain; Dupré's design later influenced the imagery on U.S. dollars (see figure 1.5). This medal depicted a new view of Liberty with novel features, presenting her in profile, her hair flowing behind her. A short staff rested on her shoulder, hanging off its end, a liberty cap, based on a Roman *pileus* (cap), a symbol of manumission.[7] When slaves in ancient Rome achieved freedom they received a *pileus* to symbolize their new status as freemen, while also reinforcing their identity as former slaves. By the eighteenth century, Europeans and Americans embraced the cap as a popular symbol of freedom.

Figure 1.5. The face of the Liberty Medal, commissioned by Benjamin Franklin in 1782, celebrated the year of the U.S. Declaration of Independence with the date 1776. The profile of the goddess Liberty and the Roman pileus symbolized America's republican freedom. On the reverse of the medal, the goddess Minerva fights the British lion, while an infant United States strangles two snakes, symbolizing colonial victories at Saratoga and Yorktown. This medallion served as the inspiration for the design of the first coins produced by the U.S. Mint.
Source: "Libertas Americana Medal," by Augustin Dupré (Paris, 1782). Photographic image courtesy of Yale University Art Gallery. Public Domain.

As evidence, Jefferson, Franklin, and John Adams all included a liberty cap in their respective designs for a national seal. The goddess and the cap became mutually reinforcing symbols of liberty from tyranny and the personal freedom of all men. This connection, however, presented a problem for U.S. citizens who owned slaves.

The institution of slavery lay at the heart of conflicts that emerged between the states as soon as independence was secured. The Roman goddess and the cap represented liberty, but many citizens found the cap's association with the manumission of slaves unacceptable. It seemed to suggest that Britain had granted Americans their freedom, like a master to his slave. So the liberty cap disappeared. The design of the first coin also likely excluded the liberty cap because the question of black slavery remained unresolved in the "land of the free." In this fraught environment, it was best to represent liberty simply as a woman with flowing hair (see figure 1.6).[8] Unfortunately, the image of Lady Liberty on the first coin was a poor copy of Dupré's original. With a startled expression and hair that seemed to be standing on end rather than gracefully flowing, Lady Liberty appeared to be gazing into the future with alarm.

22   ~   Chapter One

Figure 1.6. Dupré's original 1783 design was poorly copied on the front of this early U.S. coin. Liberty's head was misshapen, and rather than flowing, her hair billowed out behind her as though blasted by a stiff wind. As she wears a rather surprised look, this coin has earned the unfortunate nickname "Liberty in Fright." On the reverse, an unflatteringly portrayed bald eagle is misshapen and appears to have only one leg. Thankfully this first design was quickly replaced by more attractive alternatives.

Source: "Half-Disme" (1792). Princeton University Numismatic Collection, Department of Rare Books and Special Collections, Firestone Library, bequest of Charles Cass, Class of 1902. Courtesy of Princeton University. Reproduced with permission.

In contrast, the design on the coin's reverse side raised few concerns. The eagle's presence was never questioned. Popular myth suggests that Benjamin Franklin advocated for the wild turkey as a better national symbol, but he never actually suggested it for the coin. Franklin did write in a letter to his daughter that is was good fortune that the bird on the back of the first U.S. dollar looked more like a turkey than an eagle, since he thought the turkey a much nobler bird than the bald eagle. His comment was partly a criticism of the coin design's quality. The eagle was indeed poorly represented, badly out of proportion with undersized wings, a squat body, and just one leg. All the deliberations over symbolism had failed to produce a beautiful coin. It is perhaps an artistic mercy that the nation was ill equipped to produce very many of them.

The U.S. Mint

In passing the 1792 Mint and Coinage Act, the U.S. federal government conferred upon itself the sole legal authority to mint U.S. coins. Actually creating the coins, assuring their value, and placing them into circulation was another issue altogether. Indeed, Congress recognized that minting sufficient coinage to meet the daily needs of commerce would take time. The law that established a national mint in January 1792 permitted the free circulation of foreign coins for one year after the mint began production. If need be, certain foreign coins, including the Spanish dollar, would remain legal tender for an additional year or two. After three years, however, only coins minted by the United States would be considered valid currency within its borders. The legislation was at best optimistic. It would take no less than sixty-four years before the United States produced sufficient coinage of its own to at last ban the circulation of foreign currencies.

The U.S. Mint opened with hand-powered equipment and only produced fractional coins (valued at less than a dollar) for its first two years. The production of silver dollars, theoretically the benchmark of the U.S. currency, had to wait. The mint had no stockpiles of specie on hand, so it could only make coins when bullion arrived at the facility for minting. The Bank of Maryland was the first entity to bring in bullion for manufacture into U.S. coins. In the summer of 1794, its bankers deposited "94,532 ounces of silver in the form of French coins."[9] Unfortunately, the mint machinery for striking coins was insufficient for the task: production took three months, and in the first run of two thousand coins, more than 10 percent were deemed too poor in quality to enter circulation. It was evident that better equipment would have to be purchased. In 1795 the mint finally acquired a more powerful press and in that year produced 160,000 silver dollar coins as well as the first gold coins.

While US$160,000 was a tidy sum, it was nowhere near the volume required to make the U.S. currency practical for regular commerce. In fact, the mint could not actually meet the demands of the U.S. economy for years. Repeatedly chided by Congress for its weak output, the mint was hampered by both a lack of bullion and its location in Philadelphia. In the 1790s the mint regularly closed each autumn as yellow fever burned through the city. The expense of just maintaining the facility prompted some government leaders to propose closing the mint entirely and farming out coin production to private contractors.

The U.S. Mint at last began to produce coins in meaningful quantities in the early 1800s. Their appearance was also substantially improved. Lady Liberty lost her fright wig and now wore attractive flowing locks (see figure 1.7). A noble bird clutching arrows representing war and an olive branch symbolizing peace replaced the scrawny eagle. This new eagle, set behind a shield and a banner reading E PLURIBUS UNUM (out of many, one), conveyed national strength.

Figure 1.7. By the turn of the nineteenth century, the United States was producing high-quality, attractive silver coins. On the front of U.S. silver dollars, the "Draped Bust Liberty" image far surpassed the appeal of the earlier "Liberty in Fright." In the late 1790s the U.S. Mint began portraying an eagle with a shield on the reverse of the coin. This more noble-looking bird clutched arrows, symbolizing the power to make war, in one claw and the olive branch of peace in the other. The one-dollar coins were so popular for foreign trade that by 1803 Thomas Jefferson ordered the mint to cease production of them to prevent the export of specie. The mint did not resume regular production of one-dollar coins until 1836. Most "1804" silver dollars were actually produced in the 1830s and later.
Source: "Type I 1804 Dollar." Wikipedia Commons. Photograph courtesy of National Numismatic Collection, National Museum of American History.

These attractive new dollars were slightly heavier than the worn Spanish dollars circulating in the country, although brand-new Spanish dollars remained heavier. As a result, when U.S. residents came into relatively new Spanish dollars, they brought them to the mint as bullion in order to have them recoined as U.S. dollars, pocketing the difference in silver. The new U.S. coins, which had a legal tender value equal to a Spanish dollar, would then be used to pay for goods overseas, particularly in the West Indies, where they were accepted as having the same worth as the heavier Spanish coins. The same coins rarely returned because foreign merchants mainly used their own country's coins to purchase U.S. goods. As a result of this maneuvering, old Spanish dollars rather than U.S. coins remained in domestic circulation. The U.S. Mint found itself making coins that largely made their way outside the country and thus had begun adding a new face to global currency circulation: that of Lady Liberty.

Conclusion

The process of designing the United States' first coins embodied the ideals that guided the nation's leaders. They determined to imprint their coins with symbols that would highlight the principles of republican liberty and to reckon the new nation's currency using a new system, creating the first decimal-based currency. Though the nation's lawmakers managed to create all the legislation required, a shortage of precious metal thwarted production of these new coins. The debates over how the United States would make them and what they should look like tells us what hopes American lawmakers held for this new country. The difficulties they faced in producing them, and putting them into circulation, highlight how difficult it can be to transform such goals into realities.

The U.S. dollar conceived in the 1790s was based on both tradition and innovation—just like the nation. By using the coin of an empire as its standard, the dollar tapped into the long-established and accepted value of Spanish money. It also finally introduced the novel method of decimal denomination. The dollar was also particularly American in that it was to equal in value the coins minted in Spanish America, specifically Mexico. But unlike Spain's colonies, the United States still lacked the silver necessary to make these coins in sufficient numbers. The coins had rich symbolism, but the new nation was not yet able to establish its own worth by producing reliable currency on a large scale.

The U.S. government experimented with a banking system in the next few decades, creating the Bank of the United States as a means of securing the financial stability of the nation. The next chapter discusses this period in the context of another war with Great Britain and the emergence of independent republics in North and South America that confronted similar challenges: how to pay for independence and how to build a nation that embraced the ethos of the Age of Revolutions.

Notes

1. Page's speech was recorded in the *"Journal of the First Session of the Senate of the United States of America, Begun and Held at the City of New York, March 4, 1789"*; T. Schwarz, *A History of United States Coinage* (San Diego, CA: A. S. Barnes, 1980).

2. R. Garson, "Counting Money: The U.S. Dollar and American Nationhood, 1781–1820," *Journal of American Studies* 35, no. 1 (2001): 21–46.

3. The law also enacted a bimetallic system, which set a 15:1 ratio for the relative value of silver to gold.

4. J. P. Ambuske, "Minting America: Coinage and the Contestation of American Identity, 1775–1800" (master's thesis, Miami University, 2006).

5. T. Schwarz, *A History of United States Coinage* (San Diego, CA: A. S. Barnes, 1980).

6. Ibid.

7. The pileus is often mistaken for the Greek Phrygian cap. The latter, with its longer, curved top, initially symbolized outsiders, particularly the people of Phrygia, and was sometimes used as an indication of captivity. By the eighteenth century, the two images were both accepted as symbols of liberty.

8. In 1854, U.S. secretary of war and future president of the Confederacy Jefferson Davis rejected an architectural plan for the new U.S. Capitol that included a statue of the goddess Liberty wearing a Liberty Cap. The designer ultimately substituted a helmet for the proposed cap. Y. Korshak, "The Liberty Cap as a Revolutionary Symbol in America and France," *Smithsonian Studies in American Art* 1, no. 2 (1987): 52–69.

9. D. W. Lange and M. J. Mead, *History of the United States Mint and Its Coinage* (Atlanta, GA: Whitman Pub., 2006).

CHAPTER TWO

The Ghost of a Dollar

In a cartoon from circa 1808, a fictional American banker named Stephen Graspall (a thinly veiled reference to real-life banker Stephen Girard) stands before the ghostly vision of a "real dollar" (see figure 2.1). The caption describes the banker as a "shaver," someone who profited from buying promissory notes at less than their face value. The "real dollar" floating just beyond Graspall's reach is a Spanish dollar bearing the image of Charles IV of Spain. The banker entreats the coin to drop into his empty vaults. He is being sued for payment on banknotes redeemable only in specie, which he lacks, having sold off all the dollar coins in his bank at an 18 percent profit. The cartoon's primary message: Graspall (aka Girard) is a banker solely interested in personal profit, who greedily offers valueless banknotes backed by no real coin money. How do we explain this cartoon? And what does it tell us about money and banking in the first decades of U.S. independence?

The protagonist of this chapter is Stephen Girard, an exceptionally wealthy Philadelphia banker and philanthropist (see figure 2.2). The money is the U.S. and Spanish dollars he amassed as a ship owner and then global merchant during the Age of Revolutions (1775–1848), as well as the paper notes he issued from one of the most powerful private banks in the United States. His life illustrates the financial upheaval that characterized the Early Republic. The story is about the challenges faced by the young nation as the government attempted to establish a sound currency, a reliable banking system, and the political security to ensure prosperity. Girard bore witness to

Figure 2.1. Here, a usurious banker (Stephen Girard) gazes covetously at a Spanish milled dollar, having no silver left in the vaults of his own bank. Bankers in the Early Republic were often viewed as unscrupulous and greedy, charging too much for their loans and issuing paper notes with little specie on hand to back them.
Source: "The Ghost of a Dollar or The Bankers Surprize," by William Charles (Philadelphia, 1808). Prints and Photographs Division, Library of Congress, LC-DIG-pga-05635. Public Domain.

Figure 2.2. This portrait of Stephen Girard presents a much more flattering picture of the banker than the double-chinned character in the cartoon. Girard had been blind in his right eye since childhood. The blind eye, which some accounts describe as "grotesque," is turned away from the artist. Here we see simply an image of a prosperous man.
Source: "Portrait of Stephen Girard," etched by A. Rosenthal (from a posthumous portrait by B. Otis in the Grand Lodge of Pennsylvania, circa 1903). Prints and Photographs Division, Library of Congress, LC-USZ62-123051. Public Domain.

the successes and failures of fulfilling these difficult objectives in the first four decades of the nation's history.

In an era when banking in the United States was barely regulated, specie scarce, and paper money unreliable, the public regarded bankers with great distrust. Well into the second decade after independence, U.S. citizens had

Figure 2.3. This Spanish dollar, like the one in the cartoon, bears the face of King Charles IV. U.S. citizens who looked upon him were heartened by certainty that coins with his likeness and minted in his colonies could be trusted and would be valued across the globe.
Source: "Spanish Silver Peso (8 *Reales*)" (Mexico, 1796). Photo by Yale University Art Gallery. Public Domain.

little faith in the lenders of their day or even the money they traded in. The U.S. Mint and the U.S. Treasury could not yet produce and manage the currency necessary for true economic independence. State-chartered banks and private lenders faced little consistent oversight and issued paper notes of often dubious value. Thus, the only trusted currency was the coin of a foreign country (the Spanish dollar in the cartoon) (see figure 2.3). The new republic may have thrown off the yoke of monarchy, but it still remained dependent on coins bearing the image of a European king. The United States lacked the silver mines necessary to end its reliance on coins endorsed by Spain and produced in Mexico and Peru. The experience of Steven Girard—a maritime trader, sometime smuggler, merchant, banker, and ultimately the new nation's first millionaire—opens a window onto the major challenges of the early years of the new nation and its money.

In this chapter, the reader follows Girard's rise from ambitious young sailor to banking magnate. By the time the United States had ratified the Constitution in 1788, Girard was settled in Philadelphia and well on his way to becoming one of the richest men in the country. Girard supported Secretary of the Treasury Alexander Hamilton's proposal that Congress create a national bank—the Bank of the United States—and witnessed this controversial institution's creation in 1792. When a divided Congress closed the bank in 1811, Girard purchased it to create the Bank of Stephen Girard. When war with Britain and financial calamity soon followed, Girard was among a trio of wealthy Americans who loaned the government money to conduct the war; when that war was over, he was among those who led the cry for the resurrection of the national bank. His financial success and influence on economic policy tell us about the open commercial landscape of the early nation, when potential profit was extraordinary but also involved considerable risk. The rules of American commerce were only then being written.

Fortune from the Sea: Girard the Mariner

A passionate devotion to work (later generations might identify him as a workaholic) fueled Stephen Girard's journey from junior officer on a trading vessel to owner of a powerful global shipping empire. Born in 1750 in Bordeaux, France, to a family with a long tradition in maritime trade, Girard took to the sea at fourteen on a voyage to France's colony of Saint-Domingue (later Haiti) and immersed himself in trading dry goods and small-scale luxury items. Within a decade he commanded a vessel, allowing him to trade on his own accord. By 1773, Girard, not yet twenty-five years old, had amassed enough capital to buy a two-thirds share in a sloop (a small sailing vessel). A year later he partnered with New York–based shipper Thomas Randall to trade between New York, Saint-Domingue (now known as Haiti), the Dominican Republic, and New Orleans, broadening his network to the colonies of Britain and Spain. Soon there were more ships. Misfortune struck in 1776 when a British naval vessel intercepted Girard's *La Jeune Bebe* (the young child), which had barely survived a terrible beating in a storm. The British sought contraband shipments destined for American revolutionary forces, and although they found none, they seized the ship's best sailor for service in the British navy. They released Girard because he was a French citizen.

With his vessel battered and undermanned, Girard sheltered in Philadelphia's harbor, where he decided to stay and begin anew. Soon after, he opened a shop to capitalize on the war with Britain, knowing that the conflict would result in shortages of common trade goods, which he could supply at high prices. Within a few years, he was a wealthy shop owner, an independent merchant, and a member of a maritime insurance syndicate.

The first three decades of Girard's life reflect the obstacles and opportunities that characterized trade in the western Atlantic during the 1760s through 1780s. Girard realized commercial opportunity in seas beset by foul weather and revolutionary upheaval. He found his commercial and national home in the rebellious colonies, swearing allegiance to the state of Pennsylvania in 1778 and becoming a U.S. citizen by war's end.

Preparation for WAR to defend Commerce.
The Swedish Church Southwark with the building of the FRIGATE PHILADELPHIA.

Figure 2.4. This engraving depicts the USS *Philadelphia* under construction in 1799. Built to defend U.S. commercial shipping, the frigate became famous when Barbary pirates captured her off the coast of Tripoli. She was sent as part of an effort to end extortion of U.S. shipping. The Barbary states had been demanding barrels of silver dollars and other gifts to permit U.S. trade in the Mediterranean. Pirates in the Caribbean and elsewhere similarly hampered Girard's shipping business, so he supported this military effort.
Source: "Preparation for War to Defend Commerce. The Swedish Church Southwark with the Building of the Frigate Philadelphia" (William Birch & Son: Philadelphia, 1800). John Carter Brown Library Archive of Early American Images.

Girard's mercantile trading interests increased considerably during the 1780s and 1790s, which coincided with the early stages of the Age of Revolutions. His shipping empire grew despite British threats to seaborne traders, such as interdiction, seizure of cargo and vessels, and even imprisonment. He expanded his trade networks in the West Indies, shipping rice, flour, cornmeal, and other North American products south. His vessels returned north carrying sugar, coffee, molasses, and Spanish silver. To ensure smooth commerce, Girard ordered his captains to evade customs inspections and pay bribes, skirting both the spirit and the letter of international trade regulations. Such extralegal tactics were common practices at the time, and Girard used them to great effect. He also capitalized on long-standing relationships he maintained with French compatriots in Saint-Domingue. To his frustration, in 1791, the Haitian Revolution (1791–1804) brought mayhem to the colony and impeded his trading efforts. On its heels, the Napoleonic Wars (1803–1815) further endangered freedom of trade in the Caribbean.

Girard, recently naturalized as a U.S. citizen, had no patience for threats to his commerce. When war between France and Britain spilled into the Caribbean, U.S. shipping fell under threat. Like many Americans attempting to maintain trade with colonial ports in the West Indies, Girard was frustrated by the belligerents' refusal to recognize President George Washington's 1793 declaration of the neutrality of U.S. ships. He responded by equipping his vessels with various national flags and false cargo manifests and continued to urge his captains to use bribery when favorable. Despite these efforts, no fewer than five of his vessels were seized between 1793 and 1797.

Not one to dwell on misfortune, Girard chose to refocus his trading ventures farther afield, in the less politically roiled waters of the transatlantic and transpacific trades. During the 1790s, Girard sent ships to Europe and built substantial credit lines in London, Amsterdam, Antwerp, Hamburg, and St. Petersburg. By the end of the eighteenth century, American trading vessels were engaged in commerce across the globe, and Girard was a leader among this new class of international merchants. Having secured independence, the United States sought to challenge trading empires that had dominated seaborne commerce for centuries.

To insinuate themselves into global trade, U.S. merchants needed attractive commodities to sell abroad, and everyone wanted Spanish American silver, especially the Chinese. U.S. commerce with China began when the first American trade vessel arrived in the harbor of Canton in 1784. Soon afterward Girard commissioned a Philadelphia shipyard to build a ship specifically outfitted for trade with China. U.S. traders sought to supplant English merchants as the main suppliers of Chinese luxury goods to the American consumer market. However, in exchange for items like tea and silk Chinese merchants demanded silver bullion, normally in the form of Spanish dollars. The Chinese used silver as a monetary standard but had insufficient deposits of their own, historically acquiring it first from the Japanese and then, starting in the late 1500s, from the Spanish. Centuries later, English and then U.S. merchants would be the ones shipping Spanish silver coins to China.

Like China, the United States had little in the way of silver deposits, so U.S. merchants had to secure silver through a complex process of sequential trading. Girard briefly summarized his involvement in this lengthy sequence in an address to both houses of Congress in March 1812: "These several years past I have been in the habit to ship, on my account, cargoes consisting of produce of the United States, and other articles of India, West Indies and et cetera to the continent of Europe. Those shipments have been disposed of at their respective destinations by the consignees, and in many instances, the greatest part of their proceeds were invested in Spanish milled dollars, et cetera, and shipped on board my ships or vessels for the Isles of France, Bourbon, Java, Madras, Calcutta, and Canton, and back to this port."[1] Girard, in other words, engaged in global trade to secure the silver coins he needed to purchase superior Chinese merchandise, which he could then sell at a substantial profit in the United States.

Finding this system of trading around the world to acquire silver rather arduous, U.S. traders like Girard looked for an alternative commodity to trade with China. They found Turkish opium, which they purchased in Smyrna or other Mediterranean ports and then resold in China at a 500 percent profit. The Chinese prohibited this trade, but both U.S. and English traders ignored the ban. Americans soon monopolized the Turkish opium trade. In 1805 Girard wrote to two of his agents, "I am very much in favor of investing heavily in opium. While the [Napoleonic Wars] last, opium will support a good price."[2] Girard quickly made that heavy investment. In 1806, he ordered one of his supercargoes to buy twenty thousand pounds of opium to sell in either Macao or Canton. The scheme was a great success; by 1816, he was one of the largest U.S. shippers of the product.

Girard continued to have little difficulty skirting the law in international dealings through bribery, customs violations, and traffic in questionable commodities. His trade practices were typical of other merchants who sent American-flagged vessels across the oceans. Merchants' readiness to engage in illegal commerce in China speaks to their occasional disregard for the laws of their trading partners, as well as their successful intrusion into the old European mercantilist monopolies that had governed overseas trade in recent centuries.

While aggressively expanding his position as the leader of a global trading empire, Girard was also committed to his adopted home city of Philadelphia. His commercial success brought him to prominence in the community, and Philadelphians considered him a civic leader—a role he willingly embraced. In 1793, for instance, when Philadelphia faced the worst outbreak of yellow fever in U.S. history, Girard remained in the city to oversee the response. By contrast, most of his rich associates fled to the countryside to avoid the contagion. When the disease returned in 1797 and 1798, he again led the effort to help the afflicted. He worked at the hospital at Bush Hill, exposing himself directly to the sick. That the U.S. Mint in Philadelphia shut down each autumn during the epidemics indicates the persistent danger posed by the disease.

Girard's labors on behalf of others during Philadelphia's time of crisis raise some questions about what exactly he valued. Why did he push himself relentlessly to make a fortune? Indeed, he cared little for the comforts that money could bring him. He was famously tightfisted, particularly eschewing luxuries. At a time when a carriage symbolized success, Girard walked everywhere, eventually only permitting himself a two-wheeled buggy, which he drove himself. The house he had built in Philadelphia was no larger than practical to accommodate his business, which occupied the ground floor. When money could easily have allowed him to evade pestilential threat, he chose to remain in the city.

Girard appears to have valued money as a measure of accomplishment rather than as a means to acquisition. He considered work an end unto itself. A famous anecdote illustrates his belief that labor was its own satisfaction. The story goes that a poor immigrant approached Girard for work. Having nothing that he needed done, Girard offered to pay the man to move a pile of bricks from one side of his yard to the other. Once that task was completed, the man asked what Girard would like him to do next, and Girard told him to move the pile of bricks back. The immigrant protested against such wasteful labor and left with just half a day's wages. Girard was reputedly shocked that a man looking for work would not accept an offer of it, whatever the end product might be.

Fortune from Usury: Girard the Banker

Girard eventually expanded his commercial operations into money lending. In so doing, he entered into yet another growing sector of the new U.S. economy: banking. Banks then, as today, were far more than mere repositories for their customers' savings. They eased and accelerated the movement of money in the economy, in part by offering loans and extending credit. Girard's involvement in this financial world, which began with short-term loans from his counting house in Philadelphia, connected him to a broader national debate about the nature of the banking industry and the role of the federal government in the national economy.

Public concern centered on the common practice of issuing paper banknotes, which were supposed to represent a certain amount of "real money" (i.e., specie) on deposit in the bank's vaults. A banknote was not in itself money but rather a promise to pay money and, not unlike a personal check, was much easier to use. In theory, a person could take a banknote bearing a particular value, say US$100, to the issuing bank, or perhaps even other banks, and redeem it for that same value in silver or gold. Banks, however, normally extended more notes than they could redeem at any given time with the specie on deposit in their vaults because customers would not normally all come in at once to redeem their notes.

To avoid the potential for that occurrence, many banknotes had fixed periods before they "matured," which staggered when customers could redeem them. In the meantime, people could trade these notes as a substitute for cash. As long as everyone had faith that the note would be honored at face value, it effectively served as a fiduciary currency, meaning a currency based on its trusted value rather than on an inherent value. In this way, banks actually increased the supply of money circulating in the economy. This system relied on people trusting that the banks would cover the paper that they put into circulation. In the Early Republic, banks found this trust hard to come by, especially because devalued paper money was an endemic problem. Many citizens thus felt that the government needed to step in to regulate banking and ensure the value of paper currency in order to ensure the nation's financial future.

What role, if any, did the federal government have in the economy of the republic? The debate over the Bank of the United States revolved around this question. For Secretary Alexander Hamilton, the government had an essential role to play in the economic stability of the country. He argued in 1791 that the United States needed to charter a national bank tasked with facilitating the saving and expenditure of government money, printing paper currency, and acting as an example of responsible banking to other American banks. As Hamilton pointed out, many nations across Europe had long-established public banks; the Bank of England, for example, served as an "engine of state."[3] Hamilton proposed that the Bank of the United States be a private rather than a governmental institution, with government appointees filling a minority of seats on its board. Having witnessed the disastrous history of the Continental, Hamilton deemed it essential to entrust the production of paper currency to a bank rather than to the government itself. Banks, argued Hamilton, would issue notes on the basis of their ability to redeem them in specie, whereas a government would be prone to printing money on the basis of necessity, leading to an inevitable devaluation of the currency. As a single producer of paper money, a national bank could eliminate the confusion and insecurity produced by various independent banks issuing notes of questionable reliability. Whatever practical advantages a national bank might potentially offer, to many the Bank of the United States raised a constitutional question regarding the powers of the federal government.

Supporters and opponents of the Bank of the United States reflected sectional differences regarding the power of the federal government that defined the political landscape for much of the nineteenth century. Hamilton, a New Yorker, argued that chartering a bank in service to the national economy and the government itself was within the "implied powers" conferred by the Constitution. The representatives of the northern states, where support for a strong federal government was greatest, generally agreed. To others, particularly in southern and western districts, a federal bank posed a threat to state sovereignty. Such an institution would surely form an alliance with wealthy northern merchants, rendering the central government beholden to their interests. Virginian secretary of state Thomas Jefferson supported greater autonomy for the states and argued that the language of the Constitution prohibited the government from chartering the bank, as any powers not specifically ascribed to the federal government by the Constitution devolved to the states. If the Constitution did not provide for the creation of a nationally chartered bank, the federal government had no power to establish one.

In the end, the arguments of the Federalists, who advocated for a strong central government, prevailed. In February 1791, President Washington signed a twenty-year charter for the Bank of the United States. In this early phase of U.S. sovereignty, when the Constitution was undergoing its first political interpretations, those who supported a strong central government secured a role for that government in the domestic economy. Although normally a great supporter of Jefferson, Girard disagreed with him on the idea of the Bank of the United States. For Girard, economic efficiency outweighed political ideology.

The establishment of the first Bank of the United States in Philadelphia did not reduce opposition; nor did it automatically curtail the risky practices of other banks (see figure 2.5). Individual states chartered their own banks, resulting in weak and inconsistent banking regulation and continued issuance of questionable paper. Some states eventually limited the amount of credit banks could offer to two, three, or four times the amount of specie they had on hand. Such regulations, however, came only over time and in response to much bad experience. On August 5, 1809, the Vermont *Reporter* complained about the insecurity of that state's banks: "Indeed, one of the branches had in circulation bills to more than *fourteen times* the amount of specie." Other banks, known as private unchartered banks, operated with still less control.

Figure 2.5. Girard purchased the building depicted here to establish his own Bank of Stephen Girard. It previously housed the first Bank of the United States, which acted as a centralized lender for the U.S. government from 1791 until 1811, when its charter was not renewed. Many U.S. leaders felt that the federal government had neither the responsibility nor the right to maintain a central bank.
Source: "Bank of the United States, in Third Street Philadelphia" (Philadelphia: William Birch & Son, 1799). John Carter Brown Library Archive of Early American Images.

Opposition to the Bank of the United States grew over the course of its twenty-year charter. Some reiterated the claim that the Constitution did not provide for the creation of a central bank, which, as a privately owned institution, had no legal right to print money. Others were deeply concerned about the level of foreign investment in the Bank. By 1811, Britons had purchased 70 percent of its stock, and as relations with Great Britain degraded in the years before the War of 1812, many feared that the Bank would serve as a means to funnel specie out of the country. Opposition also came from state banks, which resented the competition. Bank of the United States–issued notes circulated more widely and were more highly valued than the notes of any of the smaller state banks. As the nineteenth century dawned, much of the American public disputed how a federal bank might be essential to a successful economy or a reliable currency. So when the Bank's charter came up for renewal in 1811, Congress permitted it to expire.

When the first Bank of the United States was closed, Girard bought its building and the majority of its assets to establish his own bank. Competing Philadelphia bankers deeply resented the immediately powerful Bank of Stephen Girard and tried to undermine it by amassing government notes and then demanding immediate payment in specie. The more credit banks extended beyond the specie in their vaults, the more likely they were to be found wanting when customers arrived to cash in those loans. In the cartoon in figure 2.1, Graspall/Girard finds himself at precisely this juncture, having been caught without enough specie to redeem his notes. The real Girard never actually faced such a crisis. He was a conservative lender, only loaning for short terms to those who could provide collateral. Yet, while the cartoon was wrong about the man, its basic characterization of bankers in general was not unfounded.

After the closure of the first Bank of the United States, the U.S. economy confronted significant inflation. The absence of a central bank further destabilized currency. The number of small banks rose sharply after the Bank's closure: in 1811, there were 90 banks in the United States; just five years later there were 260. Many issued notes backed by very little actual specie, and much of their profit stemmed from the printing of notes that borrowers could use for speculation, particularly in western territories. As people lost faith in paper currency, they hoarded the little specie available, forcing most banks to suspend payments of specie by 1814. The different notes printed by the various banks were the only paper currency in circulation. The use of potentially valueless paper for questionable investments had great potential to produce an economic bubble that, when pierced, might cause severe problems. Such calamity was not far off.

The Price of War

Long-festering animosities between the new United States and Britain erupted into open warfare in 1812, in part due to British obstruction of U.S. commercial objectives. The conflict dated back to the early Napoleonic Wars, when merchants like Girard confronted British and French navies that refused to recognize American neutrality. The Royal Navy interdicted American merchant vessels, often seizing sailors and impressing them into naval service, as had happened on Girard's ship in 1776. The illegal impressment of American sailors and occasional instances of naval assault on U.S.

vessels fomented anger toward the British and even calls for war. In an effort to starve the belligerents into respecting U.S. neutrality, in 1807 President Thomas Jefferson had forbidden American ships from engaging in transatlantic trade.

Unfortunately, Jefferson and his secretary of state, James Madison, overestimated European dependence on U.S. goods. The embargo had little effect on France or Britain and instead debilitated the U.S. trade economy. Within a year U.S. exports dropped to less than one-fourth their previous levels (from US$103 million to US$22 million).[4] In 1809, the newly inaugurated President Madison ended the embargo, which had not achieved its goals, and British vessels continued to interdict U.S. vessels and impress sailors. Girard, frustrated in his capacity as a maritime trader by such assaults on U.S. sovereignty and commerce, supported war against the British. Based on his previous experience, he likely understood as well as anyone that nations rarely engage in a costlier enterprise than warfare.

Citizens on the western frontier were also irritated by British support for Native Americans in the Ohio River valley fighting to prevent U.S. government expansion into their territory. Congressional leaders from the southern and western states advocated taking over western lands occupied by Native Americans. Americans had already come to believe that the future lay in continued westward expansion. If military conflict was necessary to open economic opportunity along the country's western border, then the United States was willing to fight. Thus began a policy that the United States would return to in the following decades.

Finally, in the summer of 1812, the United States declared war on Great Britain and promptly launched the first of three failed invasions of Canada. From the outset, the government was on the back foot and in need of a great deal of money to finance the war. It had begun the war with little in the way of either military or financial resources, and the lack a national bank to extend credit began to tell. To carry on, the government was forced to turn to the public. In 1813, it offered a bond issue to raise US$16 million but only found buyers for US$6 million.

At this crucial time, Girard, along with John Jacob Astor and David Parish, subscribed a US$10 million loan, which enabled the U.S. government to continue to fund the war. The loan was meant to save the United States from defeat and possible recolonization by Britain. However, it was also meant to earn money for the lenders. If the United States won the war, Girard, Astor, and Parish stood to earn a tidy profit for their efforts. The conflict raged for another two years, with neither side gaining advantage or making territorial gains.

Figure 2.6. Here a U.S. vessel captures the British frigate *Macedonian* off the Azores in October 1812—a victory in a war that was partly a response to perceived British obstruction of U.S. commerce. This struggle, fought in eastern North America and in both the Atlantic and Pacific Oceans, required massive increases in military spending by the United States, particularly to maintain a global naval presence. The United States spent an estimated US$90 million during the War of 1812.
Source: "The U.S. Frigate *United States* Capturing H.B.M. Frigate *Macedonian*: Fought, Octr. 25th. 1812" (New York: N. Currier, c. 1835–1856). Original in Prints and Photographs Division, Library of Congress, LC-USZC2-3120. Public Domain.

When the war ended in 1815, territorial boundaries remained exactly where they had been beforehand. Nonetheless, several acts of martial valor, such as Andrew Jackson's victory at the Battle of New Orleans, were woven into a growing mythology that fueled a sense of American military might. Though the war had produced heroes for the young nation, the economic effects were disastrous. In 1814, imports fell to one-tenth prewar levels and exports to one-fifteenth. The U.S. national debt nearly trebled, and U.S. treasury notes were sold at deeply discounted rates. With no territorial gains, the estimated US$90 million cost of the war went essentially uncompensated.

The conflict revealed the U.S. government's need for a reliable means of securing credit in times of crisis. The country's commercial aspirations required repeated military action. From 1801 to 1805, the United States had gone to war with the Barbary states of North Africa to end the extortion of

American commercial shipping in the Mediterranean. During the War of 1812, the United States fought both Native Americans and the British to end harassment of U.S. shipping and to end British militarization of Native Americans in the Mississippi Valley. Through these conflicts, the United States established itself as a commercially and territorially ambitious nation, determined to become a major player in global trade and to continue the country's expansion westward across the continent. These ambitions proved costly militarily, and the government could not continue to rely on the largesse of its wealthiest citizens. After the War of 1812, some in the federal government began once again to call for national bank.

The Second Bank of the United States

Girard, Astor, and Parish began planning for a second Bank of the United States in 1814. Girard's desire for this institution rested on both personal and public interest. Having received U.S. treasury notes in exchange for the wartime loan of the previous year, Girard and his two partners held a financial stake in rebuilding the U.S. economy. The financial weakness of the federal government had depreciated those treasury notes. A federal bank, backed by strong regulation, with a legal responsibility to maintain specie on hand, would go a long way toward ensuring the value of those treasury bills. At the same time, experience had taught Girard that profits were best made through careful, conservative investment. The proliferation of state-chartered banks had resulted in various notes of dubious value flooding the market, casting doubt onto the value of all paper money. When the war was over, the government needed a regulated institution as the repository for the tremendous debt incurred. By 1816, Congress was ready to authorize the Second Bank of the United States.

Even before it opened, the Second Bank stimulated the economy, eased trade, and increased the value of Girard, Astor, and Parish's treasury notes. Silver poured back into the economy as buyers of Bank stock dipped into hoarded silver supplies to purchase shares. The public bought 80 percent of the Bank's stock (the government purchased the remainder) prior to its opening. To purchase these shares, buyers needed to pay at least 20 percent in specie; they could pay the remainder in U.S. securities. This meant that during the subscription period, investors turned over US$7 million in silver. Unfortunately, simply returning some of the nation's supply of silver to circulation was not enough to shore up the economy against impending disaster.

No sooner had the Second Bank gone into operation than the United States and Britain entered a trade war. While the War of 1812 had been punishing for the U.S. economy overall, certain sectors had benefited from the blockades. Small-scale manufacture in the United States had expanded to fill some of the needs that could not be met from overseas. The textile industry in the Northeast, for example, had grown. But when open trade resumed, foreign goods arrested much of that development. In 1817, U.S. cotton manufacturers convinced the government to enforce limits on the importation of finished goods from Britain. A year later, Britain closed off U.S. trade to all its West Indian colonies, leading to a collapse in the price of U.S. wheat.

This blow to the economy was heightened when news broke of scandal in the Second Bank of the United States. Even though Girard sat on the board of directors, he was unable to impose his own ideals of conservative lending on the other members. He was appalled, in fact, by what he considered very risky lending policies. So, just months after it opened, Girard resigned from the bank he had helped found. Afterward, the Second Bank became even more involved in highly speculative loans. By the winter of 1818, public accusations surfaced that it had extended loans on little or no collateral, had accepted deposits in currency other than U.S. notes or specie (as required by its charter), and was beset with graft.

These accusations were well founded. The Bank had engaged in very risky lending to other banks. Banks across the country had been extending very loose credit to a population eager to buy public land in the Southwest and Northwest, and the Second Bank held much of the debt of those smaller banks. As of 1818, it had liabilities almost ten times in excess of the specie in its vaults, so it attempted to purchase specie from overseas. When this measure proved insufficient, it began demanding a 12.5 percent specie payment from those smaller banks that sought to renew their loans. This sudden contraction of credit exacerbated an economic slowdown already in progress. In November 1818, the president of the Second Bank resigned. That same month, Spanish dollars, as perhaps the most trusted currency in the country, traded for 6 percent above face value.

In order to regain control, the new Bank president, Langdon Cheves, ordered state banks with significant liabilities to the Second Bank of the United States to redeem those debts. The policy worked to shore up the national Bank, but numerous smaller banks across the country failed when faced with demands for specie they could not produce. Prices for all manner of goods began to fall, and with them, wages and employment.

The United States entered into its first nationwide economic depression: the Panic of 1819. Credit disappeared, taking specie with it. No one wished to find him- or herself holding paper notes worth less than their face value or called upon to settle a debt with silver he or she did not have. The banks that survived amassed all the specie they could and tucked it away in their vaults, wiping the U.S. economy clean of much of its circulating money. In some areas, currency became so scarce that people returned to a system of barter.

The turbulent years after the War of 1812 demonstrate the fragility of the early U.S. economy. The trade war with Britain had a crippling effect on American producers. The country was still short on trustworthy coin money, and as a consequence people turned to paper currency. The national focus on westward expansion provided terrific opportunity for land speculation fueled by optimism rather than capital. Even the federally chartered Second Bank of the United States succumbed to the lure of issuing paper notes valued at far more than it could redeem. Girard had argued for restrained lending policies, and the Bank's own rules prohibited such risky practices, but top leadership provided poor guidance. The costs to the nation were severe.

Girard, who remained true to his conservative lending principles, avoided the sufferings of 1819 to 1821. His own bank maintained a high level of specie to back his notes, and short-term loans ensured that the bank was never exposed to too much risk. While the Second Bank of the United States stumbled badly in its first few years, Girard's bank endured and helped him continue his rise to become one of the wealthiest citizens of the United States.

Conclusion

Independence is a political achievement, but once the kings are deposed and the laws are enacted, the real work begins. The U.S. government tried to create a currency that would represent its nation and permit free commercial trade. At every turn, leaders reiterated that currency must be based on specie, but the government could never meet its own demands. American traders traversed the globe to secure "real" Spanish dollars, but few of those found their way into use in the United States, getting spent instead in the growing China trade.

Major positions on the nature of governance and national financial policy were still evolving in the republic's early years. Commercially, the nation was expanding, with U.S. traders like Girard entering markets previously monopolized by European colonial powers. Militarily the nation was precocious, if not quite fully prepared to meet its own ambitions. Production of a steady precious-metal currency was still beyond the country's ability. Paper, of varied and dubious reliability, was still used in an attempt to supply the day-to-day needs of U.S. citizens. The nation had tried to create a central banking system, abandoned that idea, and soon returned to it. At the start of the 1820s, the United States remained wholly dependent on foreign silver, predominantly that of Mexico. With the financial crisis of 1819, even that currency was in short supply. The end of the second decade of the nineteenth century found the United States in a challenging position, with a weak economy, high unemployment, and low wages. In the failing Spanish colony of New Spain, conditions were far more unsettled.

The cartoon in figure 2.1 tells us much about the money, banking, and economy of the early United States. Bankers like the fictional Stephen Graspall, or the real-life Stephen Girard, provided a valuable resource, credit, to an economy nearly bereft of reliable precious-metal currency. But in an economy like that of the new United States, where wars frequently impeded trade, currency was rare, and paper notes could quickly lose their value, bankers became frequent targets of public frustration. Even though rich men like Girard had the capacity to bail out their nation in a time of crisis, they still charged interest and influenced national policy to their own ends. At a time when bankers and their unreliable notes were subjects of public ridicule, the Spanish dollar remained the United States' only "real dollar."

Notes

1. Stephen Girard, "Explanatory Statement: To Accompany the Memorial of Stephen Girard, Dates the 9th Day of March, 1812, and Addressed to the Senate and House of Representatives of the United States of America," in Stephen Simpson, *Biography of Stephen Girard, with His Will Affixed Comprising an Account of His Private Life, Habits, Genius, and Manners: Together with a Detailed History of His Banking and Financial Operations for the Last Twenty Years: Accompanied with Philosophical and Moral Reflections, upon the Man, the Merchant, the Patriot, and the Philanthropist* (Philadelphia: T. L. Bonsal, 1832), 102.

2. Quoted in Jacques M. Downs, "American Merchants and the China Opium Trade, 1800–1840," *Business History Review* 42, no. 4 (1968): 422.

3. Quoted in Richard H. Timberlake, *Monetary Policy in the United States: An Intellectual and Institutional History* (Chicago: University of Chicago Press, 1993), 5. The book offers an overview of U.S. monetary policy from independence through the twentieth century.

4. Jeffrey A. Frankel, "The 1807–1809 Embargo against Great Britain," *Journal of Economic History* 42, no. 2 (1982): 294.

CHAPTER THREE

Minting Mexico's Independence

In 1827 José Ignacio Esteva sat down to pen an account of his time in office as the first secretary of the Treasury of the United Mexican States (*Estados Unidos Mexicanos*), with two main objectives. One was to give his successor a kind of primer, detailing the Treasury's operations and its numerous subministries; the other was to defend his own time in office and in this way warn his replacement of the troubles ahead. Esteva presided over Mexican finances during a time of great political upheaval, with the national Treasury in near collapse. Anyone short of a miracle worker was destined to come under fire for the state of the Mexican economy. Congressmen challenged Esteva on his judgment and even his patriotism. With this missive, he hoped to clear his name and prepare the next treasurer for the challenges ahead. He wrote, "There is no law that forces me to provide you these instructions on the state of the Treasury, but perhaps in the future, the legislature will oblige its ministers to do so, to ensure the health of the republic."[1] What does Esteva's commitment to fiscal policy reveal about establishing infrastructure in a postcolonial context?

The protagonist of this chapter is Mexican statesman José Ignacio María Hesiquio Esteva, who served intermittently as secretary of the Treasury (*ministro de hacienda*) from 1824 to 1829, during Mexico's first decade of independence (see figure 3.1). The money is the silver dollar coins that the new nation struggled to produce, while trying to fund first an empire and then a republic. The story is about the challenges the young Mexican nation faced as government officials like Esteva attempted to establish a sound currency, a reliable banking system, and the political security necessary to

Figure 3.1. This lithograph depicts Esteva as a staid statesman, with deep-set eyes and a broad forehead, gazing forward with a seriousness of purpose: to ensure the republic's fiscal stability.
Source: "José Ignacio Esteva, Ministro de Hacienda, litografía" (circa 1930). Original in Archivo Casasola © (14832) Secretaria de Cultura. INAH.sinafo. fn.mexico. Reproduction authorized by the Instituto Nacional de Antropología e Historia, México.

ensure a prosperous economy. These objectives were in many ways similar to those of U.S. statesmen a few decades earlier. Esteva's efforts to balance the national budget and increase the output of silver pieces-of-eight, now known as Mexican dollars, illustrates the challenge of creating a currency and fostering a sound economy in a new nation. His experiences also serve as a window into the parallels that unite the histories of Mexico and the United States.

This chapter traces Esteva's political trajectory from local government official in the city of Veracruz to secretary of the Treasury. Along the way the reader observes the rise of Mexico as an independent nation and federal republic. In 1821, Mexico's eleven-year struggle for independence at last concluded with the creation of the First Mexican Empire (1822–1823). This conservative government, modeled on Spanish monarchical rule, lasted just eighteen months, before being replaced with a constitutional republic.

Though republican government prevailed for the rest of the decade and beyond, it too faced deep divisions. Esteva worked for both types of government, first under Emperor Agustín Iturbide and then under President Guadalupe Victoria (1824–1829). This experience situates him as a key witness to the fundamental political shifts of Mexico's early years and to the economic difficulties faced by a new nation racked by war debt and thus desperate to mint currency.

Early Years

Esteva grew up during the waning years of the Spanish Empire in the Americas. As an adolescent, he witnessed the hemispheric expansion of enlightenment philosophy and struggles for independence. His experiences during these formative years shaped his political outlook and commitment to liberal government. Esteva was born in 1782 in Veracruz on the Gulf of Mexico, which for centuries served as the main point of entry and departure for New Spain. His family's business was connected to Atlantic commerce, as were most other enterprises in Veracruz. When he reached adulthood, Esteva joined his family's ventures, specializing in the import of books. He also had a responsibility to maintain his family's social connections, which required that he participate in local government. By 1809, Esteva was an important municipal council officer.

Esteva's business and political associates avidly followed the events that swept through the Revolutionary Atlantic, and they harkened the call for liberty, equality, and fraternity. Even though Esteva served in the loyalist local militia during Mexico's fight for independence, he later insisted that he had quietly supported the rebels' cause from the beginning, likely having backed the insurgency with financial assistance. For merchants like Esteva and his colleagues, the cause of liberty meant free trade and popular sovereignty, much as it had in the original thirteen colonies. During the colonial era, the Spanish Crown had restricted trade greatly in New Spain, prohibiting Mexican merchants, with few exceptions, from trading with any country other than Spain. Even trade between New Spain and Spain's other American kingdoms was generally proscribed. Independence portended an end to colonial monopolies and an expansion of local industry and commerce.

This chapter focuses on the last decade of Esteva's life, from Mexican independence in 1821, through his years as secretary of the Treasury, to his premature death in 1830. During the war for independence, Esteva, like many other local government officials, remained in the service of Spain. Toward the end of the war, for example, Esteva protected the Fort of San Juan

Ulúa from the forces that supported the soon-to-be emperor Iturbide. When driven from Veracruz, Esteva's militia were no longer bound by their mission to defend the city for the Crown. At this point Esteva saw that revolutionary change was truly possible and switched his allegiance to the independence cause.

A political survivor, much like his fellow statesman from Veracruz Antonio López de Santa Anna (the protagonist of chapter 5), Esteva remained an important figure even as the political environment shifted from Spanish, to imperial, to republican control. By January 1822, his hometown of Veracruz had elected him deputy to the First Constituent Congress, where he helped run the national government during Iturbide's short reign. Then, after proclamation of the federal republic in October 1824, Congress appointed him secretary of the Treasury with the support of Guadalupe Victoria, the first president of Mexico.

Historians have tended to overlook the similarities between the wars of independence in the United States and Mexico, often suggesting that the thirteen British colonies were far more radicalized than the provinces of New Spain. In reality, "rebels" in both nations followed similar trajectories and pursued the same goal: acquiring and wielding political and economic sovereignty. Just as many in the British colonies were content with monarchical politics and conservative trade, royalists in Mexico balked at supporting the revolutionary movement led by Father Miguel Hidalgo y Costilla, who gave his famous "Cry of Dolores" in the summer of 1810: "Long live our Lady of Guadalupe! Death to Bad Government! Death to the Peninsular Spaniards!" This moment was akin to the opening volleys at Lexington and Concord. While the movement for independence swept a vast number of colonists into the fight, just as in the United States, many Mexicans, particularly among the elite, held firm to their loyalty to their king. In the end, Mexicans from all levels of society fought Spanish troops for eleven years with the ultimate end of securing their freedom from monarchy, just as the American rebels had during their war for independence. And like delegates to the earlier U.S. Continental Congress, insurgent Mexican leaders struggled to fund their fight. In both conflicts, patriots ultimately fell back on the same tactic: they simply made money.

Wartime Money

Prior to the war, Mexico had been the largest producer of silver coins in the world, averaging slightly more than 20 million Spanish pesos annually between 1801 and 1810. The war for independence put a stop to this kind of output. The mines surrounding the city of Guanajuato, for example, which produced silver and gold to the value of MX$5.3 million per annum prior to the war, afterward yielded just MX$1 million per year. Mines were left unmanned as residents were called up to fight in the war or forced to flee in the face of encroaching armies. Pumping equipment, left untended, allowed the shafts to flood, ruining mining equipment. Some mines were intentionally destroyed in an effort to deny their treasures to the enemy. Mexico's ability to extract silver and produce coins plummeted. Nor were great stockpiles of silver on hand. Before the ouster of the Spaniards, the colonial economy had been largely extractive, designed to get money back to Spain rather than keep it in the colony. Additionally, much of the specie not sent directly to Spain was either directed elsewhere abroad to pay for imports, or hoarded by wealthy institutions. A shortage of money quickly became a problem for all sides, but especially for the insurgent movements.

With little access to silver, the insurgents issued fiat coins made from nearly valueless metal. Fiat coins have a legal face value but no inherent value (i.e., contain no precious metal). Insurgents simply declared that their coins had to be accepted as though they were made of silver or gold. The coins operated on the same principle that underlay Continentals during the war for independence in the United States. The insurgents made a promise of their future strength, insisting that holders would be able to trade in their fiat coins for specie after the war was over. Wartime promises, however, are hard to keep. As readers will remember, Continentals lost their value, and the government failed almost entirely to redeem them in silver. The same was true in wartime Mexico, where locals were never certain if the coins they received in exchange for goods needed by the army would ever have their promised value.

The various insurgents issued coins similar to Spanish coins in order to borrow on the trust held by pieces-of-eight. Hidalgo, for example, set up a provisional mint in the city of Valladolid to make silver pesos but obviously not backed by Spain. Father José María Morelos, who succeeded Hidalgo, similarly decreed the issuance of insurgent currency. Morelos, however, lacked silver (Hidalgo had seized some bullion early in the war), so he had the coins made of copper. Morelos also ordered that they be as close in size as possible to the silver coins in circulation (see figure 3.2). His decree stated, "In order that this copper money receive the same exchange value as that of gold and silver, it must meet the following requisites: each piece must conform as to size and thickness with the current silver coins of similar face value."[2] Morelos knew that part of what confers faith in currency is its reliability and that matching the size and shape of the Spanish coins made

Figure 3.2. Morelos's eight-*real* coin carried none of the imagery of Spanish dollars. The face bore a bow and arrow above the word SOUTH to announce that it was the coin of Morelos's insurgent army. On the back, a simple design of curled lines, the coin's value, and the date were far more austere than the pillar dollars of the Spanish Empire. Yet these coins were deliberate copies of the size, shape, and feel of valuable currency, even down to the reeded edge stamped into the face of the coin, despite the fact that there was no risk of anyone clipping copper from the edges.
Source: "Moneda de Morelos tipo SUD (8 reales, cobre)" (1814). Original in Casa de Moneda de México. Museo Numismatico Nacional. Photography by T. Seijas. Reproduction authorized by the Secretaría de Hacienda y Crédito Público, México.

his own feel like real money. Unlike Hidalgo, Morelos openly decreed that the insurgent's money was not Spanish but revolutionary. It might feel like Spanish money but was not meant to look like it. On one side of the coin there was a bow and arrow with the word SUD (south), indicating the directional origin of his army; on the reverse were inscribed the coin's value of eight *reales* and the year.

Mexican royalists controlled the mint (*casa de moneda*) in Mexico City, but they also required more coinage than they could easily produce. The insurgents often prevented them from accessing the silver mines. As a result, ten provisional branch mints opened during the war to allow the coining of Spanish dollars in places where silver was available. The general upheaval of the war and the royalists' desperate need for money pushed the regional mints to produce coins of highly varied quality. The provisional mint in Chihuahua, for example, had to cast rather than stamp its coins because it lacked the proper machinery. Poorly regulated mints, acting under emergency conditions, also produced coins with varying silver content. As war upended life in the country, it also weakened the trustworthiness of all coins.

Starting from Scratch: 1821–1823

Mexico at last secured its independence from the Spanish Empire in 1821 under the leadership of Agustín Iturbide, a classically conservative leader born to wealth and privilege. Iturbide had been a successful commander in the Spanish army, much like George Washington had been in the British army. Like Washington, Iturbide also shifted his allegiance from the king to the patriot cause. The comparison, however, ends there. Iturbide only changed sides to fight for independence after Spanish junior officers, tired of fighting in the Americas, forced Ferdinand VII to accept a liberal constitution. Iturbide's revolutionary intention was to preserve a conservative monarchy. After the restored Spanish king Ferdinand VII declined Iturbide's offer to trade the rule of Spain for that of Mexico, he had himself crowned emperor. Iturbide succeeded in securing independence for Mexico but made a terrible mistake that wreaked havoc on the new nation's economy. He permitted Spanish loyalists to leave the country with all of their wealth, including the cash value for the land that they could not take with them. The new emperor would face an enormous challenge in holding together a government with no money.

Among Iturbide's first efforts to garner support for his reign was the issuance of new coins that adhered to the stylistic traditions of Spanish colonial coins. Engravers simply substituted a bust of Iturbide for that of the Spanish king and preserved the absolutist sentiment that a leader "appointed by god" led Mexico. The words AUGUSTIN I DEI O PROVIDENTIA (Agustín I by divine providence) encircled the face of the coin (see figure 3.3). On the reverse, Iturbide replaced the Pillars of Hercules with a much more Mexican image: an eagle perched on a cactus, which drew on Mexican native mythology. This eagle wore an imperial crown, reinforcing the message that independent Mexico remained a centralized monarchy, as it had been under Spain.

In Mexico and the United States national symbols on coins unintentionally reflected the weakness of the newborn states. Benjamin Franklin derided the first U.S. dollars for their unflattering image of an eagle. The same criticism held true for Iturbide's coins. The eagle was rather scrawny and poorly proportioned and thus unable to convey the strength of a powerful new state. In the case of Mexico, the first imperial eagle was prescient, as Iturbide's government survived less than a year after the coin was issued. No matter what the coins looked like, the Mexican government simply could not make enough of them, a problem faced by our protagonist Esteva over the decade to come.

Figure 3.3. The eight-*real* coins issued by Iturbide pictured above followed many of the conventions of Spanish dollars. Iturbide's profile was substituted for that of the Spanish king. The Mexican coins retained the use of Latin, proclaiming Iturbide to be divinely ordained to rule Mexico. The reverse of the coin, on the other hand, bore distinctly Mexican imagery, with an eagle perched on a cactus. The eagle wore a crown to emphasize the monarchical system of government, and the legend MEXICO'S FIRST CONSTITUTIONAL EMPEROR encircled the image.
Source: "Agustín I. 8 Reales" (1822). Original in Queens College Loan Collection, CM.QC.4927-R. Reproduction by permission of the Syndics of the Fitzwilliam Museum, Cambridge, United Kingdom.

A country that had once minted millions of coins found itself unable to make enough of them to pay the costs of running the government, to say nothing of repaying the enormous foreign debts incurred during the war. The Mexican Treasury acknowledged a debt of MX$45 million in 1822. Financing government payment of debts had similarly plagued Mexico's northern neighbor decades earlier; the U.S. government had an estimated national debt amounting to more than US$54 million in 1790. Gaining independence obviously incurred heavy costs.

In the case of Mexico, Iturbide's administration turned to printing money as a fix for the new nation's severe cash shortage. In December 1822, the emperor authorized the issuance of paper notes (see figure 3.4). These first bills were very simple, printed only on one side. Denominated in one, two, and ten pesos, they were meant to supplant the insufficient production of silver coins, which simply could not meet the demands of daily commerce. To many, the issuance of paper money demonstrated that Iturbide was ill equipped to lead the nation. In 1823, numerous generals once aligned with the emperor, including Santa Anna, led a successful rebellion against him. Unfortunately, ousting the emperor and reconstituting the government failed to repair the country's desperate financial situation.

Minting Mexico's Independence ~ 55

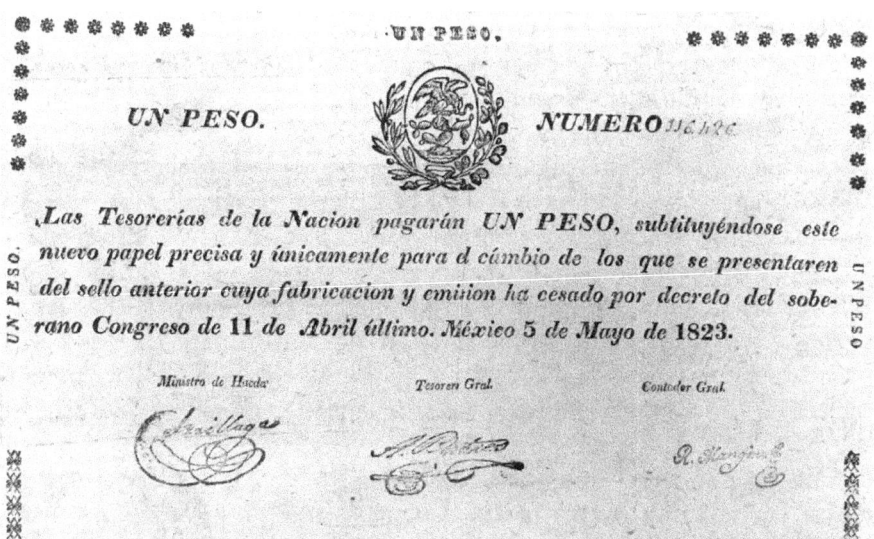

Figure 3.4. The first paper notes issued by an independent Mexico were very simple certificates, printed only on one side. They bore an image of the Mexican eagle and stars at the margin to impart some sense of authority. Congress approved the printing of thousands such notes, each individually numbered to prevent fraud. According to the Mexican Treasury, they held the value of one silver peso.
Source: "Un peso, numero 116,426. Exhibición sobre el papel moneda." Original in Casa de Moneda de México. Museo Numismatico Nacional. Photography by T. Seijas. Reproduction authorized by the Secretaría de Hacienda y Crédito Público, México.

Minting Coins in Republican Mexico: 1823–1829

The provisional government that replaced Iturbide established a republic comprised of the United Mexican States. Ideological divisions that plagued Mexican politics for the next half century appeared during the war for independence and gained traction afterward during debates regarding the establishment of a federal form of government. The national citizenry was not even unified in support of a republic. Conservatives of various stripes (called Centralists) sought to maintain Spain's system of highly centralized authority, to the point that some even called for a restoration of the monarchy. Liberals (called Federalists), on the other hand, advocated for a broader distribution of powers. Readers will note that the names and allegiances of these constituencies differed somewhat from those in the U.S. political context, where the Federalists (party of Alexander Hamilton) of the early national period favored a strong central government and good relations with Great Britain, while the Jeffersonian Republicans supported republicanism (a federative relationship between the national and state governments), which left more power in the hands of the individual states.

In Mexico, Centralists argued that the move toward federalism stemmed from thoughtless emulation of the United States. In addition, they feared that federalism would lead to tensions between the Mexican states, where allegiance to Mexico City varied, especially on the frontiers. In the worst-case scenario, peripheral states, if given too much authority, might seek to separate from the country—which indeed happened in the case of Texas. Despite such criticisms, the Federalists' position held sway, though frictions remained. The First Federal Republic, proclaimed in October 1823, ushered in a period of great political instability.

The provisional federalist government sought to express the republican nature of the United Mexican States by redesigning the country's coinage. Iturbide's bust was removed. After a long debate, much as had happened in the United States, the Mexican Congress voted to place a representation of liberty on the country's coins. The image was both abstract and unmistakably clear. A liberty cap sat at the center, with the word LIBERTAD (liberty) across its brow (see figure 3.5). The face of the coin also included two distinct and important features.[3] One was the value of the coin, 8R, or eight *reales*. Republican Mexico chose to use the same denominations as Spanish coins. Unlike the United States, the provisional government felt no need to revolutionize the way Mexico's coins were counted. A new system of rule would suffice. The other notable feature on the face was a pair of numbers, such as 10D 20G, which indicated the fineness of the coin's silver content.[4] On the reverse, Iturbide's imperial eagle gave way to a considerably more robust one that no longer wore a crown. The more powerful looking bird extended its wings beneath the phrase REPUBLICA MEXICANA (Mexican Republic).

The United Mexican States now had attractive coins, but the provisional government still lacked revenue to meet its expenses. The printing of paper notes had to continue as an artificial replacement for real revenue. But first, the provisional government denounced Iturbide's paper notes, denied all responsibility for redeeming them, and issued new notes. To confer greater legitimacy to these bills, the backs bore copies of papal bulls. Regardless, Mexico's new paper money garnered little trust among the public, much like banknotes in the United States. The production of paper money ceased by 1824. No matter how short the supply of silver, paper was clearly not the solution.

Figure 3.5. Sunbeams radiate from behind the liberty cap on the face of this republican coin, suggesting that the power of the state emanated from the promise of liberty. The imagery is an example of the kind of monetary nationalism that characterized the first coins of both the United States and Mexico. The numbers on the left announce the silver content of the coin.
Source: "Resplendor republicano, 8 reales, plata" (Zacatecas, 1833). Original at the Museo Zacatecano, Zacatecas. Photography by T. Seijas. Reproduction authorized by the Secretaría de Hacienda y Crédito Público, México.

Mexico looked abroad to remedy its money crisis. During Iturbide's reign, the government had opened negotiations with London banking houses to secure loans to run the country and keep up with existing foreign debt payments. Iturbide was out of office before the first loan came through, but the provisional government saw the same need for outside money. Though harshly critical of its high-interest terms, Esteva, as member of Congress's Treasury Commission, voted to accept the loan based on absolute necessity—the government had to pay its bills. In the summer of 1824, the London banking house of Goldschmitt and Company loaned Mexico MX$3.6 million. In August that same year, the Mexican government negotiated another loan of an additional MX$16 million. These two first English loans hung over Mexico for decades, haunting the government as late as 1862. The two banking houses that issued them both failed within a few years, but the debts survived and later justified the occupation of Veracruz by English, Spanish, and French forces.

Federalism and the Treasury

Despairing of the economy, the provisional government gladly completed its handoff to the new constitutional state in October 1824, with Guadalupe Victoria elected as Mexico's first president. A Federalist, Victoria fervently opposed the centralism that had governed New Spain and Imperial Mexico. According to Victoria, "The treasury in all countries is the barometer of its wealth and aggrandizement," meaning that the institution was a symbol of the nation's strength and future potential.[5] Its direction had to rest in the hands of a capable statesman. At this point Esteva joined Victoria's efforts to straighten out the Mexican economy, accepting the position of secretary of Treasury. Esteva undoubtedly hoped that his months in the provisional government would guide his path.

Esteva faced a tremendous task. The records of the Treasury itself were woefully incomplete, and the few he found were dispiriting. In January 1825, he issued a fairly bleak report on the current state of Mexican finances. His preamble began, "Our political situation this year has dawned as dark as the last one closed."[6] The overcast dawn metaphor drew attention to the economy. The net revenues for the nation were less than one-half of expenditures. Beyond the lack of income, Esteva also reported that poor management and outright corruption plagued government finances.

Esteva's belief in a strong central government aligned him with similar thinkers beyond the borders of Mexico. His political identity as a Federalist dovetailed with his membership in a particular branch of Freemasonry. Fraternal associations, popular among elites on both sides of the Atlantic, were deeply political in Mexico.[7] Freemasons who held to conservative/centralist political beliefs claimed membership in a branch of Freemasonry known as the Scottish Rite Order; those who favored the liberal/federalist model, or more decentralized government, belonged to the York Rite Order. President Guadalupe Victoria's appointment of Esteva to lead the Yorks signaled his trust and suggests the importance that this society played in Mexican politics.

Liberal Masons like Esteva had ready-made connections with similarly minded Freemasons in the United States. Esteva, for example, was good friends with Joel Roberts Poinsett, U.S. minister to Mexico and a liberal Freemason, who secured charters from the New York Grand Lodge to found the York Rite Order in Mexico. Both Esteva and Poinsett employed their connections with this Masonic organization to coalesce support behind the Federalist government. Esteva's alliance with Poinsett, however, came to an end during negotiations for the Treaty of Amity, Navigation, and Commerce between the United States of America and the United Mexican States, which began in 1826. The United States, to Esteva's way of thinking, had an unfair advantage in demanding terms. The two men, once joined by republican ideals and Masonic fellowship, fell out over their own national allegiances.

Esteva's liberal/federalist philosophy shaped his decisions at the Treasury Department from the outset of his tenure. During the reign of Emperor Iturbide, former colonial officials ran the Treasury and initially sought to maintain, albeit unsuccessfully, the highly centralized system of the royal Treasury, which controlled all state revenue. As a Federalist and functionary of a new republican government, Esteva pushed for a less integrated model.

Esteva was a pragmatist rather than an economic theorist, so his greatest contribution was to organize the Treasury's administrative structure and make it a truly federal institution.[8] Quite dramatically, his first initiative was to call for a completely new organization of the Treasury system; all existing Treasury offices were eliminated and replaced with new positions. General commissioners in new regional offices were charged with implementing changes at the state level. These officials reported to both the state governor and the ministry in Mexico City as a checks-and-balances measure.

At the same time, Esteva recruited experienced accountants and other fiscal administrators to work at the national Treasury, where they staffed newly revamped offices, including the federal accounting department, national mint, and several other departments. Esteva was a hands-on leader throughout the implementation of this new administrative structure, writing a vast number of letters and notices to his officials, both in Mexico and at the offices of the general commissioners, to whom he provided detailed instructions on their individual duties and responsibilities. No detail seemed to escape his notice.

The federalist/liberal model also required that the nation's revenue be divided between the federal government and the states. The problem for Esteva and the national Treasury, however, was that general commissioners (at the state level) collected and administered a much larger percentage of that revenue, derived mainly from local rents and taxes. The federal government, by contrast, primarily relied on trade tariffs, as well as internal custom/transport duties (such as tolls on canals and certain roads). These revenue sources mirrored those of the federal government of the United States.

Political fractures in Mexico, however, did not allow for the economic activity (a high level of imports, for example) that enabled the U.S. federal government to raise significant revenue (so much so that it had paid off the national debt by 1835).

In the postwar context, Mexico's imports and exports remained quite low, requiring additional measures to augment revenue. Esteva attempted to restore taxes on foreign mining operations. His brand of liberalism promoted individual economic autonomy, while also favoring restraints on private interests for the sake of the greater good. Taxing businesses would be a means of securing public funds. Esteva's opponents, however, argued that foreign companies had to be exempt from taxation before they would invest in reopening Mexico's mines. Given these constraints, Esteva spent much of his time in office figuring out how to secure other revenue streams to pay for the Treasury's main responsibilities: covering the costs of the federal bureaucracy and strengthening the standing army.

Revealing the fierce partisanship that gripped Mexico in the 1820s, Esteva published an autobiographical essay titled "Analytical Expression" in 1827, with dozens of accompanying documents that sought to defend his work at the Treasury.[9] The work begins with a quotation from Cicero about the rectitude of reflecting on one's conduct, not for praise, but to vindicate one's actions. The essay responded to newspaper editorials in the *Sun* questioning his administration of the national patrimony. Esteva's self-defense, articulated in the most patriotic of terms, shed light on his fiscal priorities as well as contemporary conceptions about the role of the Treasury.

Esteva prioritized the creation of a strong military—a justifiable position given that the Spanish government refused to acknowledge Mexican independence and retained control of the Fort of San Juan Ulúa in Veracruz. During his first year in office, Esteva employed Treasury funds in an effort to secure Mexico's claim to its territorial waters. His enemies, however, quickly denounced this spending, especially the purchase of warships from England and the United States. At one point, Esteva left Mexico City for Veracruz to marshal men from merchant ships to help sustain a blockade of the fort, but his critics saw even this decision as suspect, interpreting his concern for Veracruz as a signal that he felt a stronger allegiance to his home city than to the welfare of the federal government. Spain's capitulation and the ouster of Spanish troops from the fort later that year in 1825 vindicated Esteva's decisions but also demonstrated that Mexico had to continue to invest in defense. The threat of foreign interventions remained a constant in Mexico through the 1860s.

Esteva took an active part in drafting the legislation that established the Mexican Treasury and detailed the secretary's responsibilities: mainly securing revenue, supervising expenditures, and overseeing the production of currency. In terms of this last task, Esteva directed that the federal mint in Mexico City would have complete jurisdiction over its branches, from dictating the quantity of coins produced to naming the regional assayers. In the United States, by contrast, the foundation of the federal mint in Philadelphia predated the opening of branch mints by three decades. Esteva instituted this surprisingly centralized model (from the perspective of a political federalist) because the coinage minted in the provinces during the war had suffered greatly from a lack of oversight. Coinage needed to be uniform. It was additionally essential for the federal government to control the production of money.

Esteva understood that mints were money factories and required hands-on management to ensure quality control. In this regard he also valued maintaining the loyalty of men who worked at the mint. As such, Esteva advocated secure retirements, for example, at a time when the government was struggling even to pay military pensions. In December 1824, the Mexican Congress agreed to grant employees "who had faithfully served the Mint" for twenty years one-third of their salary in disability. Making coins was a fine art and delicate business, so encouraging future employees with this kind of benefit was a necessity. In addition, Esteva felt that the nation had to uphold its obligations and look after those who had served it well.

Esteva also sought to increase production of the liberty cap coins so necessary to paying the nation's bills, for example by purchasing new mint presses from France. But these additions were never enough. Mexico's national infrastructure was underdeveloped and damaged by years of war. The cost of supporting a military to prevent the return of the Spanish ate up much of the little money available. Necessity raised the national debt. By 1827, the Treasury was unable to service its foreign debt, marking Mexico's first default.

Conclusion

Esteva died prematurely in 1830 at age forty-seven, having lived through the most dramatic events in early Mexican history. He witnessed a reversal of fortune of almost unimaginable scope when the war turned Mexico from the world's silver mine into a country reliant on paper money. The transformation even shocked Mexico's northern neighbor, which depended on Mexican bullion to support its own economy. On August 2, 1823, the *Niles' Weekly Register*, a national magazine out of Baltimore, ran the headline "'Paper money in the land of silver!' Yes, because domestic industry does not prosper."[10] The implication, of course, was that it would take U.S. entrepreneurs to make Mexico prosper. Esteva's conservative colleagues would no doubt have agreed, as they lobbied the liberal government to grant concessions to foreign mining interests. Esteva, by contrast, pushed for domestic initiatives.

When Mexico secured its independence, like the United States before it, the nation had to confront monumental challenges. The countries' constitutions enshrined republican democracy, and both designed coins that broadcast liberty as their guiding principle. Unfortunately, the sister republics were only too soon at odds. Readers will learn about their first major crisis in Texas in the following chapter.

Notes

1. All quotations are from J. I. Esteva, *Apuntaciones que el ciudadano José Ignacio Esteva al separarse del despacho del Ministerio de Hacienda entrega a su succesor el ecsmo señor D. Tomás Salgado* (México: Imp. del Aguila, 1827).

2. Quoted in A. F. Pradeau, *Numismatic History of Mexico from the Pre-Columbian Epoch to 1823* (Los Angeles, CA: Western Printing Company, 1938).

3. The face of the coins also showed the year and location of minting, as well as the initials of the assayer.

4. D stood for *dineros* and G for *granos* (a *grano* was the equivalent of 1/24 of a *dinero*). Twelve *dineros* was a means of representing pure silver. In the example, 10D 20G indicates 902.77-thousandths fine.

5. Quoted in L. Ludlow, ed., *Los secretarios de hacienda y sus proyectos: 1821–1933* (México: UNAM, 2002).

6. Quoted in W. F. McCaleb, *The Public Finances of Mexico* (New York, Harper & Bros., 1921).

7. Father Hidalgo y Costilla and many other independence leaders were Freemasons. Freemasons date their history from fifteenth-century Europe; the fraternal organizations arrived in New Spain during the colonial era, when the Holy Office banned them as anti-Catholic.

8. L. Jáuregui, "Control administrativo y crédito exterior bajo la administración de José Ignacio Esteva," in *Los secretarios de hacienda y sus proyectos: 1821–1933*, ed. L. Ludlow (México: UNAM, 2002).

9. J. I. Esteva, *Rasgo analítico* (México: Imprenta del Aguila, 1827).

10. "Foreign News," *Niles' Weekly Register*, August 2, 1823.

CHAPTER FOUR

North America's Third Republic

On December 13, 1844, former president of the Republic of Texas Sam Houston turned over a pay warrant to the secretary of the Texas Treasury. The check, written out to him for $1,623.89 (Texas dollars), represented about one-third of Houston's annual salary.[1] It was an exceptional transaction because Houston was actually able to cash it and receive the amount in gold. In theory, all notes, warrants, checks, bills, and other paper instruments issued by the Republic of Texas were redeemable in gold or silver. The reality on the ground was quite different. During its brief nine years as an independent nation, Texas was bereft of hard currency. There simply was nowhere near enough bullion in the country to pay the expenses of nationhood, much less for the government of Texas to produce its own coins. Despite various efforts, the government of Texas ultimately failed to mint a nation.

The protagonist of this chapter is Sam Houston, two-time president of the Republic of Texas (see figure 4.1); the money is a series of paper promises. When it secured its independence in 1836, Texas became the third nation in North America to embrace republican governance. What can this short-lived country tell us about the importance of creating a reliable currency? And what does it reveal about the developing relationship between Mexico and the United States?

Figure 4.1. Sam Houston, pictured here in his fifties, had already been a U.S. congressman, governor of Tennessee, and twice president of the Republic of Texas—an extraordinary political career. His expression is that of an accomplished man, satisfied with the course he has helped chart for Texas.
Source: "Sam Houston" (circa 1848). Print. Prints and Photographs Division, Library of Congress, LC-DIG-pga-03993. Public Domain.

Sam Houston: Tennessee Days

Sam Houston's childhood in Virginia and Tennessee during the birth of the United States provided the conditions that honed his political mind and military talent, both of which served him well as a leader in Texas. Houston was born in Virginia on March 2, 1793, two days before fellow Virginian George Washington was inaugurated as president of the United States for the second time. Houston's father (also named Samuel) passed on his own patriotism, having served as an officer in a rifle company during the American Revolution, but was otherwise a problematic role model. In the early 1800s, after going bankrupt, he decided to leave his debts behind and relocate the family to Maryville, Tennessee, near his kin, on the western side of the great Smokey Mountains. Regrettably, the elder Houston died soon after, leaving his young family to make the move alone to their new home. Decades later, when the younger Sam emigrated from the United States to Texas, he followed in his father's footsteps, leaving behind unpaid debts in his homeland and also taking a position of command in a war for independence.

Houston's historic future was hardly preordained, though as a young boy he did nurture a romantic fascination for the exploits of the heroes of the Trojan War. Biographers repeatedly echo the claim that young Houston memorized Homer's *Iliad*, often wandering into the woods to read it in solitude. As a young man, Houston wandered further afield. Disinclined to work as a clerk in the family store, he would instead disappear into the woods for days at a time. Then, when he was sixteen, he ran away from home to live with a Cherokee community roughly eighty miles southwest of Maryville. Adopted by Cherokee chief Oo loo te ka, he stayed for three years. Houston later was sympathetic toward Native Americans—a sentiment notably absent among many of his contemporaries.

Houston took his first steps toward leadership in 1812, when he joined to fight in the U.S. war with Great Britain. He entered the army as an enlisted man and left the service as a lieutenant, having distinguished himself for his bravery and military prowess. Following a brief and successful career in law, Houston turned to politics, which would occupy most of the rest of his life. By 1822, he was a U.S. congressional representative from Tennessee and in 1829 became the governor of that state. Houston was only thirty-four years old when his trajectory intersected with that of Texas.

Texas before and after Independence

Texas's history as an independent nation must be understood in the context of Spanish colonialism and Mexican independence. Located on the remote northern frontier of the Viceroyalty of New Spain, the region then known as Tejas never attracted a significant number of settlers, partly due to the political strength of native societies, which openly resisted the colonists. Instead, Spanish colonists preferred to concentrate in urban centers to the south. In the late seventeenth century, the Spanish Crown funded missions and presidios in eastern Texas to convert and "civilize" the indigenous population and also to prevent other European powers from encroaching on the territory (see figure 4.2).

Despite Spanish hopes, the region never developed strong commercial or political ties to the colonial capital at Mexico City. Instead, it grew increasingly separate from the national center, developing its own cultural identity;

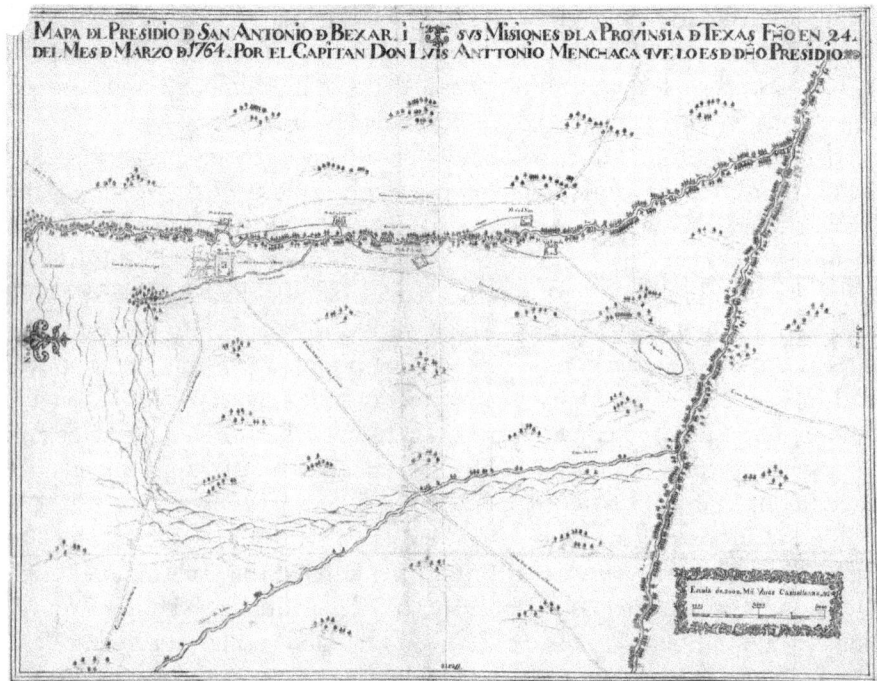

Figure 4.2. This map shows the topographical orientation of San Antonio de Bexar presidio and connected mission churches. The Spanish government had a number of such fortified outposts built during the second half of the eighteenth century to shore up New Spain's northern frontier. The presidio was meant to protect Catholic missions from Native American raids, as well as to discourage encroachment by the French, English, and eventually the United States. The mission, later known as the Alamo, was the site of various battles during the Texas Revolution.
Source: "Plan del presidio de San Antonio de Bejar, de la Provincia de Texas," by Luis Antonio Menchaca (1764). Map Collection. Courtesy of the John Carter Brown Library at Brown University.

residents also became ever more frustrated with the central government, which did little to integrate the region. After Mexican independence, this political dissatisfaction turned Texans inward, as residents sought to find local solutions to problems like the constant shortage of hard currency.

Texas's geographical isolation from major Spanish settlements meant that the territory only ever received small amounts of national currency, be it Spanish or later Mexican. The royal mint was hundreds of miles away in Mexico City, and much of the coinage produced there soon exited the country. Consequently, underpopulated and peripheral regions like Texas were chronically short of cash.

During Mexico's fight for independence, nine additional mints opened across New Spain, but all available currency at that point went to meeting the extraordinary costs of war. By 1821, the newly independent Mexican national government was bankrupt. The nation held enormous mineral wealth, but the extraction of silver was almost at a standstill. This shortage of hard currency and the overall precariousness of Mexican finances had a debilitating effect on local economies in outlying regions like Texas, Upper California, and New Mexico.

The lack of money in Texas, as elsewhere, necessitated substitutes for coins. In 1822, the governor was forced to issue paper currency to pay soldiers. This regional scrip was Mexico's first paper money. Apart from these provisional notes, the few coins in use consisted of old Spanish dollars, or pieces-of-eight, circulated widely in Mexico, sometimes with a counterstamp marking them as Mexican rather than Spanish, sometimes not. Notably, Spanish dollars also remained legal coinage in the United States, from where they also found their way into Texas, as did southern U.S. banknotes and a small number of gold coins. Texans nonetheless conducted daily commerce primarily through credit and barter.

Mexico experienced grave challenges in the years immediately following independence, including the task of joining disparate regions into a federal republic and warding off U.S. territorial expansion. The republic's 1824 Constitution theoretically bound its nineteen states into the United Mexican States, but it also limited the power of the executive and provided considerable autonomy to the states. States like Texas and New Mexico held fiercely to that independence over the course of the next decade, thwarting efforts in Mexico City to strengthen the national government. The growing United States also represented a persistent menace to Mexico's national territory.

To defend its claim to Texas and the northern frontier, the Mexican government resolved to give much of it away to foreign settlers. Like the United

States, Mexico sought to rectify the demographic problem of having an underpopulated frontier through immigration. Native Americans, of course, lived in the region but were not Mexican citizens; nor did many of them wish to become so. Thus, Mexico passed new immigration laws in 1823 and 1824 to increase the population of "civilized" people on its northern frontier. It aimed to develop the agricultural potential of the region, expand commerce, and remove the indigenous population. Through these measures the government intended to establish a buffer zone between northern Mexico and the United States. Foreign immigration had augmented the population of the United States quite effectively since independence, so officials hoped the same strategy would work for Mexico.

The idea of bolstering the Texas population through U.S. immigration dates to the last days of Spanish control in New Spain. Moses Austin, a onetime resident of the United States who had previously attempted a settlement scheme in Missouri when it was under Spanish control, negotiated a new program with the Spanish government in 1820. Austin had planned to oversee the settlement of Anglo-Americans in Spanish Texas but died of pneumonia within the year. At this point, his son Stephen took up this role, organizing a party of settlers. By the time they arrived in the region, however, Spain no longer controlled its North American colony. Fortunately, Mexico was equally interested in populating its northern territory.

Mexico sanctioned a colonization program based on individual settlement zones overseen by *empresarios* (settlement agents or recruiters)—organizers who would contract to settle families in the Texas territories. The settlement law granted a unit of 177 acres (called a *labor*) of farmland to each married man and as much as 4,251 acres (a *sitio*) to those who wished to raise cattle. In return for this land, the Mexican government required that the settler pay US$2.50 per unirrigable *labor* or US$3.50 per irrigable *labor* within six years of settlement (roughly 1.4 to 1.9 cents per acre). *Empresarios*, for their part, were paid in land, receiving a premium of 23,025 acres for each group of one hundred families brought to Texas. All settlers were required to become citizens of Mexico and to prove that they were Catholics of good moral character. All business in these settlements was to be conducted in Spanish. It fell upon the *empresario* to ensure that he brought in only people who would respect the cultural and legal norms of the nation of Mexico.

The foreign-settlement policy worked to the extent that it swelled the population of Texas. Tens of thousands of settlers from the United States entered the territory during the 1820s. The Panic of 1819, and the depressed economy left in its wake, spurred Americans westward, particularly those interested in escaping debts in the United States. Settlers and their *empresario* leaders were all too happy to capitalize on the opportunity for cheap land, so they gladly swore to uphold the laws of their adopted country.

Immigration did not end up bolstering Mexican claims to Texas, contrary to the Mexican government's hopes. Instead, the influx of immigrants from the United States created an Anglicized population tied more closely to New Orleans and the United States than to the national capital in Mexico City. Few of the settlers from the United States spoke Spanish; most were Protestants of some form.

Texas became an Anglo-dominated territory. Tellingly, *empresario* Green DeWitt issued paper notes for his colony denominated in U.S. dollars rather than Mexican pesos.[2] His paper money, while indicative of *empresarios*' U.S. ties, also underlined Texas's coin shortage. The region's tendency was to fall back on printing paper rather than minting money.

Mexico had supported foreign immigration as a means of securing its northern border, intending for settlers to transform this underpopulated region into a productive Mexican state that could stimulate the economy and act as a bulwark against challenges to Mexico's national sovereignty. Unfortunately, the policy of welcoming immigrants from the United States had exactly the opposite effect. Texas became even more disconnected from the capital in Mexico City and came to identify quite strongly with the greatest threat to Mexico's northern territory: the United States.

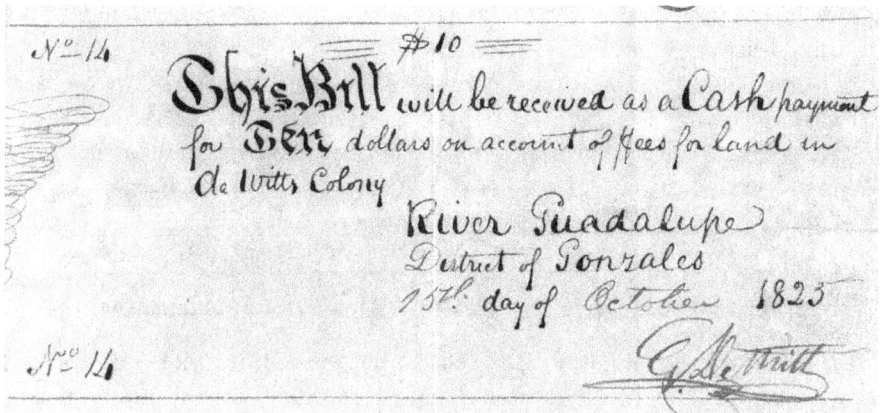

Figure 4.3. This ten-dollar note was handwritten for use in the Mexican settlement of empresario Green DeWitt. These simple notes, each numbered and signed by DeWitt himself, were denominated in U.S. dollars rather than Mexican pesos—one of several indicators, including the presence of black slaves (in violation of Mexican law), that U.S. immigrants did not sincerely embrace their new Mexican citizenship.
Source: "Green DeWitt Ten Dollars Private Scrip" (River Guadalupe, 1825). Original in the Rowe-Barr Collection of Texas Currency, DEG1791. Courtesy of the DeGolyer Library, Southern Methodist University.

Texas Leaves Mexico

Anglo-American settlers in Texas and the Mexican government became increasingly suspicious of one another as the 1820s wore on. Mexico's 1824 Constitution joined Texas with Coahuila to make one large northeastern state, irritating Texan settlers who felt little historical or cultural allegiance to this new political unit. Anglo-Americans, in fact, felt little loyalty to Mexico as a whole. In 1826, Haden Edwards, a former U.S. senator who had migrated to Mexico, led a rebellion near Nacogdoches, Texas (close to the Louisiana border), to found the independent state of Fredonia. The Mexican army easily put down the rebellion, but it was a worrying sign that Texans might seek to become part of the United States. The U.S. government's offer to purchase Texas from Mexico twice during this period, highlighting the vulnerability of the northern border region, added to suspicions.

Anglo settlers openly ignored the laws of Mexico and served as a destabilizing force as well. Slavery was abolished at Mexican independence, but persistent Texan violations of this prohibition led President Vicente Guerrero to decree the end of slavery once again in 1829. Texans took this act as a direct threat to their commercial practices, which included the production of cotton. By this time Anglo-Americans outnumbered Hispanics by four to one, and Texas was home to more than one thousand slaves. Mexico responded to this demographic reality by passing a law in 1830 banning further immigration from the United States and organizing a countersettlement plan to bring Mexicans and Europeans into the region.

Political and economic ties between Texas and Mexico City were at a breaking point, as Anglo residents, who now referred to themselves as Texians, made all too clear when they began to openly call for independence. The threat to Anglo-Americans' capital, held as slave property, was arguably among the most significant factors that led to Texan succession.

Houston Fights for Texas with Guns and Money

Sam Houston's participation in Texas's final break from Mexico illustrates our protagonist's political astuteness and also points to the inherent danger of funding a war with debt. Houston arrived in Texas in December 1832—two years after Mexico had banned immigration from the United States—amid a regional crisis. That summer, Texian militias skirmished with Mexican forces near Galveston and then drove them out of East Texas after the Battle of Nacogdoches. Texian delegates also held a convention, calling for a repeal of the law banning further U.S. immigration and proposing that

Texas become its own state (apart from Coahuila). Houston was immediately drawn into this political storm. The residents of Nacogdoches elected him as their representative to a second Texas convention in April 1833, where he helped to draft a constitution for the new state of Texas.

Meanwhile, partisan turmoil plagued the Mexican capital, which gave Texas some respite. Mexican troops were occupied with fighting a series of coups that eventually brought General Antonio López de Santa Anna (the protagonist of chapter 5) to the presidency in 1833. A year later, Santa Anna's Plan of Cuernavaca curtailed the autonomy of the states and eliminated regional militias; Texians found both measures intolerable. Next, Santa Anna rescinded the Constitution of 1824, galvanizing eleven of Mexico's nineteen states to openly oppose the man many now considered a dictator. Texas was at the vanguard of this opposition.

In 1835, Nacogdoches sent Houston to San Felipe de Austin as its representative to the Consultation, the representative body of the Texas resistance. The Consultation formally condemned Santa Anna and joined Mexico's other states in demanding the restitution of the Mexican Constitution. The Consultation was not yet calling for Texan independence, but all official reports were notably conducted in English rather than in Spanish (Mexico's official language). Texians were clearly more culturally aligned with the United States than with the country to whom many had sworn fealty only a decade earlier. The Consultation also created a provisional resistance government, with a treasury department that opted to denominate all money in U.S. dollars instead of Mexican pesos. These measures, which so clearly articulated Texians' sense of separateness, were also predictive of what came next.

As had been the case in the U.S. Revolution, fighting began in Texas before the insurgency officially declared its independence. The conflict erupted into war in October 1835, when a detachment of Mexican soldiers arrived at the town of Gonzales to retrieve a cannon left there to fight Comanche raids. Some 140 locals refused to hand it over, reputedly offering the now famous reply, "Come and take it!" in open rebellion. Mexican forces withdrew to the garrison at San Antonio de Béxar (see figure 4.2). War had begun.

While the conflict was unfolding, the nascent Texas government scrambled to secure provisions—from gunpowder to corn—for the fighting forces. The Consultation, again consisting of representatives from the different Texas municipalities, gathered at Austin. The meeting opened with an unfortunate report from the general council: "You may consider that at this moment, the council is out of funds." To pay for the needs of the war, the provisional government voted to secure loans out of New Orleans for

US$200,000 at 8 percent interest. Texas had no silver or gold, so the loans were redeemable in land—the only available resource. As the Consultation noted in an open letter to the people of New Orleans, "Any who embark in our cause, in the army or navy, shall be liberally rewarded in land and money, and in the blessings of a grateful and redeemed people."[3] Lenders received the right to Texas land at fifty cents per acre. Within a week, the Consultation had subscribed loans worth US$7,000. Additionally, the Consultation agreed to pay 640 acres to all men who enlisted for the duration of the conflict and half that amount for those who signed on for three months.[4] Texas soldiers were paid in treasury warrants and headright certificates for land. The new country paid for war with its own territory.

In early 1836, Mexican president Santa Anna crossed the Rio Grande with an army of four thousand men to pacify the area; in doing so, he instigated a Texian call for complete independence. During the most famous battle of the war, Santa Anna defeated the Texians in a twelve-day siege of the Alamo mission, killing 187 men. The Consultation responded to the calamity by declaring Texan independence in March 1836, followed by the adoption of a constitution and the creation of an interim national government. In April, our protagonist, Sam Houston, now a major general of the Texan army, captured Santa Anna at the Battle of San Jacinto. Houston then extracted a treaty from the Mexican president guaranteeing Texan independence. The government in Mexico City, however, quickly deposed Santa Anna and repudiated the treaty in short order. The war was over, but Texas's fate as a republic was altogether unclear.

Houston feared that the nascent republic could not survive on its own, partly due to very real economic concerns. Houston sent a letter to President Andrew Jackson expressing his hope that the United States would annex Texas—a desire that Texan voters overwhelmingly endorsed in a referendum. In fact, many in Texas hoped that independence from Mexico would be just one step on the road to becoming part of the United States. The admission of Texas into the Union, however, was enormously problematic for the United States. Northerners feared that admitting the territory would tip the balance of power in favor of the southern slaveholding states. Southerners, on the other hand, worried that slavery might be banned in Texas territory, thus containing its spread and ultimately reducing the political voice of slaveholding states. Additionally, since Mexico did not recognize Texan independence, U.S. admittance of the rebellious state would surely spark an international conflict. Annexation would not occur until years later. In the meantime, the U.S. government did recognize the independence of the

ANTI-TEXAS MEETING
AT FANEUIL HALL!

Friends of Freedom!

A proposition has been made, and will soon come up for consideration in the United States Senate, to annex Texas to the Union. This territory has been wrested from Mexico by violence and fraud. Such is the character of the leaders in this enterprise that the country has been aptly termed "that valley of rascals." It is large enough to make *nine* or *ten* States as large as Massachusetts. It was, under Mexico, a free territory. The freebooters have made it a slave territory. The design is to annex it, with its load of infamy and oppression, to the Union. The immediate result may be a war with Mexico—the ultimate result *will be* some 18 or 20 more slaveholders in the Senate of the United States, a still larger number in the House of Representatives, and the balance of power in the hands of the South! And if, when in a minority in Congress, slaveholders browbeat the North, demand the passage of gag laws, trample on the Right of Petition, and threaten, in defiance of the General Government, to hang every man, caught at the South, who dares to speak against their "domestic institutions," what limits shall be set to their intolerant demands and high handed usurpations, when they are in the majority?

All opposed to this scheme, of whatever sect or party, are invited to attend the meeting at the Old Cradle of Liberty, to-morrow, (Thursday Jan. 25,) at 10 o'clock, A. M., at which time addresses are expected from several able speakers.

Bostonians! Friends of Freedom!! Let your voices be heard in loud remonstrance against this scheme, fraught with such ruin to yourselves and such infamy to your country.
January 24, 1838.

Figure 4.4. In 1836, newly independent Texas voted to seek annexation by the United States. U.S. public opinion on the annexation was divided. Those opposed believed it would expand the power of slaveholders in the United States and start a war with Mexico. The broadside above called upon Bostonians to meet at Faneuil Hall to oppose "that valley of rascals" who sought to bring new slaveholding territory into the Union. President Martin Van Buren, likely as a result of pressure from abolitionists, chose not to entertain annexation; Texas withdrew its petition in 1838.
Source: "Anti-Texas Meeting at Faneuil Hall! Friends of Freedom!" (1838). Broadside. Original in Prints and Photographs Division, Library of Congress, LC-USZ62-57792. Public Domain.

Republic of Texas—a country that now had to mobilize its few resources to build up military defenses.

Money and Nationhood in North America's New Republic

Texas began its history as an independent nation with severe money problems—a reality that Houston, the republic's first president, lacked the resources to alter. During Houston's tenure, the young country acquired additional and crushing debt. Houston, like his father, was not averse to taking

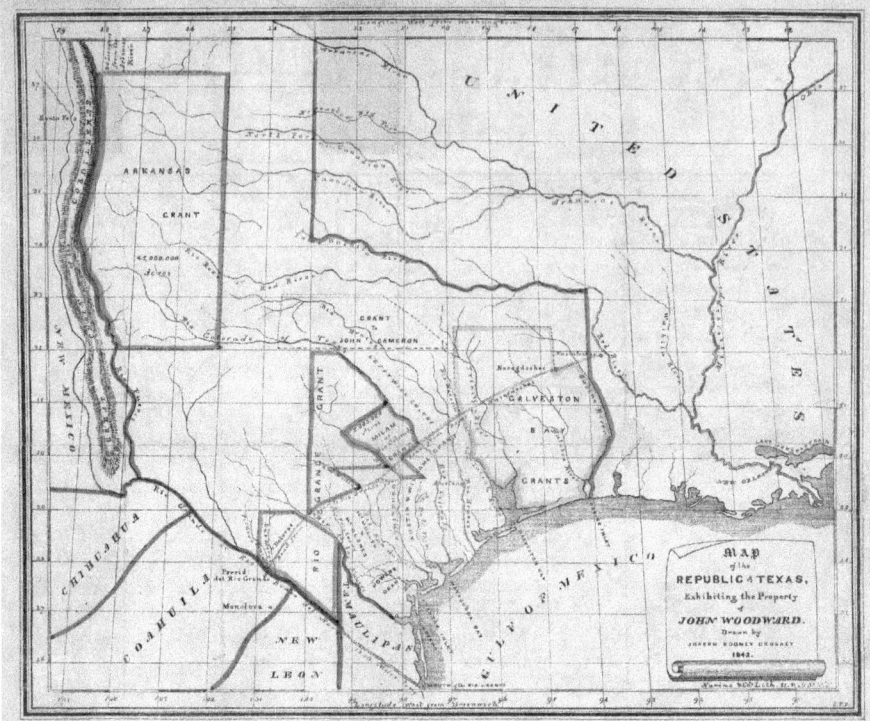

Figure 4.5. This map shows the borders claimed by Texas after its war with Mexico. Major land grants, like those shown here, were often parceled and sold in eastern markets rather than directly issued to settlers. When Texas secured its independence via a treaty with Santa Anna, the new republic claimed it extended to the Rio Grande. The Mexican government never formally recognized the independence of Texas, but it considered the Nueces River (over one hundred miles northward) to be the boundary of Texas territory. Mexico did not dispute this boundary until ten years later, when U.S. troops moved into the territory between the Nueces and Rio Grande Rivers.
Source: "Map of the Republic of Texas, Exhibiting the Property of John Woodward. Drawn by Joseph Rodney Croskey" (1842). Perry Castañeda Map Collection, Courtesy of the University of Texas Libraries, The University of Texas at Austin. Reproduced with permission.

loans. Paying them back, however, was a different matter. At the end of the war, Texas had incurred a relatively small debt of US$267,534 in fighting for independence.[5] Yet the threat that Mexico might seek to reconquer the territory remained very real. So the government's first order of business was to fund a standing army and navy, in addition to defraying all the other expenses associated with a government bureaucracy. To meet these financial obligations, Houston, under congressional authority, sent commissioners abroad to the United States and Europe to secure loans of up to US$5 million (at an interest rate as high as 10 percent).[6]

The government's other fiscal strategy was to incorporate the Texas Railroad, Navigation, and Banking Company, to be capitalized at US$5 million. This company would help build the Texan economy by serving as a trustworthy national bank and by investing in the construction of infrastructure. It never came into operation, however, failing to meet the requirement that it hold at least US$1 million in specie.

Texas, as already noted, had no gold or silver and only foreign coins in circulation. Nonetheless, Article II of the Texas Constitution prohibited establishing as legal tender anything other than gold or silver coins, which were pegged to the coins of the United States. Thus, the monetary standard for the Texas Republic was the U.S. dollar, just as Spanish pieces-of-eight had once been the standard in the United States. No matter—Texas never issued a single coin. Lacking circulating coinage, the day-to-day economy of Texas continued to function largely on barter.

Texas's economic standing also suffered from the region's lack of infrastructure and an extremely limited productive sector. The country manufactured little beyond agricultural products, such as cotton and cattle; consequently, its imports far outweighed its exports, a trade imbalance that continuously drained Texas's specie reserves, as coins left the region as payment for foreign goods. To make matters worse, the U.S. economy collapsed in 1837. Texan exports had predominantly targeted the U.S. market, specifically New Orleans, for years. Due to the U.S. recession, which persisted through most of Texas's history as an independent nation, foreign capital investment was not forthcoming.

Texas's remaining recourse for stimulating the economy was to print paper money. For example, in November 1837, the government authorized the printing of money to cover military expenses related to ongoing conflicts with indigenous groups. At the same time, Texas Congressmen understood the inflationary dangers associated with paper money, so they prohibited individuals or corporations from circulating promissory notes. It was the beginning of an unending process, wherein Congress prohibited the circulation of valueless currency, while simultaneously covering the costs of governance with paper money based on little more than a promise of future payment.

The imagery on these government notes, printed in New York and Philadelphia, illustrated Texas's national aspirations. The allegory of liberty was a standard, just like on the coins of the United States and Mexico, marking the countries' shared republican ideals (see figure 4.7). The notes also bore representations of the Roman goddess Minerva, typically associated with

Figure 4.6. The Republic of Texas issued numerous series of paper notes, like this early one signed by Sam Houston. The notes used popular symbols of liberty, such as a liberty cap atop a pole. They were meant to accrue 10 percent interest, but every issue suffered depreciation.
Source: "June 1, 1838, Republic of Texas $1 Note, Serial #88." Courtesy of the Texas State Library and Archives Commission. Reproduced with permission.

commerce, industry, and education, in an attempt to project Texas's future as a fully functional state based on trade and human capital. Images of machinery, tools, steamships, and wildlife similarly spoke of the new Texan republic's resources and promise. The one-dollar note, for example, bore an image of Minerva holding a liberty cap atop a pole and bearing a shield emblazoned with the Texas star. Allegorical ideals on paper money, however, could not sustain a nonexistent economy. Upon issuance in 1838, the notes experienced a precipitous fall in value, as they did every time Texas printed money during the remaining years of its short existence.

During Houston's first term as president (1836–1838), Texas accumulated foreign debt and printed paper money to keep the government afloat. His successor, Mirabeau Lamar, faced a similarly dire economic situation, but his fiscal vision ran somewhat contrary to Houston's. Unlike his predecessor, Lamar opposed annexation to the United States and felt certain that Texas could persist as an independent nation. He had two primary goals: to secure Texan sovereignty by acquiring European recognition of the republic and to strengthen the national currency by creating a national bank of Texas (following the U.S. model).

Texas had to become an enduring nation, which required drastically increasing government spending. So Lamar, for instance, pushed for congressional approval to move the capital from Houston to Austin, which

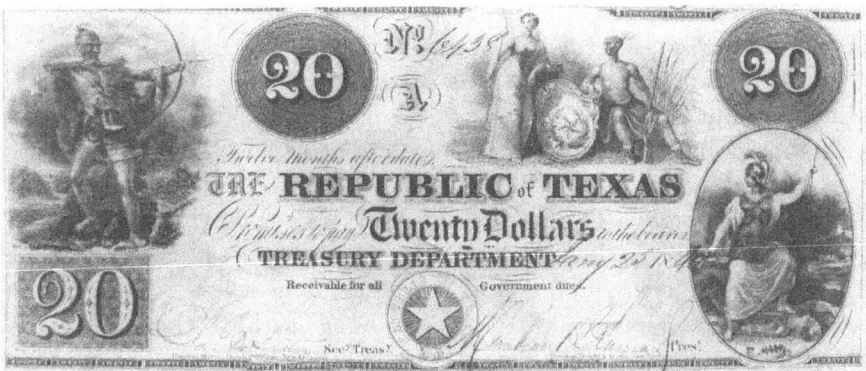

Figure 4.7. This 1840 twenty-dollar Republic of Texas note is signed by the second president of Texas, Mirabeau Lamar. The notes issued by the government celebrated various attributes of the state, including resources such as crops and industrial potential. The image of a Native American on this bill appears respectful, if not romanticized, which is incongruous with Lamar's efforts to remove Native Americans from Texas.
Source: "$20 Republic of Texas Note" (1840). Photography by J. Frederick. Private collection of Phillip R. Rutherford. Reproduced with permission.

also included commissioning the construction of many new and arguably unnecessary government buildings. To receive the recognition of countries with capitals like London and Paris, in Lamar's view, Texas could not run its government out of dreary single-story buildings. Overall, annual government expenditures during Lamar's administration were four times higher than

Figure 4.8. The distinctive "redback" notes were issued under Texas president Mirabeau Lamar from 1839 to 1840. Like other Texas paper money, redbacks immediately lost value. By 1842 the Texas government itself was unwilling to accept the bills.
Source: "Verso of Republic of Texas Red Back." Courtesy of the Texas State Library and Archives Commission. Reproduced with permission.

under Houston. Lamar's fiscal policy was apparently to spend as though the Texas economy was already as sound as he hoped it would become.

Lamar illustrated his optimism for Texas's future on a new series of notes, which continued to combine allegorical images from classical mythology with aspirational visions of future Texas industry. The bills issued in early 1839 were known as redbacks for the red ink used to depict a star with the letters of the word TEXAS printed between its five points (see figure 4.8). Like Mexico and the United States during their wars for independence, Texas simply ordered currency into existence. Redbacks were not loan receipts; they were money. Unlike previous notes issued by the government, they bore no interest (unlike typical banknotes). People had to accept them as money despite their not being backed by gold or silver. Tellingly, when the government issued redbacks, the Texas Treasury was long overdue on paying its bill to the printers for previous notes, a fact that highlights the ephemeral nature of Texas currency.

To encourage Texans' faith in the new bills, the government relied on artistry. The printing contract specified that the bills required the highest production value. In other words, they had to look like real money. Allegorical and mythological figures decorated their fronts, including Lady Liberty, of course, and the Greek god Zeus. Native Americans appeared on the bills as noble warriors, a recognition and respect not granted them by the government. Lamar aimed, in fact, to remove Native Americans from western Texas—a military process that cost quite a bit of money.

Redbacks depreciated at an alarming rate, just like the one-dollar notes from 1838. Within months their value fell to 37.5 cents on the U.S. dollar; a year later, in 1840, they were down to 16.6 cents. By 1842 they were worth just 2 percent of their face value, which the government never enforced. Instead it paid them out at the prevailing market rates, meaning that a government official, for example, had to receive nearly 98 redbacks to equal US$1 of his salary. Inflation spun out of control.

In the face of this economic crisis the government could only borrow more real money from foreign banks to remain solvent. Under Lamar's presidency, Texas's national debt more than tripled, from less than US$2 million to over US$7 million. His policy of spending to legitimize the Republic of Texas had some political success: France, Holland, and Belgium all recognized it as an independent nation. These diplomatic ties, however, failed to produce commercial relations that could prop up the republic's failing finances.

By the end of Lamar's term, the Texas economy, never strong, was wrecked. Voters returned Sam Houston to the presidency in December 1841, hoping for a miracle. Trade had not improved since independence;

nor had production increased much. Texas had less hard cash than ever before. Houston responded to the crisis by reversing many of Lamar's policies, especially his endorsement of government spending, which Houston cut by 90 percent. The economy would have to be stimulated by other means. Additionally, Houston had to figure out how to bring specie into the country. So like the United States and Mexico, Texas established high customs duties (25 percent) to create a revenue stream. Finally, Houston took on the problem of worthless paper money. The Texas government resolved to repudiate all its previous paper currency and issued a new series called "exchequer Bills," swearing to recognize them at face value and this time printing far fewer of them. The exchequer bills proved more resilient than the previous issues, so even though their value fell immediately, it rose once again before U.S. annexation.

During the nine-year history of the Republic of Texas, money posed a constant and nearly insurmountable problem. Lacking hard currency, the country could only ever pay for its operation with paper currency. Houston sought to keep spending low and simply tried to preserve the integrity of the nation, hoping the United States would one day sweep Texas into its protective arms.

Lamar, on the other hand, thought that he could legitimize Texas as an independent nation by spending lavishly on the trappings of state. Among his greatest expenditures was the Texas navy, which did successfully prevent further assault from Mexico. Ultimately, the United States absorbed Texas, whose financial future thus became tied to another country altogether.

Conclusion

By 1845, Texas was at last attracting small amounts of specie back into its economy, which permitted the government to ban any further issuance of paper money. Nine years after its creation, Texas was ready to make good on its national promise to adhere to the use of hard money, but it very soon ceased to be a country at all. It had set out as an independent republic, the third such nation to appear on the North American continent in fifty years. Texas, however, always faced the risk of reconquest by Mexico or absorption by the United States. Its worth to the two countries with the power to determine its future remained to be determined.

Sam Houston's paycheck symbolizes the difficult economic environment that plagued the Republic of Texas and the government's ultimate failure to mint a nation. His ability to cash his pay warrant speaks to Texans' optimism that the United States would annex the young nation. There was finally a little money in the coffers as investors expected it to become another state. In addition, the story shows the significant role Sam Houston played in the creation and direction of an independent Texas. During its entire existence as a nation, Texas rarely managed to make good on its debts in genuine hard currency. In this way Houston's paycheck tells another story: that of a nation hamstrung by debt, bereft of precious-metal resources, and struggling to pay its bills with little more than optimism about a prosperous future. The third North American republic ultimately could not stand on its own—a vulnerability that turned Texas into a central arena in the future of U.S.-Mexican relations.

The value placed on Texas varied wildly between the 1820s and 1840s. The Mexican government had considered Texan land to be worth less than two cents per acre. Then, investors in the independence effort sometimes valued it at as much as fifty cents per acre. In the next chapter, the reader will learn that the United States eventually came to value Texas as well, primarily as a gateway to the Pacific Ocean, which instigated the Mexican-American War.

Notes

1. *Laws Passed by the Sixth Congress of the Republic of Texas* (Austin, TX: S. Whiting, Public Printer, 1842).

2. The most common currencies in *empresario* settlements were Old Spanish silver pillar dollars, portrait coins with the image of Charles IV, Iturbide's imperial coins, hammered Mexican coins, and U.S. banknotes.

3. W. M. Gouge, *The Fiscal History of Texas. Embracing an Account of Its Revenues, Debts, and Currency, from the Commencement of the Revolution in 1834 to 1851–52. With Remarks on American Debts* (Philadelphia: Lippincott, Grambo, and Co., 1852).

4. Notably, many soldiers sold their pay certificates at a discount for gold and silver because the land was far away and required the cost of surveys.

5. W. M. Gouge, *The Fiscal History of Texas. Embracing an Account of Its Revenues, Debts, and Currency, from the Commencement of the Revolution in 1834 to 1851–52. With Remarks on American Debts* (Philadelphia: Lippincott, Grambo, and Co., 1852).

6. Ibid.

CHAPTER FIVE

Buying Mexico

Antonio López de Santa Anna must have been well pleased as he watched American emissary Alexander Slidell Mackenzie embark on his nine-mile journey back to Havana, Cuba. It was July 6, 1846. The deposed Mexican president, now fifty-two years old and living in exile, had just concluded a secret three-hour meeting. That afternoon Mackenzie had informed Santa Anna that U.S. President James K. Polk would help him return to power by giving him safe conduct through the American naval blockade presently off the coast of Mexico. In turn, Santa Anna had vowed that upon reclaiming the presidency, he would negotiate the sale of territory in northern Mexico to the United States. Surveying the palatial estate where he was living, in what was then one of Spain's last remaining American colonies, Santa Anna turned his mind to plans for the weeks ahead. Soon he would once again be at center stage, determining Mexico's history.

The protagonist in this chapter is lifelong soldier and frequent president of Mexico Antonio López de Santa Anna (see figure 5.1). The money is the MX$15 million payment made by the United States to acquire half of Mexico's national territory after the Mexican-American War (1846–1848), or the United States Intervention (*Intervención Estadounidense*), as it is known in Mexico. Santa Anna was president and commanding general during the height of this conflict.

Santa Anna's experiences illustrate how neither Mexico nor the United States has ever fought a more important war in terms of territories lost and won. The Treaty of Guadalupe Hidalgo that ended the conflict, signed on

Figure 5.1. In this print from circa 1847, President Santa Anna directs his steady gaze forward, proudly bearing on his chest the colors of the Mexican flag and his military insignia. Here is a man who lived to see the creation of a new nation and the loss of nearly half of its territory to its sister republic.
Source: "General D. Antonio López de Santa Anna, President of the Republic of Mexico." Original in Prints and Photographs Division, Library of Congress, LC-DIG-pga-07113. Public Domain.

February 12, 1848, ceded more than five hundred thousand square miles of Mexico's national territory to the United States (see figure 5.2). In compensation, the United States agreed to make five annual payments of MX$3 million "in the gold or silver coin of Mexico."[1] Even though the money theoretically reimbursed Mexico for its lost land, many on both sides of the border saw the war as nothing more than an American landgrab. This perception, still common in Mexico today, has ever since tainted relations between the two countries, optimistically called North America's "sister republics" in the nineteenth century.[2]

The war began in April 1846 with a skirmish between Mexican cavalry and an American patrol near Brownsville, Texas, but its origins go back to the founding of the United States. It was the product of a national vision that supported unobstructed expansion from the Atlantic states toward the Pacific. U.S. westward aspirations increased in the early 1840s, nurtured by fears that European powers would lay claim to the Pacific coast. Many felt that the United States had to act preemptively, before another power beat it to the riches of the West.

An 1840 editorial expressed a common view: "The Editor of the *Arkansas Star* at Little Rock strongly urges the purchase of California by our Government. . . . This country [is] rich . . . and most valuable from its natural resources."[3] The piece continued, "Mexico finds difficulty in paying her bonds for various loans from individuals and companies in England," alluding to rumors that the British Crown would force Mexico to cede California in lieu of loan payments. Mexico's foreign debt represented a threat to both Mexican and U.S. territorial interests. Adding to these murmurings, the Texan secession in the previous decade had starkly proven that territory could be wrested from Mexican control.

President Polk was arguably the most vocal and active proponent of western expansion. His election in 1844 provided him with the opportunity to fulfill a lifelong dream: to extend the United States across the North American continent and claim the West, a desire he articulated in a diary entry from June 30, 1846: "We must obtain Upper California and New Mexico."[4] Polk believed deeply in America's natural right to western land and the wealth of the Pacific. And he meant to clear away the one obstacle to U.S. Manifest Destiny: Mexico.

The immediate pretense for seizing Mexico's northern territory, which extended from Oregon to Texas, grew out of the founding of the Republic of Texas in 1836 (see chapter 4). Largely run by U.S. expatriates, Texas was never destined to persist as an independent land between Mexico and the United States. Its government had solicited admission to the United States

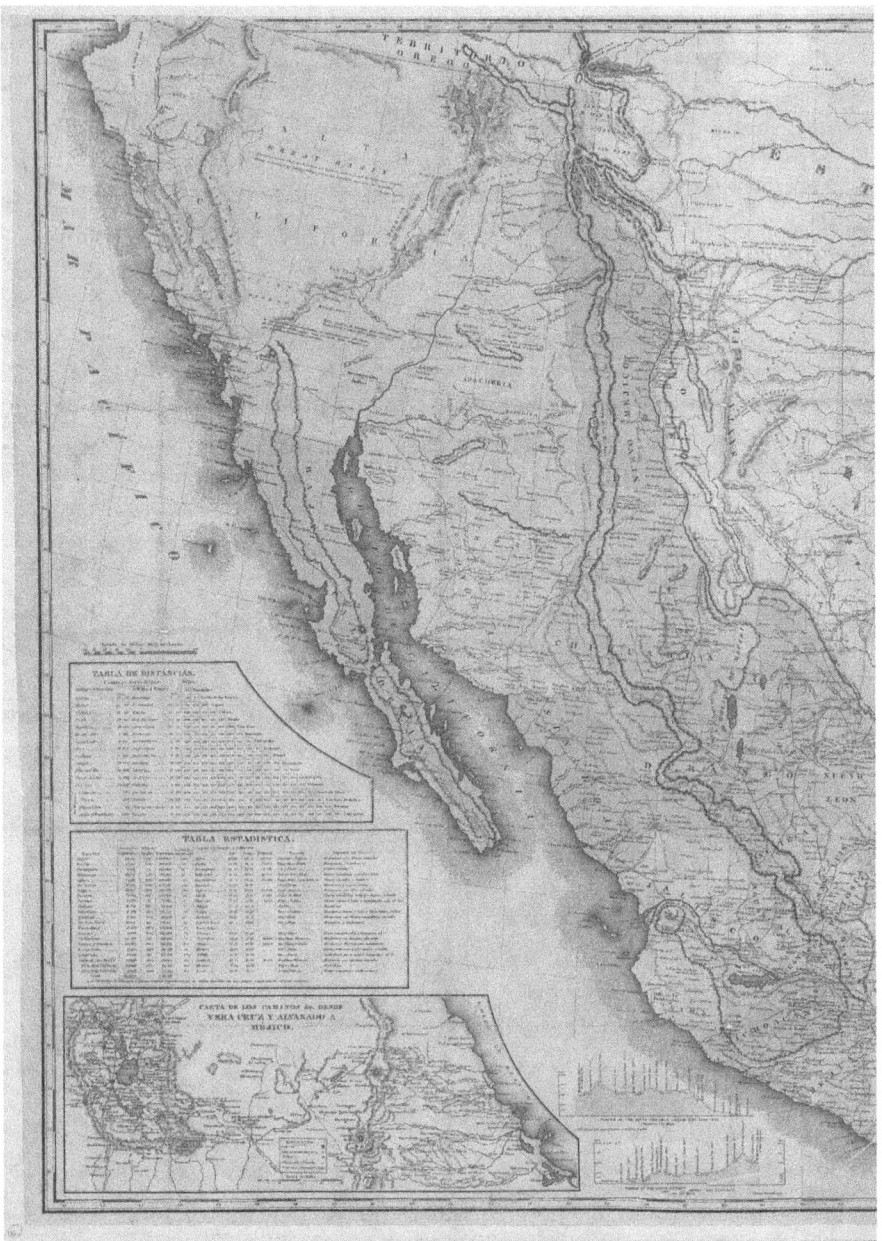

Figure 5.2. In this prewar map, the Mexican nation reaches along the Pacific Coast as far north as Washington State and includes the "American Southwest." This rendering of Mexico's borders prior to the Mexican-American War helps us envision the immensity of its territorial loss.
Source: "Mapa de los Estados Unidos de Méjico: según lo organizado y definido por las varias actas del congreso de dicha república y construido por las mejores autoridades" (New York: J. Disturnell, 1847). Geography and Map Division, Library of Congress, LC- 2004627240. Public Domain.

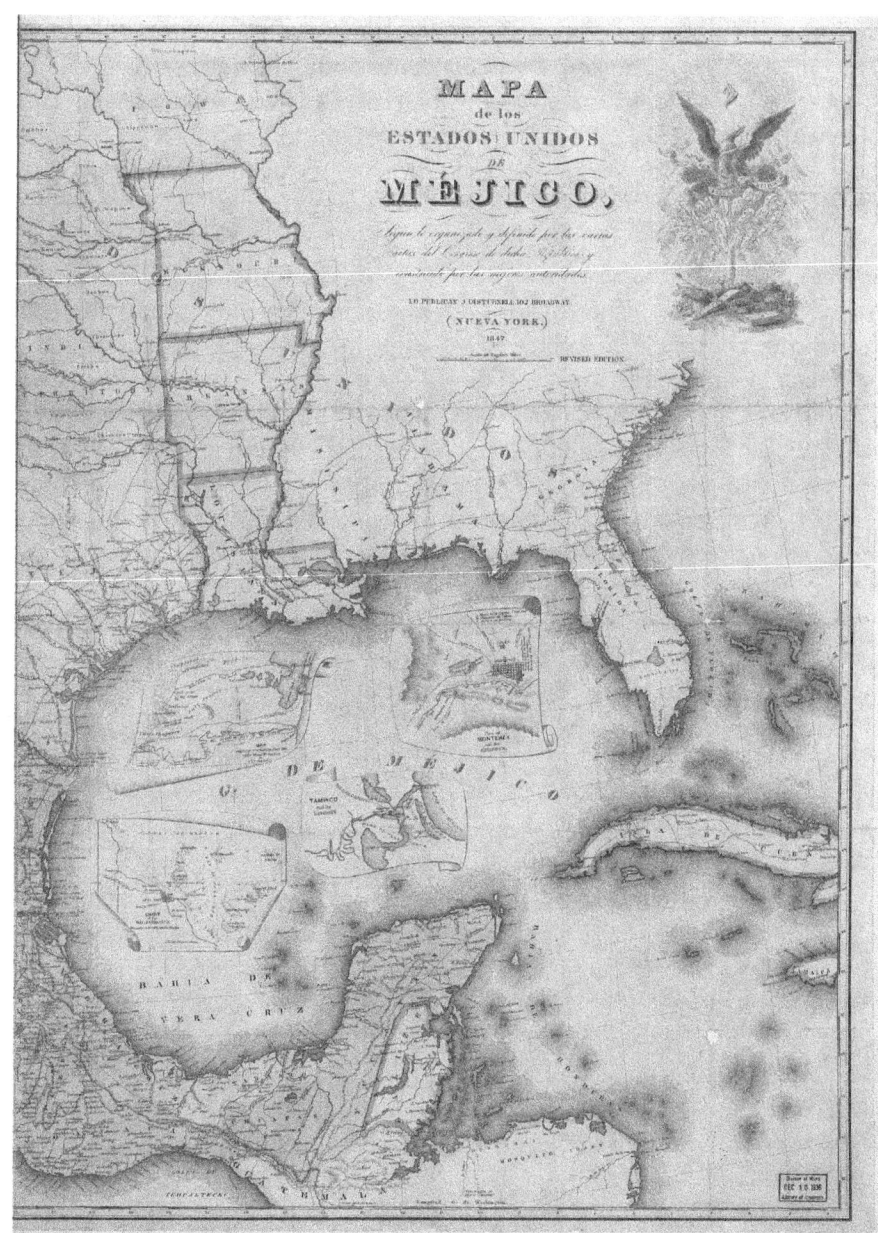

as soon as Texian rebels defeated General Santa Anna (a central player in that war as well). Annexation was not forthcoming at that moment due to North-South divisions related to slavery, but the issue resurfaced ten years later.

The shift toward favoring the acquisition of Texas was intimately connected to a desire to possess California. Many Americans, including Polk, believed that western resources were underutilized in Mexican hands. A traveler who spent the winter of 1842 in Upper California rhapsodized about an untapped Eden: "[California] is possessed of the some of the finest harbors in the known world. . . . Apples, peaches, pears, oranges, figs, cherries, etc., etc. come to fine perfection. . . . The valleys are entirely destitute of timber, they are covered with oats, clover and grass, the most luxuriant the eye ever beheld."[5] This ecstatic description conveyed the message that California needed the diligent attention of American settlers. In the traveler's words, "Such a country, in the hands of an industrious and enterprising people, would at no distant day, compare with the most flourishing countries of the globe." Between the United States and the riches of California lay Texas.

President Polk saw admitting Texas into the Union as a first step in acquiring California. He had campaigned for territorial expansion and was eager to build on Democratic Party momentum after taking office. Congress had already passed a resolution admitting Texas under the previous administration, so Polk pressed the Texas government to accept annexation, finally signing the bill in December 1845. This action also indicated the U.S. government's commitment to acquiring Mexican territory by one means or another, be it a payment scheme or possibly war.

As we saw at the beginning of the chapter, Polk was prepared to install a leader in Mexico who would sell the land to the United States. Our protagonist Santa Anna intersected with Polk's plans at this juncture. For the U.S. president, enabling Santa Anna's return to Mexico from exile promised two possibilities: an avenue to carry out this purchase or to instigate formal war. The latter would provide an outlet for Polk's best generals, and possible political opponents, Zachary Taylor and Winfield Scott. Their certain victory in Mexico would secure the Democratic Party's ascendancy.

Santa Anna and the Defense of Mexico

Santa Anna's eventful career began with a meteoric rise in the military (see figure 5.3). Born in 1794 in Veracruz, then a Spanish colony of New Spain, Santa Anna became a cadet in the Veracruz infantry in service to King Charles IV of Spain at age sixteen. Promoted three years later for bravery,

Figure 5.3. This engraving of Santa Anna as a young officer astride a horse evokes his boundless energy. To contemporaries it seemed like he was always on the move, ready to fight for his country. He is represented here with the cactus of the Mexican flag in the lower right.
Source: "Equestrian Portrait of General Santa Anna," by W. H. Dodd (no date). Original in Prints and Photographs Collection, Briscoe Center for American History, University of Texas, Austin.

he became an officer working to put down the independence movement and soon became a lieutenant colonel in the Spanish military. In March 1821, however, he switched sides to support Agustín Iturbide's conservative independence movement, the first of his frequent changes in political allegiance.

Following independence, Santa Anna returned to Veracruz. Devoted at heart to the soil of his birth, he spent much of his time acquiring property and investing in agriculture. Yet when Spain made its last attempt to reconquer Mexico in 1829, Santa Anna led an outnumbered force in a successful defense against the Spaniards at Tampico, becoming a national hero. He then retired from public life once again and returned to his haciendas.

Santa Anna could never resist the lure of the military limelight and political power. When his old allies called on him in the early 1830s to stabilize the fractured government in Mexico City, he marched to the capital at the head of an army. In 1833, Santa Anna was elected president for the first time. The office, however, held little interest for the man sometimes referred to as "the Savior of the Fatherland," so he swiftly appointed a vice president to govern in his stead.

Santa Anna was an enigmatic public servant—a devout patriot but a mercurial leader who apparently felt little love for the strictures of elective office. He officially held the title of president six times and actually served in the office a total of eleven times between 1833 and 1855, a period in Mexican history characterized by recurring coups and failed governments. Yet he essentially remained an absentee president. Santa Anna delighted in military glory but chafed at political responsibility.

By March 1845, when Polk assumed office, Santa Anna had been in and out of the presidential office eight times and was currently living in exile in Cuba. Remarkably, his reputation as a heroic defender of the nation meant that, exile or not, he could always return to power. Polk made use of this fact as he made plans to acquire northern Mexico. The U.S. president understood from the outset the potential unpopularity of a war against Mexico, so he initially sought to make his land acquisitions by peaceful purchase. That said, there was no guarantee that the Mexican government would welcome his overtures, especially as it continued to reel from internal divisions.

In the six months prior to Polk's inauguration, the Mexican presidency changed hands four times, and it did so again during Polk's first year as president when Mexican conservatives seized power in a coup. This unrelenting conflict and the resultant political instability meant that Polk had to stack the odds in his favor if Mexico was going to respond positively to his overtures. So, Polk began secret negotiations with Santa Anna in Cuba, seeking to arrange a deal—a kind of preemptive truce—in which the United States would help Santa Anna return to Mexico, and he in turn would convince the Mexican government to sell northern Mexico to the United States. Santa Anna agreed to this proposal, promising that, should he return to power, he would accept the Rio Grande as the Texas border and sell California to the United States for US$30 million (the market value of dollars and pesos was roughly equivalent at this time).

While Polk and Santa Anna negotiated through proxies, Polk made sincere but obviously unacceptable overtures to purchase California and New Mexico from the sitting Mexican government. The Mexican Treasury was continually empty, so a cash influx from the United States might stabilize government finances. No government leader, however, could possibly permit the loss of half of Mexico's territory without committing political suicide. So Polk's offers were repeatedly rejected, whatever the amount offered, and yet he continued to look for a deal while also preparing for war.

President Polk needed a pretext for war. He had succeeded in getting Congress to accept Texas as a new state, giving him the legal right to protect American territory at the Mexican border. Texans (now U.S. citizens) allegedly had reasons to fear an attack from Mexico, so in March 1846, Polk sent U.S. troops to defend them. The ulterior plan was to instigate a border conflict, which U.S. soldiers carried out by marching southward to the Rio Grande beyond the existing boundary between Texas and Mexico at the Nueces River. Mexico had never accepted Texan independence but endured it down to this northern line. As such, U.S. troop movements beyond this boundary constituted an undeniable invasion of sovereign Mexican territory. The results were predictable. Mexican troops retaliated against U.S. forces, resulting in the death of eleven American soldiers. In response, Polk requested and received a formal declaration of war against Mexico on May 13, 1846.

Here we return to the Cuba episode in early July 1846, when Santa Anna was approached to negotiate the sale of Mexican territory. At this late moment purchase was still more economical than war. Reaching out to Santa Anna, however, involved an alternate possibility. His return to Mexico had the potential of finally galvanizing the Mexican Congress to declare war against the United States. Back in May, the president of Mexico had manifested a need for defensive military action, but Polk still needed a formal declaration from the Mexican Congress to legalize the campaign according to the constitutions of both countries and international law, which did not happen until July 7, 1846.

Mexico delayed because it was in no position to mount a meaningful defense against the United States, having never recovered economically or politically from the convulsions of the war for independence. Ongoing warfare, foreign interventions, and often self-interested leadership had depleted the national Treasury. The Mexican military was underequipped and overextended, and most troops were already occupied with internal insurrections, including a war in Yucatan. The U.S. military, by contrast, benefited from half a century of stable political rule and economic growth, making it larger, better trained, and more amply supplied than Mexican forces. This military imbalance allowed U.S. troops to march beyond Texas and occupy New Mexico, taking the territory almost unopposed, followed by California in summer 1846.

Mexico faced catastrophe: foreign troops occupied much of its territory, and its ports were under blockades. Political factionalism prevailed, making it nearly impossible to mount a unified national defense. Santa Anna saw this opportunity to return to Mexico's political stage and entreated the government to accept his help to fight off the foreign invaders. The Mexican government relented and invited the ousted leader to return. Santa Anna, a political genius, used his prior secret agreement with the U.S. government to bypass the American blockade, landing in Veracruz in August 1846.

By this point in Santa Anna's career, the Mexican Congress understood the man's strengths and weaknesses: he was an excellent general but an unpredictable politician. When they declared him president of Mexico later that year, it was with the proviso that he remain in the field in control of the army, constitutionally prohibiting him from wielding political power back in the capital. This arrangement suited Santa Anna just fine, as his main objective was to ready his forces to confront General Zachary Taylor, whose army was then south of the Rio Grande near Monterrey.

One might wonder if Santa Anna ever truly intended to arrange the sale of Mexican territory or simply planned to use the deal with Polk to return home. Santa Anna always maintained that he was devoted to his homeland above all else, and his spirited defense of Mexico during the war certainty

Figure 5.4. This print is a view of Monterrey under U.S. occupation, created by an officer in the 7th U.S. Infantry under General Zachary Taylor. The guard at the bottom right overlooks the main plaza lined with artillery. Santa Anna's troops rushed northward but were unable to prevent Taylor from seizing the city.
Source: "Monterey, as Seen from a House-Top in the Main Plaza, October, 1846," based on a topographical sketch by D. P. Whiting (New York: G. W. Endicott, 1847). Original in Prints and Photographs Division, Library of Congress, LC-DIG-pga-06723. Public Domain.

Figure 5.5. This marble plaque commemorates Santa Anna's 1842 presidential order to renovate and expand the Mexican Mint *(Apartado General de la Nación)* in Mexico City, in order to increase output. Construction took years to complete and the building was not occupied until after the withdrawal of U.S. troops from Mexico City.
Source: Marble plaque, located in the main staircase of the Museo Numismático Nacional. Photography by T. Seijas.

supports his patriotic claims. Criticized for his opportunism and tyrannical tendencies and for switching positions to suit his political goals, Santa Anna has even been accused of treason and only pretending to defend Mexico during the Mexican-American War. For all of his numerous flaws, a lack of determination in the military defense of his country was not one of them. Repeated defeat plagued Santa Anna's campaigns against American troops, but they lacked resources, not resolve.

A lack of money severely hampered Santa Anna's ability to prepare for combat. In late 1846, the Mexican Treasury had less than Mex$2,000 to offer the general. That amount, equal to the same in U.S. dollars, would have bought fewer than seventy rifles.[6] Over the next few months, Santa Anna sent increasingly desperate requests from the front to Mexico City for funds to provision his army.

The Mexican government's only recourse was to secure funds from the one institution left in the country that had considerable wealth: the Catholic Church. In January 1847, Vice President Valentín Gómez Farías pushed Congress to authorize the seizure of MX$15 million from ecclesiastical coffers. The move immediately touched off a riot among conservatives and church supporters, which prevented the government from accessing the money that Santa Anna so desperately needed to fight U.S. troops. Left without resources, he mortgaged his own properties to supply his men. At this moment of national crisis, the church offered only a loan of MX$2,000,000, contingent on the government's repeal of recently passed anticlerical legislation.

Santa Anna's military leadership during this crisis, as well as his generosity relative to the church's parsimony, redeemed his image as the nation's savior.

Santa Anna's return to Mexico was a political blow for Polk. He was an undeniable force, and though he never vanquished U.S. forces, his men did considerable damage. The loss of U.S. lives was a critical consideration; Polk's opponents used mortality rates to call for the war's end. Then, within months of Santa Anna's return to Mexico, the press revealed Polk's secret alliance with the now enemy leader. An editorial in the *Milwaukee Journal Sentinel* voiced a common national concern: "Let time decide whether Mr. Polk, in opening the gates of Mexico to Santa Anna, did not furnish the enemy with a club, which if it do not beat out our brains, will at least deal us some hard and unwelcome knocks."[7] Senator Caleb Smith of Indiana was even less circumspect: "The administration has been engaged in a petty and wicked intrigue with our worst foreign enemy, Santa Anna."[8] Polk's plans to acquire Mexico's northern territory had progressed from offering to purchase the land, to threatening war, to secret negotiations with Santa Anna—the last came back to haunt him. Americans' disapproval of the president's actions echoed from pressrooms to the chambers of Congress. Polk could now only hope for a quick end to the war. Exhaustion with the conflict and calls for its conclusion were equally prevalent across Mexico.

Mexico had neither the military resources nor the money to defeat the United States; yet Santa Anna's troops pushed aggressively forward during the first half of 1847. He directed his men against General Zachary Taylor in the north and then turned southward to confront the U.S. occupation of Veracruz—the port of his home state, where U.S. troops under Major General Winfield Scott threatened to march inland. Santa Anna experienced numerous military and logistical setbacks during this campaign, but his political maneuverings were quite remarkable.

In early May 1847, when Scott's forces took the city of Puebla on the road to Mexico City, Santa Anna sent word with an audacious proposal. If Scott agreed to pay him MX$1 million, Santa Anna would ensure that peace negotiations began at once. Scott agreed, falling prey to another offer by the Mexican president to aid the United States. Santa Anna received a MX$10,000 down payment, and though the rest of the MX$1 million was not forthcoming, he got what he really wanted, which was to keep Scott's forces in Puebla for a little while longer so that he could shore up defenses in Mexico City. In the end, his scheme failed, as Scott once again outflanked Mexican troops and took over the capital in September (see figure 5.6). Faced with defeat, Santa Anna resigned the presidency only thirteen months after returning to Mexican soil.

THE AMERICAN ARMY, UNDER GENERAL SCOTT, ENTERING THE CITY OF MEXICO.

Figure 5.6. This print shows U.S. troops filing into Mexico City's main plaza, marching in front of the cathedral. General Scott waves a greeting to the teeming crowds. In reality the event was not nearly so orderly and far less celebratory on the part of Mexican spectators. The image nonetheless conjures the incredible military spectacle that foreshadowed Mexico's subsequent plea for peace.

Source: "American Army, under General Scott, Entering the City of Mexico," by Christian Mayr (1856). Wood engraving. Courtesy of the Picture Collection, New York Public Library, Astor, Lenox and Tilden Foundations.

With few resources and tired troops, the Mexican government's gambit in early 1848 was to incite international condemnation against the United States. Mexico had a righteous cause, as evidenced by the near-universal censure of Polk's campaign by foreign powers. A lengthy article in the *Times of London* castigated the U.S. administration for profligate spending on an unjustified war. The summation of U.S. achievement thus far was as follows: "Scott, Taylor, Worth, and a few other fine fellows are written on the page of American fame, and some ten or a dozen millions of British pounds sterling are added to the sum of American debt."[9] The reference to British financial gains from U.S. spending in the war brought home the point: the United States would surely win this war, but at what cost to the national Treasury? That very concern was in the minds of most U.S. citizens, as was the fear of worsening sectional tensions in the country. To people living in nonslave states, the war seemed a slaveholders' landgrab to be contained forthwith.

The end of the war finally came when Mexico opted to negotiate peace with the United States. Supreme Court Justice Manuel de la Peña y Peña, proclaimed interim president of Mexico, was at the front of this long and arduous process, made no less difficult by Santa Anna himself, who often undermined the negotiations by remaining on the battlefield after resigning the presidency. Nicholas Trist sat on the other side of the negotiation table. It was a stressful diplomatic mission. At one point, Trist was relieved of his post for being too sympathetic to the Mexicans, but he continued negotiations against his president's wishes. Perhaps he feared that the U.S. government would opt to annex the entire nation of Mexico if the question of its northern territory was not immediately settled. Polk had, after all, gone to war for this exact end. Finally, on February 2, 1848, U.S. and Mexican representatives signed the Treaty of Guadalupe Hidalgo, ending the war and ceding 529,000 square miles of Mexican territory. Santa Anna called the treaty an "eternal shame."

Mexico saw the loss of half of its national territory to foreign conquest as an unpardonable blow, regardless of any financial compensation. The terms of exchange—MX$15 million for more than half a million square miles of land—received considerable criticism, unsurprisingly. For most commentators the amount itself was a pittance, though it is nearly impossible to judge what an appropriate price would have been. The sale was forced on Mexico while U.S. troops remained stationed in Mexico City, which left the government little freedom to wrangle for a higher amount. Notably, Trist had initially been authorized to pay as much as US$20 million for what came to be called the Mexican Cession, which suggests that Mexican negotiators could have held out for more money. Mexico's representatives, however, knew full well that failure to secure a treaty with the United States meant the resumption of military action and quite possibly the annexation of the entire country. For them, the negotiations were not about selling off parts of the nation; they were about preventing the eradication of the Mexican state.

The price accorded to the Mexican Cession requires some comparisons to understand its ramifications. The treaty stipulated payment of the MX$15 million in exchange for 336 million acres of land, or approximately just under 4.5 cents per acre. This was far below the price land commanded in Iowa, for example, which fluctuated between US$3 and US$5 per acre during the same period.[10] The number of large purchases made by the United States during its first century reveal that there was no consistent cost structure for foreign land acquisition. The 1803 Louisiana Purchase cost the same amount—US$15 million—but secured more territory: 530 million acres (828,000 square miles). Even if we account for inflation, France arguably received a lower price (roughly three cents per acre) in this exchange than Mexico did forty-five years later. The Gadsden Purchase offers a different comparison. In 1854, the United States paid US$10 million for 18,969,600 acres (nearly thirty thousand square miles) of additional Mexican land (roughly fifty-three cents per acre)—a rate nearly twelve times greater than that in the treaty of 1848. One major difference was that U.S. troops were no longer in Mexico in 1854, which gave the government slightly more leverage to secure a larger sum. Then, in 1867, the U.S. government paid Russia only US$7.2 million for 375,304,960 acres (roughly two cents per acre), meaning that half the amount spent for Mexican land bought roughly 11 percent more land in Alaska. Periodization, market preferences, and distinct political contexts all explain the above variances in prices.

It is important to point out, however, that when the United States paid France and Russia, those empires were selling off undesirable colonial territories. In the case of Mexico, the United States was dealing with a newly independent nation that was nearly bankrupt from fending off foreign invasions, including attacks from its sister republic. Ultimately, the price of the Mexican Cession is best understood in the context of the peace it secured. The Mexican government had little choice but to concede the land, deeming that sacrificing half of Mexico was worth holding onto the remaining territory.

Debate about the price and significance of the Mexican Cession continued for years after the treaty's ratification by both countries' congresses. As noted at the chapter's beginning, the Treaty of Guadalupe Hidalgo divided the payment into five installments, with the first to be made in the "gold or silver coin of Mexico." Mexico could choose to receive the remaining four

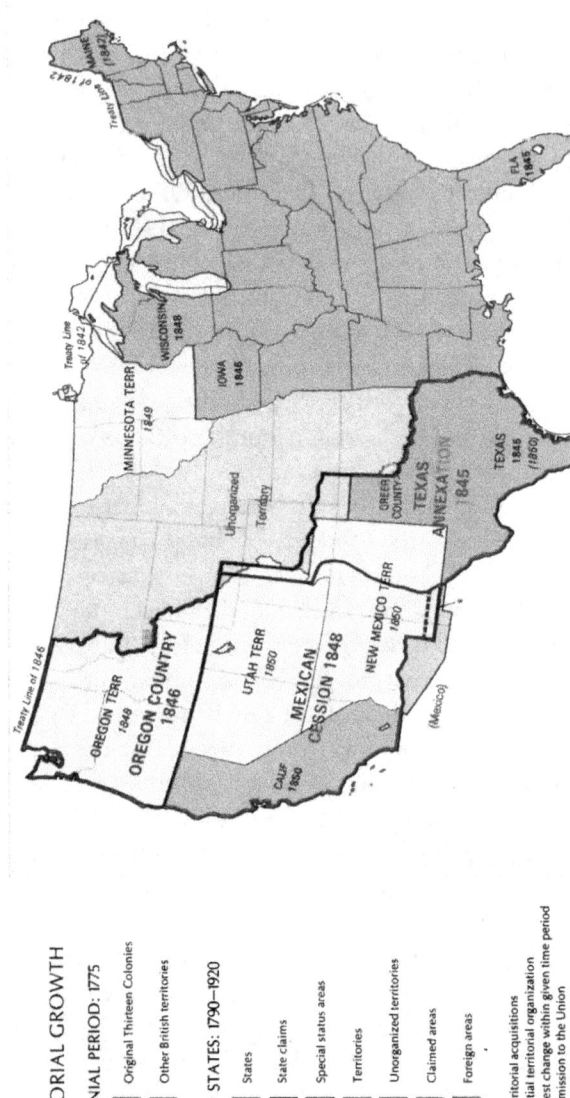

Figure 5.7. This map shows the United States in 1850 and includes the recently acquired Mexican Cession and subsequent Gadsden Purchase. The western half of the United States in this map was acquired through warfare, intrigue, negotiation, and purchase, but to many it was the fulfillment of "destiny."
Source: "Territorial Growth as of 1850," from *National Atlas of the United States of America* (Washington DC: U.S. Department of the Interior Geological Survey, 1970). Public Domain. Photography by Sion Song. Courtesy of the Pennsylvania State University Libraries.

in one of two forms. One option was to receive U.S. government stock and be paid in Washington, DC, beginning two years after the treaty was ratified. The other option was to receive the payments annually in Mexican gold or silver coins, paid in Mexico City. In both cases, 6 percent interest would accrue on the outstanding debt. Mexico chose the latter of the two options, receiving the money in coin. Hard cash—coins made of specie—was always the preferred option, even if it proved a logistical nightmare for the U.S. Treasury.

The money received from the U.S. government had the potential to stabilize the Mexican Treasury for the first time since independence. As already noted, the per-acre price of the Mexican Cession was extremely low, but MX$15 million was nonetheless a lot of money, equivalent to about 5 percent of Mexico's gross domestic product. In the decade and a half prior to the war, the Mexican government had an annual income of just MX$10 million. The annual influx of MX$3 million to Mexico's Treasury for five years could have been used to stabilize the economy and enable the government to meet its operating expenses. The annual indemnity payments did not, however, have this effect. The Mexican Treasury remained empty because the money went to servicing Mexico's enormous debt to foreign creditors, particularly London banks.

The heavy weight of Mexico's foreign debt owed in part to the political context in which the country first acquired the loans, starting with the war of independence. Like the United States and later Texas, the Mexican republic came into being because foreign investors took a bet on the revolutionaries' success and loaned them money. In the case of Mexico, additional loans that bore excessive interest rates compounded the war debt. In 1825, Mexico's estimated debt to English lenders was MX$32 million. By 1847 it was MX$58.5 million,[11] an amount so great that Mexico failed to meet its payment obligations. So in 1849 Parliament appointed William Robertson to negotiate a payment structure for Mexico's English debt. Following nearly a year of heated negotiations, Robertson secured an agreement from the Mexican government to hand over MX$4.5 million of the U.S. indemnity payments. The amount was not to retire the debt, but simply to preserve Mexico's international credit, keep it on some kind of payment schedule, and avoid more aggressive intervention by Great Britain.

Ultimately British bondholders rejected this plan in favor of another payment scheme, made up of a number of different financial instruments, that only required MX$2.5 million of the U.S. indemnity. When the British creditors asked the U.S. government to deliver the money to London, however, they were refused. The United States insisted on meeting the letter of the treaty, which stipulated delivery of the money to Mexico City. Louisiana senator Pierre Soulé was outraged by the very suggestion that the government would permit Britain to come between the United States and its neighbor, "whose quiet, her peace, her prosperity, ought to be equally dear to us." Soulé's declared, "Our wish ought to be, as our policy demands, that [the Mexicans] be a contented, happy, and powerful people."[12] British wrangling over the indemnity, to Soulé's mind and those of many others in Congress, was simply evidence that the British sought to monopolize access to Mexican specie—a significant reminder that neither the United States nor England had substantial silver reserves and thus were in competition to acquire it.

Delivering silver came with hazards; every stage of transportation brought its own risks, including theft or loss at sea. As noted, the United States made the indemnity payment delivering bullion in five installments to Mexico City. During a congressional debate in 1850, Senator John Davis of Massachusetts decried the expense of transporting bullion over such a long distance (Philadelphia to Mexico City), stating that simply delivering the money would ultimately cost the United States an additional 3 percent. Senator Edmund Badger of North Carolina countered, pushing for a motion to plan the next delivery with great care, declaring, "You cannot dispatch a messenger with the money in his pocket-book to Mexico to make the payment." After all, MX$3 million worth of silver weighed more than eighty thousand kilograms. The final payment for MX$3.18 million was made in May 1852.[13] Though U.S. officials dutifully brought the payment to Mexico City, the Mexican government immediately handed the money directly to an agent of British bondholders to cover debt payments.

The figures recorded by the Treasury secretary for the Mexican Cession indemnity do not begin to cover the price paid by the United States for this territory. The war itself cost US$71 million. And going forward, governing this expanded territory entailed considerable expense. Enforcing Article XI of the Treaty of Guadalupe Hidalgo, which required the United States to "forcibly restrain" the "savage tribes" of Indians on the northern side of the new border, was particularly costly. At the time, certain Native American groups were indeed raiding villages on the Mexican side of the border as part of their long-standing efforts to maintain territorial sovereignty over their ancestral lands. This resistance ultimately failed but did have financial repercussions for both the U.S. and Mexican governments.

Regarding the cost, a U.S. citizen made the following lament: "And it will be found, when all the expenses and blood arising from the performance of this duty come to be reckoned, that the country has paid—or is to pay—a considerably higher price for our Mexican acquisitions than has been ordinarily calculated on." This reckoning proved prophetic. The treaty placed 160,000 formerly Mexican Indians on the U.S. side of the border; the United States now had to ensure that they would "refrain forevermore, from the delightful privilege of hunting Mexicans." To prevent violations of the treaty, the U.S. military placed eight thousand troops in the area—at a cost of US$12 million in the first five years after ratification.[14]

The U.S. government sought to negotiate with Mexico in 1853 to evade the responsibilities (and costs) associated with Article XI and to gain more territory. Mexico agreed to negotiate because its government was once again bankrupt. In the five years since the end of the war, the U.S. military had wholly failed to stop cross-border raids by Indians against Mexican villages. The U.S. government was also overwhelmed and ill disposed to respond to claims made by northern Mexicans for compensation over loss of personal property. More significantly, the United States also wanted more land. Just to the south of the newly established postwar border was terrain well suited for the construction of a southern Pacific rail line, a communication route to the new western part of the United States.

At this juncture, the Mexican government was more willing to talk about selling land than it had been in 1846. On the southern side of the border, Santa Anna had returned to the helm for a final time, gaining the presidency in April 1853 through a military coup. And, once again, Mexico desperately needed funds—a problem that had deviled the country since independence. When the United States reached out, Mexico had a MX$17 million deficit from the previous fiscal year. U.S. government propositions to buy land offered Mexico a possible solution for this budgetary problem, but the threat of force was once again a major concern.

Mexico signed the Gadsden Treaty while facing overt intimidation by the United States. James Gadsden, a colonel in the U.S. Army and railroad businessman, served as the U.S. representative for the negotiations in Mexico City. His task: negotiate a renunciation of Article XI and acquire additional land for the United States. To ensure that Santa Anna understood the importance of these negotiations, the U.S. government increased its military presence on the Mexican frontier, sending an unambiguous message. The United States would have the land it wanted. Santa Anna later described this diplomatic approach as its sister republic having come "with knife in hand . . . attempting to cut another piece from the body it had just mutilated." Under these strained circumstances, Santa Anna released the United States from Article XI and conceded just enough land to build the railroad. The United States paid Mexico US$10 million in return.

Regrettably, this money never made it into the service of the Mexican government. Santa Anna pocketed most of it, and the rest went to his supporters. To Santa Anna's regret, the money did not suffice to keep him in power as a self-appointed dictator for life. A year and a half later, the Mexican people deposed him and sent him into exile for the last time. In present-day Mexico, Santa Anna is commonly characterized as having sold out the nation. He likely did not do so during the Mexican-American War, but his actions during the Gadsden affair greatly justify his infamy.

Conclusion

The Treaty of Guadalupe Hidalgo ascribed to the United States and Mexico the titles of victor and vanquished. Afterward, Texas extended to the Rio Grande, and U.S. territory spanned from the Atlantic to the Pacific coasts of North America. Mexico, by contrast, lost half its national territory. The northern provinces had been part of New Spain for three centuries but part of Mexico for less than three decades. The new republic simply did not have the resources to hold on to the territory in the face of U.S. aggression. In the summer of 1848, American troops streamed out of Mexico, and the Mexican flag was once again raised over the capital city. Just one thing remained to be done. The treaty described the new boundaries between the nations, but that line had yet to be officially surveyed. Someone had to examine this new terrain, to find the valleys and mesas, to identify the paths and roadways, and to affix in reality what the treaty could only suggest. Someone needed to go into the field and discern just what the United States had "bought." The reader will learn of this story in the following chapter.

Notes

1. U.S. Congress, *Treaty of Peace, Friendship, Limits, and Settlement between the United States of America and the United Mexican States Concluded at Guadalupe Hidalgo*, ed. Records of the U.S. Senate (Washington, DC, 1848).

2. The term was coined in N. C. Brooks, *A Complete History of the Mexican War: Its Causes, Conduct, and Consequences: Comprising an Account of the Various Military and Naval Operations, from Its Commencement to the Treaty of Peace* (Philadelphia: Grigg, Elliott and Co., 1849).

3. From the *Arkansas Star*, reprinted in *North American Daily Advertiser* (California), February 3, 1840.

4. A. S. Greenberg, *Manifest Destiny and American Territorial Expansion: A Brief History with Documents* (Boston: Bedford/St. Martins, 2012).

5. "Following communication is from a gentleman who spent last winter in Upper California, and affords some valuable information." *Easton Gazette*, February 25, 1843.

6. A newspaper advertisement in New York listed rifles for sale at US$30 and shotguns for $140. Gun sale advertisement in the *New York Herald*, February 2, 1848, 3.

7. "Mr. Polk and Santa Anna," *Milwaukee Journal Sentinel*, January 13, 1847.

8. "Congress," *Fort Wayne Times and Peoples Press*, 1847.

9. "The Americans Are Beginning to Pay for Their Whistle," *Times of London*, January 4. 1848.

10. "Valuable and Cheap Iowa Property," *Daily Missouri Republican*, April 10, 1850.

11. Interest compounded very quickly. On June 1, 1846, Mexico's English debt was about £10.241,559; by January 1, 1851, Mexico's debt to British bondholders was £12,546,021.

12. U.S. Congress, "Mexican Indemnity Bill," *Congressional Globe*, September 24, 1850.

13. The U.S. Treasury received a credit of US$66,467.42 on the exchange rate because the payment was made in Mexico City. U.S. Congress, "Report of the Secretary of the Treasury on the State of the Finances," Exec. Doc. No. 22, Washington, DC, 1852.

14. "Our Savages in Mexico," *Western Literary Messenger*, 1849.

CHAPTER SIX

Border Coppers

In May 1851, John Russell Bartlett, chief commissioner of the United States–Mexican Boundary Survey, arrived in Bacanuchi, a small, half-abandoned settlement in the Mexican state of Sonora, and dispatched his men to "scour the town" for provisions. They found "three dozen eggs—the entire stock on hand." But how would they pay for this bounty? According to Bartlett, "American coin would not pass," be it a silver half-dollar or half eagle (see figure 6.1); the sellers simply "shook their heads." When Bartlett asked, "Is it not good gold and silver?" the "universal reply" was "¿Quien sabe?" (who knows?). The townspeople also refused Mexican silver. Bartlett had to change the "few Mexican dollars" in his possession into Sonoran copper coins. Why did the locals of Bacanuchi value copper coins, with a face value of only one-quarter *real* and little intrinsic value, but not the larger precious-metal coins of the United States or their own country?[1] And what do "border coppers" tell us about the nature of money exchange in the U.S.-Mexican borderlands?

The refusal by the townspeople of Bacanuchi to accept either U.S. or Mexican gold and silver coinage hints at the complexity of the frontier economy in the years following the Mexican-American War. This chapter takes the encounter between Bartlett and the people of Bacanuchi as a starting point for investigating how people ascribed value to currency at a time of tumultuous political change. The townsfolk's rejection of their own country's currency suggests that they had a limited sense of national belonging and that citizenship had little bearing on how people regarded money. The use

Figure 6.1. This gold half eagle coin had a face value of US$5. Bartlett carried coins like this one to purchase provisions, but they were apparently worthless in small towns like Bacanuchi, where residents distrusted outsiders and managed with tokens made from local copper rather than risk accepting counterfeit money.
Source: "U.S. Gold Half Eagle." Photo by Yale University Art Gallery. Public Domain.

of border coppers, at the same time, indicates that local residents knew well the dangers of forgery and fake money. Better to have local copper than falsified gold. The story, moreover, illustrates the dynamics of the local market, which had almost no connection to the national economy centered on the Mexican capital (approximately eight hundred miles away). In contrast, the people of Bacanuchi were only some fifty miles from the United States. It was not lost on Bartlett that distance mattered. The town's future would likely be tied to the North.

This chapter is about John Russell Bartlett and the people he encountered in the early 1850s on a coast-to-coast expedition that crossed both countries. The chapter's money includes copper, silver, and gold coins, as well as other media of exchange, used on both sides of the postwar border. During his travels, Bartlett was an agent of the victorious U.S. government, charged with charting a new map of his country's territorial gains (see figure 6.2). The Mexicans he met, on the other hand, were reeling from their nation's reduced territorial sovereignty. The two countries' contrasting material and economic conditions shaped Bartlett's own experience, as well as his assessment of opportunities for market expansion and U.S. settlement. Beyond marking the new border, Bartlett was on a self-appointed mission to inform Americans about the postwar economy of the region. He took extensive notes about economic markers like the price of commodities and the cost of labor. His accounts illuminate how people on the ground conceived of money and value, including the profitability of land.

In the mid-nineteenth century, both Americans and Mexicans experienced economic insecurity, but they also expressed hope for future growth and prosperity. These contradictory emotions—uncertainty and promise—pervaded the newly divided territory. This chapter follows Bartlett on a trip from the Gulf of Mexico to California and examines through his eyes how the new geopolitical reality affected the ways that citizens of both countries made market transactions. Before beginning this transcontinental journey, we need some background to understand why this man's writings offer a unique, on-the-ground perspective of how people understood money and value in the Mexican Cession territory of the United States and further south.

The United States and Mexico Boundary Commission established the borderline between the two countries as dictated by the Treaty of Guadalupe Hidalgo (1848). The boundary line crossed two thousand miles of varied topography, so the work of surveying took years to complete and involved hundreds of men. Bartlett, appointed chief commissioner by the U.S. president in 1850, began the effort for the United States and led the process until 1853, when he was forced to step down because Congress disputed his settlement with Mexican commissioner general Pedro García Conde. The broader context for his dismissal was a congressional debate over states' rights, slavery, and the construction of a southern transcontinental railroad line. After considerable diplomatic effort, the Gadsden Purchase of 1853 resolved this boundary dispute and facilitated the railroad.

Establishing the precise location of the new border on the ground involved painstaking survey work, which continued for the next four years under different leadership. Major William H. Emory for the United States and José Salazar Ylarregui for Mexico finally agreed on the boundary survey maps in 1857.[2] Though Bartlett was in charge of the survey for less than half of its existence, his keen observer's eye offers a remarkable window into the everyday lives of people who experienced changes in territorial sovereignty.

Our story's protagonist, John Russell Bartlett, was a learned gentleman, bibliophile, and fine artist from Providence, Rhode Island, who owed his appointment as commissioner, in part, to his Whig political party connections (see figure 6.3).[3] Bartlett was the fourth nominee, ascending to the position after the previous three candidates declined, including the military man and explorer John Charles Frémont. In contrast to these experienced men, Bartlett had led a solitary scholarly life, so he perhaps overestimated his ability to survive the harsh conditions of camp life or to lead a large number of men charged with surveying an unknown landscape. On the other hand, he had a gift for storytelling and description—qualities that made him a wonderfully astute observer and recorder of history. His personal diary is filled with everyday interactions with varied people, from Spanish priests,

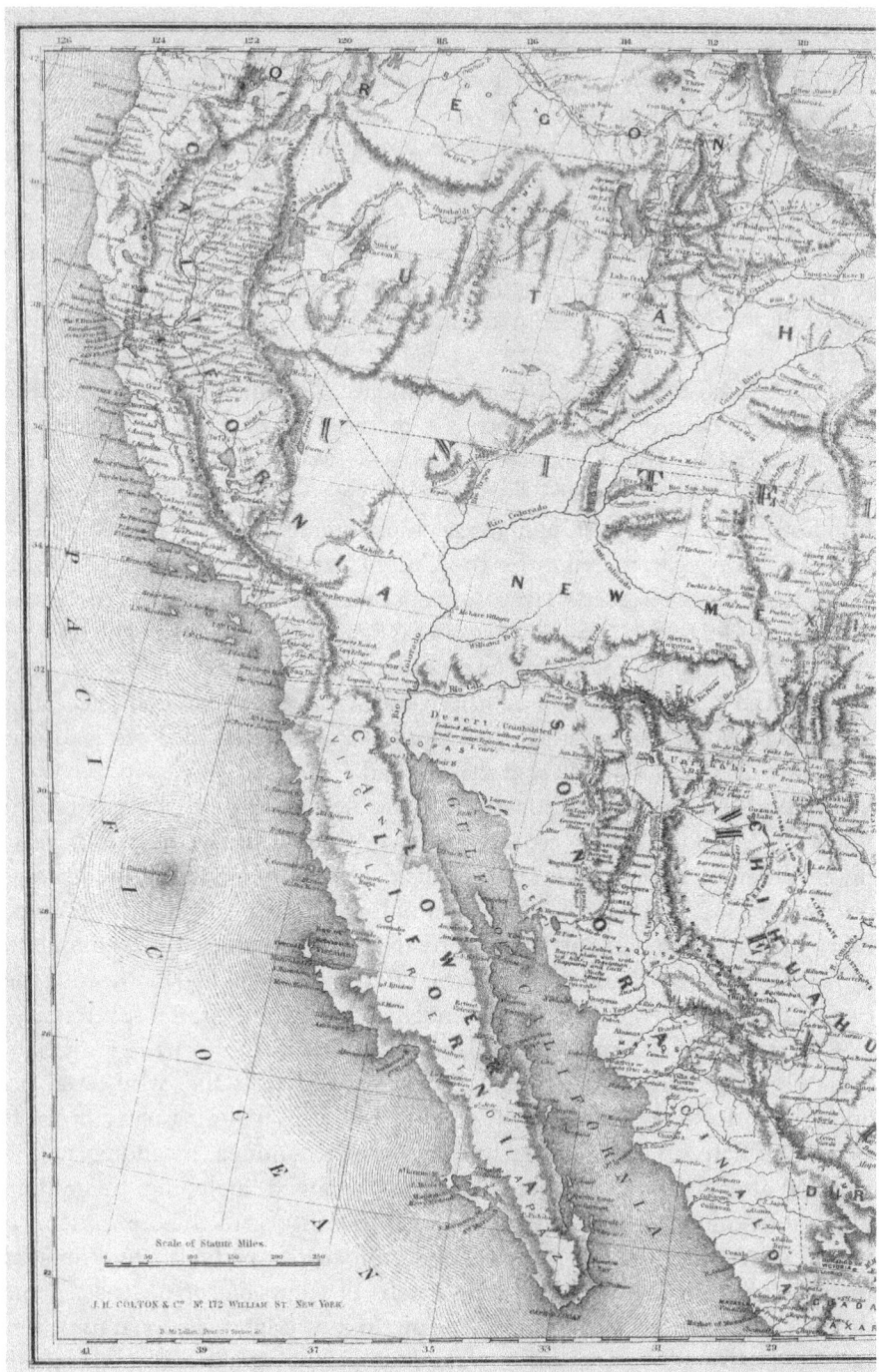

Figure 6.2. Bartlett included this map of northern Mexico and the U.S. Southwest in his *Personal Narrative*. It describes the region he explored, including rivers, mountains, settlements, and main travel routes.

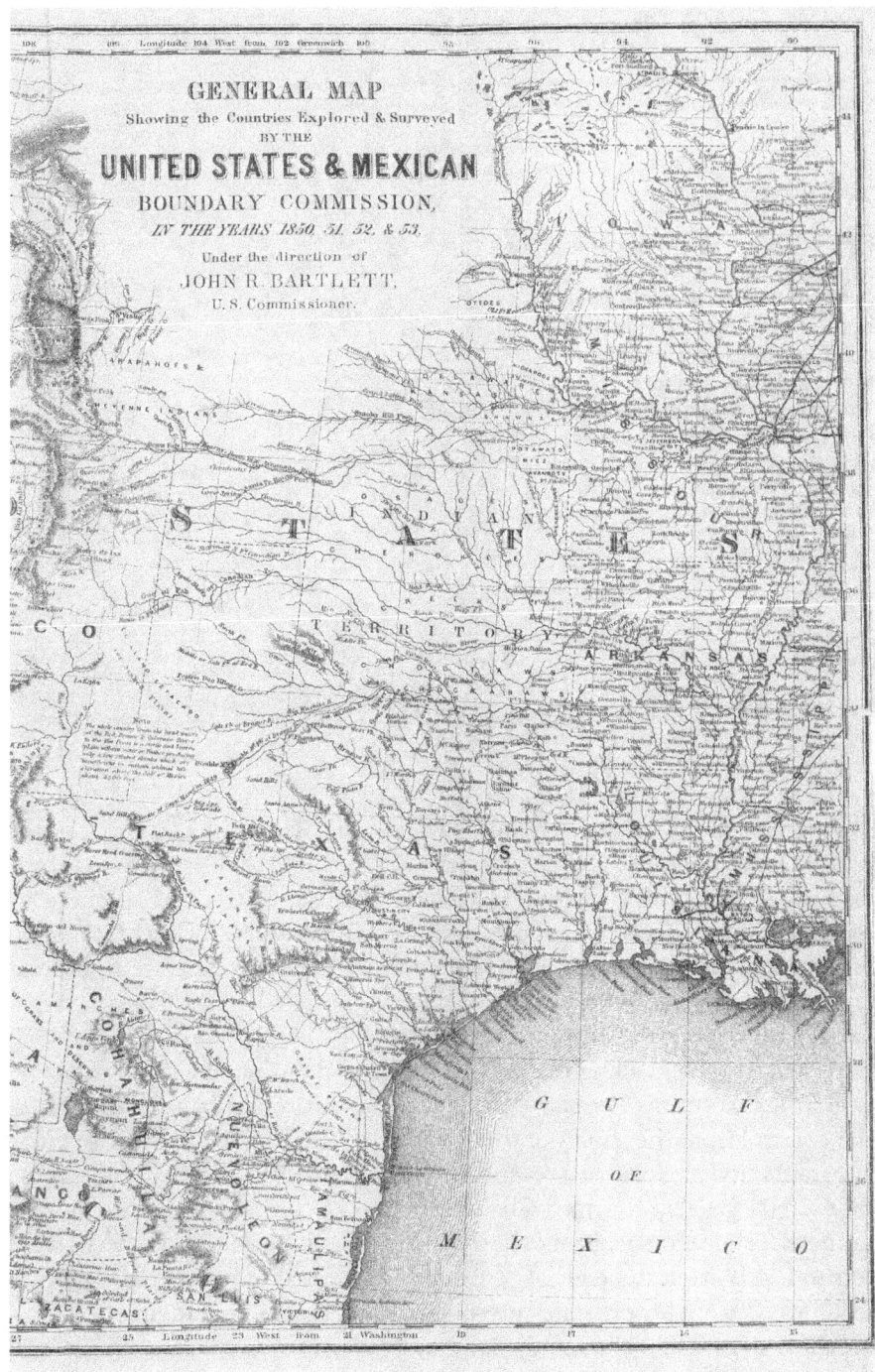

Source: "General Map Showing the Countries Explored & Surveyed by the United States & Mexican Boundary Commission, in the years 1850, 51, 52, & 53, under the direction of John R. Bartlett, U.S. Commissioner" (J. H. Colton & Co., 1854). Map Collection. Courtesy of the John Carter Brown Library at Brown University.

Figure 6.3. This portrait depicts Bartlett at work during the expedition. He might have been writing notes in his field diary or making a sketch of the landscape before him. The artist evokes Bartlett's concentration and seriousness of purpose.
Source: "J. R. Bartlett." Pencil sketch by Henry Cheever Pratt (no date). John Russell Bartlett Collection. Courtesy of the John Carter Brown Library at Brown University.

to Apache chiefs, to Mexican storeowners, with whom he conversed about politics, the economy, and the recent war. Bartlett dutifully recorded these exchanges during his travels and later used them to write a two-volume *Personal Narrative of Explorations and Incidents in Texas, New Mexico, California, Sonora, and Chihuahua*, published a few years after the expedition to great critical acclaim, receiving dozens of positive notices in East Coast newspapers. For our purposes, Bartlett's stories provide an entry point into the lives of people who lived along the boundary line and further afield.

Bartlett wrote his *Personal Narrative* to give "an accurate description of the country from the shores of the Atlantic to the Pacific" in order to guide emigrants and travelers across the newly expanded territory of the United States. His travels confirmed a belief among U.S. citizens that the country's future depended on realizing the great economic potential of the western territories. Bartlett hoped that "crowds as large as those now pressing on to California" would soon start "prospecting among the mountains of Texas, New Mexico, Chihuahua, and Sonora, attracted by similarly rich mineral deposits." Great success awaited, but people had to be made aware of these riches, which is what he intended his *Personal Narrative* to accomplish. So, apart from describing the land and its latent possibilities, Bartlett gave accounts of the products he found for purchase (or sometimes the lack thereof) and their prices. He also provided a sense of the market and the nature of economic transactions. About the town of Arispe in Sonora, for example, he wrote, "The few stores in the place are miserably furnished, their stocks being chiefly dry goods suited to the Mexican market." Such accounts were more than warnings to travelers that supplies might be hard to come by. They also implied that great prospects existed on both sides of the border, such as in Arispe, where merchants would find a paying public eager for superior U.S. products. The message of integration was clearly heard at the time, as articulated in a *Boston Post* review of Bartlett's *Narrative*: "A few revolutions of the wheels of the cars of time will almost invariably find parts of, if not all Sonora and Chihuahua an integral part of the United States."[4] The Mexican Cession was merely a beginning.

Four different accounts in Bartlett's narrative shed light on the way individuals perceived the economy and the value they placed on money, specifically coins. These accounts tell of events that took place as Bartlett crossed the country. The first is about his ongoing efforts to provide provisions for the team, with a focus on El Paso, Texas. The second is about the potential of copper mining at Santa Rita del Cobre, New Mexico. The third recounts events that took place south of the border at Magdalena de Kino, Sonora. The last report is about San Francisco, California, and nearby Napa Valley, where Bartlett documented the prosperity brought on by the California Gold Rush. Together, these four accounts capture the economic spirit that infused different places along the boundary line that newly divided Mexico and the United States.

El Paso, Texas: The Cost of Provisions

Throughout the journey, Bartlett had to acquire provisions for the men on his team and secure equipment, responsible as he was for the group's safety and well-being. This work required accounting and management, which were not his strengths, but his writings about these efforts do provide a sense of what it was like to travel through territory without banks, where stores accepted money from different nations—two conditions unheard of today. Bartlett began his supervisory duties prior to leaving from New York Harbor, where he determined "to purchase provisions, medical stores, and such other articles as would be required in a distant country, where few of the necessaries of life could be procured." Even with his preparations, maintaining stocks was necessarily an ongoing effort. Bartlett had to plan and budget carefully throughout the journey, as supplies were indeed scarce everywhere. After leaving New York, the team traveled by steamship to the Gulf Coast, landing at Indianola, Texas, in August 1850 to start on the journey into the interior. They traveled in six mule-drawn wagons to their first official destination, El Paso, where Bartlett had a prearranged meeting with his Mexican counterpart, Commissioner Conde.

In locations with military posts, Bartlett had the support of the U.S. Army Quartermasters Office, whose personnel arranged for quarters, rations, and the like (see figure 6.4). The presence of these military posts highlights the fact that the boundary commission worked along a militarized border; the war was only two years past in 1850, when Bartlett arrived in El Paso. There, he employed his government authority "to call upon the U.S. Commissaries of Subsistence for provisions." He gratefully noted that officers from this post provided for the "immediate needs" of the party. Food for the animals

Figure 6.4. This sketch of the El Paso Commissioner Quarters shows the main building flying a U.S. flag, marking the political transition of this territory. The wooden buildings in the background housed soldiers and workers. The mule-drawn cart and wagons on the left were similar to those that carried the supplies of Bartlett's expedition.
Source: "El Paso, Texas Commissioners Quarters." Pencil and sepia sketch by J. R. Bartlett (no date). John Russell Bartlett Collection. Courtesy of the John Carter Brown Library at Brown University.

who carried them was another matter—fodder "had to be purchased at the market prices." Bartlett had a U.S. government line of credit to make such purchases, which spared him from carrying around large sums. Instead, he relied on certain wealthy local residents, such as one Mr. Brodie in Sonora, who were willing to cash Bartlett's "draft on the government" and give him Mexican or American coins as need be. Mr. Brodie and others acted as an informal network of banks for Bartlett. Such wealthy individuals provided this service on the understanding that, with time, the U.S. government would pay them back through a local private bank. In this way, the U.S. government extended its own credit to the furthest reaches of its new territory. The extension of U.S. sovereignty via credit lines was a mechanism of state formation.

Bartlett's observations about the local economy at El Paso reveal his interest in that region's economic potential as well as a concern for the everyday running of his operation. On taking stock of the local market, he remarked that prices were "exceedingly high." By prices, he meant the amount he had to pay for things as opposed to their actual cost. Bartlett recorded that flour sold for US$32 a barrel; pork, sugar, and coffee were US$0.50 a pound, and corn was US$8 per *fanega* (a volume equivalent to nearly three bushels), all of which he considered excessive.

Were these prices unusually high, or was that merely Bartlett's impression? To get a sense of the local market, we need some regional comparisons or figures on the price of corn (maize) in nearby areas. According to Colonel Emilio Landberg of the Mexican army, who carried out a military inspection around the same time, the price of maize at Piedras Negras (opposite Eagle Pass, Texas) in 1852 was MX$2 per *fanega*.[5] This transnational comparison tells us that the price for corn in El Paso was indeed high (the value of Mexican and U.S. dollars remained roughly equivalent). Using a different measurement, based on U.S. annual averages, which varied a great deal, the price of corn was US$0.78 per bushel a decade later, less than one-tenth what Bartlett was forced to pay.[6] Why such high prices? In 1850, the supply of corn in El Paso was insufficient to meet the sudden increase in travelers seeking feed for their pack animals. So the few individuals who had any stock of the grain on hand raised prices to make a larger profit, which, according to Bartlett, amounted to price gouging.

Bartlett's enumeration of the prices for food provisions reflects El Paso's changing economy as well as its status as a new U.S. town. El Paso was an old Spanish colonial trading center on the Rio Grande, where travelers had acquired provisions for several hundred years. The town had considerable agriculture, so visitors usually found plenty of locally grown corn and other food for themselves and their animals at reasonable prices. At the time of Bartlett's visit, however, the town was at the very beginnings of an economic boom related to the recent arrival of American settlers and the influx of travelers passing through on their way to California. An increase in prices is typical at such moments; when a place quickly fills with people requiring food and shelter, there is more demand than supply. While the arrival of American settlers had already spiked prices in the town, storeowners and ranchers hiked rates still further upon receiving news of the commission's imminent arrival.

The conclusion of the Mexican-American War shifted the economics of the new border region. Some towns, like Bacanuchi, found themselves in a type of no-man's-land in which the currency of neither nation had yet earned the trust of the residents, an understandable concern in a place were few travelers came, other than those who were redrawing the borders. Other communities, like El Paso, experienced the change very differently. While supplies were hard to secure, and then only at exorbitant prices, Americans like Bartlett viewed that very problem as opportunity. If newly claimed towns were not yet prepared for the coming wave of travelers and settlers, American entrepreneurs were ready to step in. American ambitions had long included northern Mexico. Now that this land was in American hands, American businessmen could not be far behind.

Santa Rita del Cobre, New Mexico: The Cost of Transport and the Value of Copper

When Bartlett took possession of Santa Rita del Cobre for the United States in 1851, the New Mexico mining town lay abandoned. Native American nations had regained control of the region, forcing miners to retreat southward to towns with military garrisons. Prior to this withdrawal, Santa Rita's copper mines had made men rich—a fact that Americans from both Mexico and the United States well knew. Army officer Zebulon Montgomery Pike, of Colorado's Pikes Peak fame, had referenced the mine in a widely read report years earlier: "It is wrought and produces 2,000 mule loads of copper annually, furnishing that article for the manufactories of nearly all the internal provinces."[7] During the first decades of the nineteenth century, the owners of Santa Rita also supplied the mint in Mexico City. The purity of the copper metal in the ore mined there made it ideal for coinage. The Spanish and then Mexican governments both used metal from New Mexico to make coins in fractional denominations of *reales* (which came in coins of one-half, one-quarter, and one-eighth *real*).[8] The ore also contained traces of gold, which was sufficiently valuable to cover the transportation costs. The mine had run as a private enterprise under government contract, which paid the operator a rate of sixty-five cents for a pound of refined copper. Such prices were no longer attainable because the mint in Mexico City had since turned to sources of copper much closer to the Mexican capital. The Mexican market for Santa Rita's copper was in the past. For Bartlett, the mine was now in U.S. territory and its future lay in American industry.

Though the town's economic potential was not lost on Bartlett, he was cognizant of existing obstacles. First, men would have to be coaxed back to work at the site. El Paso had cheap labor available, but workers would have to be ensured safe transport before they ventured the 150 plus miles that lay between them and the mine. Second, there was the very real fear of Apache raids. Indians had, after all, "attacked and overcome" a wagon train some ten years earlier and subsequently cut off the mine from receiving provisions. This attack had capitalized on the third obstacle: miners had historically relied on outside purveyors for food. The area had timber and good grazing land for animals but not for planting, so crops like maize and beans had been brought in from Chihuahua and elsewhere. So what could be done about these logistical constraints? Bartlett made quick calculations: with military order and some planning, the mine could reopen and become reoriented from Mexico toward the United States through Texas. If his plan were put into action, the Santa Rita del Cobre mine could become a significant asset to the United States.

For planning purposes, transportation was fundamental. How would the metal reach Philadelphia, for example, for coining into pennies? Bartlett was not blindly optimistic and lamented that it would "hardly pay to work" the mine without a better means of transport, say by rail. In the same breath, however, he proposed a short-term solution. Wagon trains already ran the seven-hundred-mile route from the Texas port of Indianola (where his own expedition made landfall) to El Paso and returned empty. Bartlett presumed that drivers would "no doubt, be glad to carry the copper at half price," which would amount to ten cents per pound of ore. The calculation could pay off given the high dividends yielded by copper mines and the limited supply of copper in the United States at the time.[9] A willing investor would surely profit if he could arrange to deliver copper to a new market like New Orleans with its major port. By wagon and then steamship, the trip, at some twelve hundred miles, was still shorter than the route to Mexico City.

Finally, there was the question of Indian attacks, but Bartlett had hopes for a quick resolution to that problem. The Mexican government had made considerable advances in the previous five years against the "Copper Mine

Apaches," who occupied "the country on both sides of the Rio Grande." Bartlett's informants told him that the Apaches were "greatly reduced in numbers"; they could not "muster 200 warriors." It was important for Bartlett to emphasize this fact because the American authorities "placed their numbers much higher." Bartlett, however, had it on good authority that future U.S. settlers had nothing to fear. He also felt that the few Apaches who remained could be pacified, especially if the American government followed Mexico's lead and supplied them with corn. The Mexican government had at times temporarily placated Apache groups by providing them with food. Bartlett reasoned that the United States had to do the same: to pay the Apaches in order to secure the stability essential to economic growth.

For Bartlett, the mines of Santa Rita del Cobre were emblematic of American attitudes about the region that had recently been northern Mexico. Expansionist Americans felt that the Mexicans were not using the land to its proper potential. If Mexicans were no longer able to profit from the copper mines, Americans certainly would, potentially shipping the metal to the U.S. Mint and turning it directly into cash (pennies). Borderland folk like the people of Bacanuchi already accorded value to copper coins; the goal would be to expand and transfer this trust to U.S. currency. If western North America was to be fully developed, American entrepreneurs and modern technologies, like the railroad, would be essential parts of that change.

Feast Day Celebrations at Magdalena de Kino, Sonora: Coins Lost to the Catholic Church

A few months after his sojourn in Santa Rita del Cobre, Bartlett was three hundred miles to the southwest in Magdalena de Kino, Sonora.[10] It was October 1851, and the town was in the midst of a feast day celebration for Saint Francis. The lavish events prompted Bartlett, a Protestant, to comment on the traditional influence of the Catholic Church on Mexican culture. His generally negative appraisal was typical of liberal thinkers of his era, who valued the separation of church and state. As a political ideology, classical liberalism in the nineteenth century articulated the idea that religious institutions hindered social and economic progress. In the minds of many, the Catholic Church stunted economic prosperity because it encouraged believers to donate their money for festivals and church upkeep rather than using it as capital for investments and personal gain. For Bartlett, the money spent on celebrating a saint was money better used elsewhere.

Three aspects of the festivities stood out to Bartlett. First was its duration. The feast day fell on October 4 each year but merely culminated long planning efforts. Final preparations began "several days previous . . . so that the devotions and offerings, with their accompanying festivities, were in full blast a day or two in advance." To Bartlett, these days of planning and celebrating represented wasted labor, to say nothing of the cost of the festivities themselves. The Protestant work ethic demanded productive labor on all days except for the Lord's Sabbath.

Also problematic were the offerings made to the saint's image. For a Protestant, prayer and offerings to a saint amounted to worship of graven images, forbidden in Exodus 20:4–5. Bartlett could not understand why people believed that a statue made of wood and "clothed in rich vestments" had miraculous powers. According to legend, a mule led by Franciscan friars had carried an image of the saint for hundreds of miles. When the animal stopped in its tracks, the friars took it as a sign of "the Saint's pleasure" and desire that they should establish a Christian mission at the site. Though historically questionable, this story made the Church of San Francisco, in Bartlett's words, the "Mecca of devout Mexican Catholics." To Bartlett's great disbelief, thousands of pilgrims flocked to Magdalena each year from hundreds of miles away, taking still more time away from profitable labor.

Bartlett's last target of cultural disapproval regarding the festival was notably linked to money. Pilgrims made offerings with candles and coins. Catholic tradition has long supported prayer for intercession by saints. Small donations to the church often accompany these pleas. The poorest offered candles made of tallow (wax was too expensive). The majority of conveners, however, offered money in silver coins (Mexican dollars), which made a "continual jingling" sound as people dropped them into a receptacle. Bartlett, amazed by the quantity of coins, made a quick calculation based on the crowds he saw: "I state that the receipts this year, although the attendance was less than usual, were about 12,000 dollars." He learned that previously "the amount of money voluntarily given had reached the sum of 18,000." Where did all the money go? What was it used for? No priest was present to inform Bartlett, so he asked a number of the pilgrims. The usual reply, *¿Quien sabe?*—the eternal "who knows?"—tried his patience. Finally, "a gentleman" provided an answer that only confirmed Bartlett's belief that the offerings were simply a waste. The silver coins, thousands of them, went to Mexico City (the site of Mexico's main archdiocese), so that "neither the poor of Magdalena, nor the church there derived any benefit" from the money (see figure 6.5). Charity would at least have been an economic benefit that Bartlett understood, even if he did not approve. The said gentleman, however, confirmed Bartlett's liberal

Figure 6.5. The 1858 silver peso above, with liberty cap and Mexican eagle, bore the marking 10D 20G to show that it contained the set amount of silver. Yet Bartlett found that local residents in Bacanuchi did not trust that these coins really contained the silver they claimed, while residents in Magdalena de Kino unproductively donated them to the church.
Source: "Republican Coin" (1858). Original in Queens College Loan Collection, CM.QC.4930-R. Reproduction by permission of the Syndics of the Fitzwilliam Museum, Cambridge, United Kingdom.

disdain for the Catholic Church, which hoarded capital rather than using it to society's profit.

As if wasted labor and capital were not enough, Bartlett identified an additional problem. From the liberal Protestant perspective, feast days were merely occasions for profligate revelry. So Bartlett made great fuss about the lengthy festival, centered in the town's plaza, where vendors sold food and trinkets out of temporary booths. There was also a stand for music and dancing. Worst of all, gambling was everywhere. Bartlett's descriptions reveal his contempt for this "exciting amusement," which attracted crowds of Catholics "of every age, sex, and class." For Bartlett, such revelry epitomized wasteful Catholic extravagance and indulgent worship.

The gambling scenes tell us about diverging views on the value of money and its purpose. Bartlett saw children "laying down their coppers," the low-denomination coins Bartlett had previously encountered in Bacanuchi. The actual value of the children's coins was not Bartlett's gravest concern. Rather, he worried that the children followed their parents' model and learned terrible lessons about managing their finances. Soon they would be like the adults, who gambled away "their reales and dollars," mimicking the richer among them, who sat at different tables and "ventured their ounces." Money handed over in cards and other games of chance was wasted capital, just like the offerings to Saint Francis.

In Magdalena de Kino the cultural differences between nineteenth-century Mexico and the United States came into sharp focus. Bartlett's narrative contrasts faith in God with faith in the market. Embodying the myth of the Protestant work ethic, Bartlett calculated the days of preparation and celebration as labor hours lost. He recoiled against the notion of silver dollars going toward something other than clear, capital-generating enterprise.

San Francisco, California: Gold and Trade on the Pacific Coast

Many months and miles later, Bartlett arrived in San Francisco. His first remark: "There is no project too great for the Californian of the present day. He is ready for any undertaking, whether it be to make a railroad to the Atlantic, to swallow up Mexico, or to invade the empire of Japan." How prescient. The first transcontinental railroad was completed in 1869.[11] The latter "undertaking" occurred in 1945 with the U.S. occupation of Japan.

Bartlett had a grand vision for the town that corresponded with the spirit of the California Gold Rush era (1848–1855). At the same time, California's promise was equally tied, in Bartlett's mind, to San Francisco's history under the Spanish Empire—a time when the port welcomed the Manila Galleon on its way to Acapulco. This annual fleet had maintained trade links between Spain's colony in the Philippines and Mexico for nearly three hundred years. Such trade was now wide open for the United States—ships sailing in and out of San Francisco would herald a new era of Pacific commerce. The United States had at last completed its expansion across North America and would now certainly continue to spread its influence still further west.

Bartlett found evidence of Chinese riches in northern Mexico, which inspired him to imagine the great possibilities of U.S. trade with China. At the Church of San Ignacio de Cabórica in Sonora, he discovered "two Chinese figures, intended doubtless for mandarins, but here metamorphosed into saints." Those very images reminded him that the United States was now in close "proximity to the Pacific" and, beyond it, the "Celestial Empire" (meaning China), with which Mexico had once had "a flourishing commerce." Under the Spanish, Mexico had exported "silver, cochineal, cocoa, wine, oil, and Spanish wool" in return for "China silks, India muslins and cottons, spices and aromatics, jewelry, and other articles of luxury and taste." Citizens of the United States prized Chinese goods as well and had been trading for them out of East Coast ports for more than sixty years. A major U.S. port on the Pacific coast would certainly ease and expand that trade. According to Bartlett, the Spanish had limited commerce to a "single" ship, "whose cargo was estimated to be worth from £300,000 to 400,000 sterling." Under liberal economics such a limitation of commerce would be unthinkable.

Bartlett also witnessed remnants of the Manila Galleon trade at the Mexican port of Acapulco, which he visited on his way to San Francisco. At Sonora, it was easier to sail down the Pacific coast and then get on a fast steamer to reach northern California than to continue overland. Bartlett explained that Acapulco "owed its former importance to its commerce with the East Indies." Acapulco had been the official port of disembarkation for Spain's Manila Galleon (ships only stopped in San Francisco for provisions) (see figure 6.6). Now the port lay "in a more or less ruined state," which offered Bartlett further indication that the Pacific now belonged to the United States rather than Mexico. There was also little to buy at market; vendors crowded in the corner of a plaza to sell fruits and vegetables but little else. Transactions were small and bore little profit. Bartlett, in fact, saw no evidence of real money, writing, "Change being scarce, small cakes of soap are used instead, as in other parts of Mexico." This unusual currency was actually officially authorized. Only cakes of soap stamped with their town of origin and manufacturer were accepted as money. On seeing this poverty, Bartlett

Figure 6.6. This view of the harbor at Acapulco shows the town's main buildings and thatched-roof homes. The fort on the left flies the Mexican flag, symbolizing the nation's hold on this important port, which welcomed ships from newly independent republics in Latin America, the United States, and China, among other nations, during the second half of the nineteenth century.
Source: "Acapulco." Charcoal and wash drawing by J. R. Bartlett (1852). Original in John Russell Bartlett Collection. Courtesy of the John Carter Brown Library at Brown University.

could well contemplate that San Francisco would soon take Acapulco's place as North America's most important port.

The prices in San Francisco reflected the Gold Rush. Few fortunes were made from gold, but a great number of merchants and farmers grew very rich indeed from supplying the thousands of prospectors who migrated to California during this period. Miners needed tools, clothing, and food, all being sold at extraordinarily high prices. Bartlett witnessed this phenomenon firsthand. Speaking to a certain Mr. Kilburn, a farmer in the Napa Valley originally from Missouri, Bartlett learned that the farmer had profited US$8,000 in cash from selling the onions he grew on just two acres of land. At San Francisco, the market price for onions was over twelve cents apiece. Bartlett ate this delicacy "with more relish than I ever did an orange." He had paid the modern equivalent of US$3.60 for the pleasure.[12] Why such a high price? Well, it seems that onions were "the most valuable of all vegetables among the gold miners, on account of their anti-scorbutic properties," meaning that they prevented scurvy. This dreaded disease, which causes gums to bleed and great tiredness, stems from a deficiency of vitamin C. Onions contain both that vitamin and chemical compounds that help the human body absorb it. San Francisco, moreover, was experiencing an extreme version of the phenomenon that Bartlett had witnessed in El Paso. Following the discovery of gold at Sutter's Mill, San Francisco's population began growing much faster than its available resources. As a result, vendors who could provide merchandise could charge hopeful miners, on their way to try to strike it rich, exorbitant rates.

In this last segment of his journey, Bartlett traveled from Acapulco, where specie was so rare that the local population used soap as currency, to San Francisco, where miners were digging riches out of the ground. His narrative symbolically compares a town whose greatness had sailed away decades before with the last of the Manila Galleons to the United States' new El Dorado, where gold streamed from the ground into the expanding economy of an ascendant United States. A few years later, in 1857, silver was found at the Comstock Lode in the Virginia Range along the California-Nevada border. Bartlett would not have been surprised; boundless wealth was on America's horizon.

Conclusion

This chapter began with a historical query about the nature of everyday exchanges in the U.S.-Mexican borderlands. Here we have seen that the local availability of goods and media of exchange largely drove those exchanges. Commerce in these border towns was still an insular process. While national borders may have changed, communities like Bacanuchi and Santa Rita del Cobre were not yet connected to national commerce, as they one day would be by rail lines and expanding settlement. During the postwar years Bartlett witnessed the beginning of a new economic phase for the United States. The national landscape had expanded by more than five hundred thousand square miles. The country had completed its "Manifest Destiny" to span the continent and now had a coastline facing into the enormous trade potential of the Pacific Ocean. Lastly, the country had acquired deposits of gold, silver, and copper that would at last permit it to sustain adequate production of its own coins. Our next chapter discusses the consequences of minting this gold.

Notes

1. All Bartlett quotations are from John Russell Bartlett, *Personal Narrative of Explorations and Incidents in Texas, New Mexico, California, Sonora, and Chihuahua*, 2 vols. (New York: D. Appleton & Company, 1854).

2. The International Boundary Commission resurveyed the line between 1891 and 1896, which was amended in 1970 with the Treaty to Resolve Pending Boundary Differences and Maintain the Rio Grande and the Colorado River as the International Boundary.

3. At the time of his appointment Bartlett was known as an ethnologist and founding member of the American Ethnological Society, established in 1842. He was also the personal librarian and friend of John Carter Brown, founder of the John Carter Brown Library at Brown University.

4. J. Gray Sweeney, ed., *Drawing the Borderline: Artist-Explorers of the U.S.-Mexico Boundary Survey* (Albuquerque, NM: Albuquerque Museum, 1996), 64.

5. Emilio Langberg, "Itinerario de la Expedición de San Carlos a Monclova El Viejo Hecha por el Coronel D. Emilio Langberg, Inspector Interino de las Colonias Militares de Chihuahua . . . en el Año de 1851" (Beinecke, 1852).

6. We only have data on commodity prices from 1866 onward. "Table Da693-706. Corn, Barley, and Flaxseed—Acreage, Production, Price, and Corn Stocks: 1866–1999, Annual," in *Historical Statistics of the United States*, ed. Susan B. Carter et al. Millennial edition online (New York: Cambridge University Press, 2015), http://hsus.cambridge.org. These figures do not reflect the actual price paid by consumers. The calculation is further complicated by the fact that Bartlett purchased the corn for animal feed rather than human consumption, so the regional price index for food cannot be used. Philip R. P. Coelho and James F. Shepherd, "Differences in Regional Prices: The United States, 1851–1880," *Journal of Economic History* 34, no. 3 (1974).

7. Zebulon Montgomery Pike, "Geographical, Statistical, and General Observations on the Interior Provinces of New Spain," in *Exploratory Travels through the*

Western Territories of North America (London: Printed for Longman, Hurst, Rees, Orme, and Brown, 1811), 331–32.

8. Ferdinand VII of Spain introduced copper coins in the late colonial period. President José María Morelos continued to mint in copper (one *real* and one-half *real*) in the national mint (*casa de moneda matriz*), as did the state branches (*casas foráneas*) that emerged in the Republican period.

9. Michigan was the sole producer of copper in U.S. territory prior to the 1850s.

10. The town is named after Father Eusebio Kino, who died there in 1711, after founding missions throughout the region and into Baja California. The Temple of Saint Mary Magdalene is famed for holding Kino's remains. Buford Pickens, *The Missions of Northern Sonora: A 1935 Field Documentation* (Tucson: University of Arizona Press, 1993), 18.

11. The Transcontinental Railroad (also called the Pacific Railroad), laid out between 1863 and 1869, ran from San Francisco Bay to Council Bluffs, Iowa, where it joined previously built lines. For a detailed rendering of its history, see David Haward Bain, *Empire Express: Building the First Transcontinental Railroad* (New York: Viking-Penguin, 1999).

12. Measuring the worth of things in the past is incredibly complicated. Most economic historians translate prices in the past to modern equivalents by using a purchasing power calculator, which determines the relative value (in today's money) of something purchased in a prior year. The approximate worth, or relative value, of US$1 in 1852 was the same as US$31.60 in 2014. The calculation is from http://www.measuringworth.com.

CHAPTER SEVEN

Gold Recklessness

In December 1832, Professor Robert Maskell Patterson at the University of Virginia received a printed letter from the directors of Girard College in Philadelphia, offering him "a premium of four hundred dollars" to "author of a system of instruction and government" for their institution.[1] After Stephen Girard died in 1831, his will revealed that he had left the largest bequest in the nation's history to endow a school for boys in his adopted city of Philadelphia. The men charged with organizing the college addressed Patterson, a fellow Philadelphian, in the hope that he would come to their assistance. They needed a scholar like him to help them devise the proposed school's course of education. Patterson was unable to be of service. Nonetheless, this document underlines the importance given to education at this time, when millionaires like Girard held that the future of the United States depended on "intellect and knowledge." Soon after this exchange, Patterson returned to Philadelphia, where he directed his intellect toward securing that future by thinking about bullion, metallurgy, and the circulation of U.S. dollars in an era of gold strikes. How did the heightened availability of this most precious of metals alter the production of money in the United States?

The protagonist in this chapter is Dr. Robert Maskell Patterson, who served as director of the U.S. Mint from 1835 to 1851 (see figure 7.1); the money is the gold coins produced in the mint branches that opened following gold strikes in North Carolina, Georgia, and California. The San Francisco branch, which opened in 1854, minted more than US$4 million in its first year of operation. By February 1857, the outflow from the California

Figure 7.1. This portrait of Patterson's staid demeanor evokes his seriousness of purpose. His sober expression reflects his meticulous approach to managing the task of making the nation's money. Here was a determined and intelligent man who could be trusted with the orderly administration of the U.S. Mint.
Source: "Portrait of Robert Maskell Patterson," by Samuel F. Dubois (1855). Oil on canvas. Original in the American Philosophical Society. Gift of Mrs. Robert M. Patterson, April 20, 1855.

gold fields had provided the United States with sufficient bullion to end, at last, the use of foreign coins as legal tender—six decades later than planned. This chapter examines mid-century gold coin production during Patterson's tenure within the broader context of U.S. western expansion. President James K. Polk supported Patterson's advocacy for a California branch soon after the Mexican Cession. California gold had the singular potential to replace silver as the U.S. monetary standard and thus to liberate the mint from its dependence on imported silver.

This story also considers the consequences of increased gold in circulation, which inspired profligate spending and speculation that ultimately fueled a real estate bubble, drawing in lenders from across the United States and even Europe. When that bubble burst in the summer of 1857, the country plunged into its first international economic crisis. The chapter's focus on gold coins brings to light the gains made by the United States as a result of the Mexican Cession, as well as the perils of sudden and seemingly endless wealth.

Robert Maskell Patterson (1787–1854) was a medical doctor, a professor of chemistry, mathematics, and natural philosophy, a president of the American Philosophical Society, and a director of the U.S. Mint. Like John Russell Bartlett of the previous chapter, Patterson was a learned gentleman. Born into a prominent Philadelphia family, he grew up in privilege. He attended the University of Pennsylvania, where his father served as professor of mathematics; he earned his medical degree in 1808 and then continued his training among leading scientists in Paris and London. His studiousness and dedication to learning led to a distinguished career in scholarship and government service, but much of his success was also a product of birthright. His father, a man of science himself, had also held the positions of president of the American Philosophical Society and director of the U.S. Mint (1805–1824). Inherited positions were not uncommon in the Early Republic, both in science and politics. To his credit, the younger Patterson well understood his good fortune and was committed, like his father before him, to serving the new nation.

Patterson was probably not surprised when the Treasury Department, likely at the direction of President Andrew Jackson, contacted him in May 1835 to offer him the directorship of the U.S. Mint. His father had received a similar letter directly from President Thomas Jefferson back in 1805. According to a family member, the younger Patterson was greatly honored to be entrusted with the office, for he considered "the conservation of the standards and relative values of real money, and the faithful execution of monetary laws" to be fundamental to the public interest. This chapter focuses on the last two decades of Patterson's life, from his appointment as director of the mint in 1835, to his retirement in 1851, to his death three years later. During these years, Patterson led the U.S. Mint through a period of economic depression, wartime recovery, and a gold boom.

Patterson's commitment to scientific order and expertise in mathematics served him well at the mint, where he did much to streamline and modernize coin production. His first order of business was to draw up a digest of laws governing the mint's operations, which included attention to accounting practices and metallic values. The act that confirmed Patterson's new regulations passed in early 1837.² In accordance with his commitment to scientific innovation, the legislation included new standards for the fineness, or purity, of precious metals to be used in coins.³ Patterson pushed for limiting the amount of pure metal in coins to save bullion (a scarce resource in the 1830s and 1840s). Additionally, he shifted the expression of fineness from carats and fractions to the millesimal system used in France, which simplified accounting and conversions.⁴ Looking forward in time, Patterson's interest in the metal composition of U.S. coinage resurfaced at the outset of the California Gold Rush, when it seemed finally possible that the nation would have enough bullion to mint gold of the highest purity and in larger denominations than ever before.

Patterson faced a number of administrative challenges during these first years, not the least being the recent establishment of three new mint branches in Charlotte, North Carolina, Dahlonega, Georgia, and New Orleans, Louisiana. Congress approved these new facilities in 1835 prior to Patterson's appointment, but it fell to him to manage their opening and get them functioning. The branch at Charlotte was a product of the nation's first gold rush. News of gold in the region came to light in 1793, but not until the turn of the century did men stream in to make their fortunes, particularly in an area known as the Reed Gold Mine outside Charlotte, where John Reed found a seventeen-pound nugget. For the next three decades, the government had to transport gold from central North Carolina to Philadelphia for minting. This voyage was a concern, given the likelihood of nuggets finding their way elsewhere and ending up as jewelry rather than proper coins.

Then, in 1828, the town of Dahlonega, located in Georgia's Blue Ridge Mountains, became the site of the next gold rush. This gold strike, located roughly 250 miles to the west of Reed's mine, raised new worries. Apart from the increased chance of banditry given the distance, the government also had to consider the costs of transporting gold to the mint. To reduce expenses and ease turning gold from these mines into U.S. currency, the government ordered the establishment of two new mint branches in Charlotte and Dahlonega, which opened for operation in 1837 and 1838 respectively. Both produced exclusively gold coins. Patterson's experience with these two branches and the move to mint coins at mining locations likely influenced his call for the speedy approval of a new branch in California soon after the gold find at Sutter's Mill became public.

Whereas the previous two mint branches were located in gold regions, New Orleans was selected for a third branch, which opened in 1838, for its position in the Mississippi Delta, the riverine opening to the nation's interior and a main center of commerce. The New Orleans branch would convert imported bullion, primarily from Mexico, into gold and silver coins and facilitate their circulation to the states along the Mississippi River. This minting effort was extremely important to President Andrew Jackson, who decried the persistent lack of specie in circulation, which he felt limited business opportunities for the common man.

Two years into Patterson's tenure, the U.S. economy spun out of control, due in part to Jackson's relentless drive to eradicate the national debt during his presidency (1829–1837) and his desire to destroy the Second Bank of the United States (see chapter 2 for the first and second national banks). Jackson opposed debt on principle and despised elite bankers, especially those associated with Girard's Philadelphia bank. So he ordered the Treasury to withdraw federal funds from the Bank of the United States and to make deposits into smaller banks throughout the country. These actions, meant to kill the Second Bank, had an unforeseen consequence.

Small regional banks, flush with new money from these transfers, turned around and made unprecedented loans, especially to land speculators who purchased giant tracts with notes drawn on these small banks. Jackson, in turn, sought to check this trend, shuddering at such widespread borrowing. According to his 1836 executive order, the Specie Circular, the General Land Office would henceforth accept only gold and silver for the purchase of federal land. This directive had a domino effect: speculators panicked; small banks called in loans, demanding payment in specie; individual borrowers defaulted; banknotes lost their value; small banks failed; citizens hoarded gold and silver; inflation skyrocketed; factories closed; state and federal tax revenues plummeted; states defaulted (including Pennsylvania); big banks

Figure 7.2. This silver dime bears the same image by Christian Gobrecht on its face as the U.S. dollar introduced in 1836. The liberty cap on the upper right is across Lady Liberty's shield on the lower left, with the word LIBERTY—a triple confirmation that U.S. coins expressed the nation's highest political ideal.
Source: "U.S. Silver Dime" (1838). Photo by Yale University Art Gallery. Public Domain.

failed. It was the Panic of 1837, and the resulting economic depression weighed on the citizenry until 1843.

Throughout these years, Patterson worked tirelessly as the head of the mint to realign confidence in the currency of the United States. As part of this effort, he oversaw redesigns of the silver dollar, reintroduced at last in 1836. On these new dollars, the bust of Liberty gave way to a full-body image of Liberty sitting on a rock, holding a staff topped with a liberty cap (see figure 7.2). Patterson also increased the production of coins at all branches, made possible by the introduction of the steam press. Citizens needed hard currency. The creation of coins, however, remained limited by the available supply of bullion. All that changed in 1848.

California Gold Strike

The now legendary gold discovery at Sutter's Mill, ninety miles from San Francisco, in January 1848 changed how U.S. citizens perceived money. As readers well know, news of the gold strike spread within months, sparking the California Gold Rush. The timing of the discovery, just days before the signing of the Treaty of Guadalupe Hidalgo on February 2, 1848, when the Mexican government ceded this territory to the United States, has since inspired conspiratorial murmurings about the U.S. government's decision to end the war when it did. It seems ever so convenient that the greatest gold find in North American history took place in newly purchased U.S. territory. Be that as it may, the California Gold Rush was a boon for the U.S. economy, even as it also created new logistical challenges for Patterson, who needed to turn this new gold into U.S. currency.

Almost unimaginably, annual gold production in the United States multiplied by a factor of ten within a year of the discovery in California and by a factor of more than one hundred by 1852, when gold production achieved its nineteenth-century peak of 104,758 kilograms (3.7 million ounces) per year.[5] Not all of that gold, of course, reached the Philadelphia mint, but enough did to overwhelm Patterson's facility. Turning gold into coins involved a lengthy process, and the mint had a relatively small staff of twelve, with only one assayer and one smelter and refiner. It simply could not keep up with the volume. Patterson responded by lobbying for a new branch, following the precedent of those opened in gold territory some eighteen years earlier.

Immediate congressional approval of two new gold coin denominations in March 1849 points to just how quickly the government mobilized to capitalize on California gold.[6] Merely a year after the initial discovery, the nation finally had enough bullion to mint gold dollar coins (equal in value to the largest silver coin) to meet the constant need for currency. At the same time, this new denomination would help the mint absorb the gold pouring into it. The new branch coined the country's first double eagles, the largest U.S. coin denomination ever, worth US$20.[7]

Gold fever ran high in the government as well as among the citizenry, in part due to the recent victory over Mexico. A popular song, titled "California Gold, a Song for the Occasion," published in 1849 in *The United States Magazine and Democratic Review*, a Jacksonian publication that espoused western expansion, illustrates this connection:

> Gold! Gold! It was the watchword, when the Spaniard first unfurled
> The flag of conquest over the new found western world . . .
> Twas a golden dream that westward turned many a venturous prow
> . . . To build our western empire, its cornerstone was gold.
> Thus to California's valleys, gold . . .
> Lures thousands but to show what their real treasures are
> The soil, the streams and harbors, whose wealth remains untold.[8]

The song extols the nation's new role as a conquering power. The United States would replace Spain as the premier bullion empire. Spaniards had lusted for gold during their bloody American conquests and successfully built an empire based on the production of silver pieces-of-eight. Now the United States would take its place and give the world a new monetary standard—based on gold coins. And gold aside, the song praised California's other natural bounties, which would have been squandered, the lyrics suggest, if the land had remained part of Mexico. This song is but one of countless popular reiterations of the United States' Manifest Destiny—the idea, espoused by the very same publication, that the new nation had a moral responsibility and historical right to rule the Americas. The minting of coins from gold extracted from this newly acquired land perfectly illustrates the nation's unique destiny: to bring forth all the fruits of North America.

Patterson was at the heart of this gold-minting endeavor, which had to happen at the source. Transporting tens of thousands of kilos every year to mints across the continent would not do. So he used his connections to open a branch of the mint in San Francisco. Congress did not approve of this plan until July 1852, months after Patterson had retired, but he remained involved in its planning and construction through close contact with his successor, George Nicholas Eckert, who had, like Patterson, trained as a medical doctor at the University of Pennsylvania. Congress moved forward on the branch after Eckert, through the secretary of the Treasury, put forth a comprehensive plan with specifications for the building. He had this proposal drawn up by a San Francisco architect who "knew the value of materials &c. in that place."[9] The estimated cost of US$876,000, plus US$250,000 for machinery, was considerable, but the branch building, upon completion, promised to have "the ability to carry its operations on the same scale as that at Philadelphia."

Unlike the branch mints in Georgia and North Carolina, the San Francisco branch would be a large-scale operation. The gold rush in California dwarfed those in the American South, and it deserved a mint where gold could be assayed and minted on a scale commensurate with the treasure coming out of the ground. Patterson died a few months prior to the branch's opening in 1854, but the facility certainly would have met with his approval. Under the sound management of L. A. Birdsall, the first superintendent, the San Francisco branch mint produced US$4,084,207 in gold coins in its first year alone.[10]

The gold coins (see figure 7.3) pouring from the San Francisco branch precipitated a momentous boom in the U.S. economy, followed by a crisis. The availability of gold once again encouraged the opening of small banks across the country—much as preceded the Panic of 1837. These new banks extended credit through banknotes, especially to land speculators eager to buy large tracts out west. European banks jumped on the bandwagon and also made enormous loans, largely for real estate purchases in the U.S. West. Despite their difficulties recovering loans made to Mexico, London lenders were particularly eager to continue extending credit in the Americas.

Citizens spent and invested as if they had never had money before, but a lot of this economic activity was unsustainable. Western land values, in par-

Figure 7.3. This gold coin had a face value of US$1. Its unique octagonal design provided a tactile reminder of its gold (as opposed to silver) content, as did the words CALIFORNIA and GOLD on the coin's back.
Source: "U.S. California Gold Dollar" (1860). Photographic image courtesy of Yale University Art Gallery. Public Domain.

ticular, would not go up indefinitely, and small banks could not extend such vast amounts of credit without having stores of gold to back it up. To make matters worse, by the 1850s there was no longer a national bank to moderate the production of paper notes. Jackson had shut down the Second Bank of the United States decades earlier. Thus, as speculation boomed and banks printed all manner of paper notes of credit, no singular government institution existed to regulate the money supply. Once again, rather than shoring up the solidity of the U.S. economy, the presence of specie only encouraged borrowers and lenders to embrace credit.

The flow of California gold across the Atlantic only added to the problem of too much credit and too little hard currency. The Bank of England had systematically acquired U.S. gold coins because Great Britain

Figure 7.4. This dramatic depiction of the steamship *Central America*'s demise evokes the terror of the event. The caption highlights the loss of US$2 million in treasure, which primarily consisted of California gold. This lithograph circulated broadly, even in England, which points to the popularity and impact of its subject.
Source: "Lithograph by J. Childs" (no date). Original in the Robert B. Honeyman Jr. Collection of Early Californian and Western American Pictorial Material. Photographic image courtesy of the Bancroft Library, University of California, Berkeley. Reproduced with permission.

had, back in 1821, switched from silver to gold as its monetary standard (i.e., British money was pegged to the value of gold rather than silver). England needed gold to mint its own coins. To acquire it, the British demanded gold for payment in international trading, and since Queen Victoria's empire spanned the globe, Britain set the norms of exchange. Flush with more specie than ever before, the United States once again became a country that ran on credit, with an economy dictated by private banks in New York and London. British bankers, in fact, provided much of the capital used to build the U.S. West by routing investments through American banks.

In the mid-1850s, output from the gold fields leveled off, reducing the mint's output and causing some worry in the market. At the same time, western land began to lose its allure, especially as land values in California ceased to rise and even began to fall. The relatively new railroad system also experienced a loss of revenue. In this climate, bankers became wary of lending to western enterprises, and some started calling in loans in the spring and summer of 1857. In August, the Ohio Life Insurance and Trust Company failed. Suddenly, the solid-gold U.S. economy turned fragile. Grain prices fell, farmers lost their land, railroad companies went bust, and U.S. banks found their paper notes no longer accepted.

If gold had caused the problem, perhaps gold could solve it. In early September 1857, bankers in New York waited anxiously for the arrival of a ship that promised to be their deliverance. The credit economy rested on faith in gold, which a fresh infusion of bullion would restore. Thirty thousand pounds of California gold were due to arrive at the docks of New York on the SS *Central America*. Alas, the ship ran into a hurricane off the coast of South Carolina. The crew fought their way northward for a few days but eventually lost to the stormy sea (see figure 7.4). When the ship slipped under the waves on September 11, it took with it 425 passengers and crew, as well as the gold that bankers had hoped would stave off financial disaster. On February 21, 1857, Congress had withdrawn the legal tender properties of foreign coins, making U.S. dollar coins the sole national currency. After the sinking, some thought that the government had perhaps acted prematurely.

Conclusion

Robert Maskell Patterson's brother Ewing accompanied the Lewis and Clark expedition from St. Louis to the Pacific from 1804 to 1806. The director of the U.S. Mint, by contrast, never ventured west of Pennsylvania, but he probably heard tales from Ewing about the lands across the Mississippi

River. Little could he have imagined that gold would one day be found in California and that he would play a major role in its becoming part of the U.S. economy.

During the first half of the nineteenth century, the U.S. economy had not yet fully begun its upward trajectory vis-à-vis Mexico's decline. The United States staggered from crisis to crisis. Patterson witnessed the Panic of 1837 and likely hoped that such a catastrophe would not reoccur. So it was perhaps a mercy that he missed the credit crisis that gripped the country only twenty years later. In the following chapter, the reader will learn about the civil wars that further exhausted the economies of both Mexico and the United States.

Notes

1. The Committee on Girard College was made up of Roberts Vaux, James Page, and John M. Hood. Committee on Girard College, "Under Authority of Resolutions," in *Patterson Papers* (American Philosophical Society, 1832).

2. United States and Miscellaneous Pamphlet Collection (Library of Congress), *Act of January 18, 1837, Relative to the Mint and Coinage of the United States* (Philadelphia: Printed for the use of the Mint, 1837).

3. Fineness measures the ratio by weight of the precious metal to a base level. The fineness of gold used to make gold coins (the standard) in the United States has changed over time. It was first set in 1792 at twenty-two carats (equal to 917-thousandths fine), reduced to twenty-one carats (899.225-thousandths fine) in 1834, and then set at 900-thousandths fine in 1837. The fineness of silver used in Mexican coins (the standard) has similarly changed.

4. Fineness is usually expressed as a number of parts out of one thousand (with one thousand being 100 percent precious metal), which is called millesimal fineness. Before Patterson instituted the use of millesimal fineness, the purity of gold was expressed as carats (still used today for jewelry), which counts parts out of twenty-four. Pure gold is twenty-four carats, which is 99.95 percent gold by mass (counted as 999.95 of one thousand fine); the remaining 0.05 percent is another metal. Before millesimal fineness, the purity of silver was expressed in troy weight. There are 480 grains in a troy ounce and twelve troy ounces per troy pound (not sixteen like in a standard pound). In terms of millesimal fineness, sterling silver is 92.5 percent silver by mass and 7.5 percent another metal (equal to 925-thousandths fine). Under the weight system, sterling silver weighs eleven troy ounces, two pennyweights (out of twelve troy ounces).

5. "Table Db87-95. Metal Production—Bauxite, Aluminum, Magnesium, Gold, and Silver: 1834–2000," in *Historical Statistics of the United States*, ed. Susan B. Carter et al. Millennial edition online (New York: Cambridge University Press, 2015).

6. U.S. Congress, Act of March 3, 1849, Authorizing the Coinage of Gold Dollars and Double Eagles.

7. In 1997 the U.S. Mint introduced Platinum Eagles with values as high as US$100. The bullion value of these coins is much higher than their face value; therefore they do not circulate as regular currency.

8. "California Gold: A Song for the Occasion," *United States Magazine and Democratic Review* (1837–1851), October 1849.

9. Thomas Corwin, "Letter from the Secretary of the Treasury Transmitting a Plan and Specification for a Mint at San Francisco, Referred to the Committee of Ways and Means" (Department of Treasury, 1852).

10. "Interactive Timeline: History of the United States Mint and Circulating Coins since 1780," United States Mint, http://www.usmint.gov/about_the_mint/mint_facilities/?action=timeLine.

CHAPTER EIGHT

Defending the Republics

On June 19, 1867, Emperor Maximilian I of Mexico stood before a firing squad, his most trusted generals, Miguel Miramón and Tomás Mejía, at his side. It is said that the doomed emperor handed each of his executioners a gold coin, asking them not to shoot at his head, so that his mother could look on his face when his body was returned to Austria for burial. Those coins would have been among the last Mexican coins ever to bear the face of a monarch. During his short reign, Maximilian did away with the liberty cap of republican Mexico and issued coins with his own profile, echoing the old coins of Spain. Maximilian had mythologized the colonial era as a time of strong rule and sought to return Mexico to that stability. As the soldiers tucked the coins into the pockets of their uniforms and prepared to fire, the emperor offered his last words to the country he had ruled for just three years: "I forgive everyone, and I ask everyone to forgive me. May my blood, which is about to be shed, be for the good of the country. Long live Mexico! Long live Independence!"[1] Moments later, six bullets struck him. None hit his head.

The protagonist of this chapter is Ferdinand Maximilian Joseph, member of the House of Habsburg-Lorraine (see figure 8.2). The money is the coins he issued as Emperor Maximilian I of Mexico, the last to carry the image of a monarch and the first to bear the word "peso." The chapter explores the period of the French Intervention in Mexico (1861–1867), a time when Mexico confronted outside conquest, while the United States simultaneously descended into internal warfare. Republican North America was tearing

Figure 8.1. This stylized painting of the execution of Maximilian embraces a romantic, if inaccurate, vision of the Austrian's death. In Édouard Manet's version of the execution, Maximilian wears a Mexican sombrero and stands in front of Generals Tomás Mejía and Miguel Miramón, holding their hands. The firing squad stands just feet away from their first victim. Mejía's dark complexion contrasts starkly with that of Maximilian. The soldier to the right appears to be readying his weapon for the execution of one of the two other men. In reality, all three men were lined up yards apart before a wall and shot at the same time by three separate firing squads.
Source: "The Execution of Emperor Maximilian," by Édouard Manet (1868–1869). Kunsthalle Mannheim. Photographic image by Wikicommons. Public domain.

itself apart, from Yucatan to Maine. The 1860s were about young republics facing existential crises. For the United States, a fundamental conflict over the nature of government and the institution of slavery threatened to put an end to the Union. During the same decade, Mexico confronted both internal division between conservatives and liberals and external invasion by France. Both of the sister republics faced possible destruction.

Ferdinand Maximilian Joseph, born in 1832 in Vienna, the heart of the Austrian Empire, had a typical aristocratic upbringing, tutored and trained from a young age to rule in some capacity. Little could have prepared him to become emperor of Mexico, though his years in the Austrian navy were particularly instructive. There, he gained command experience, rising to commander in chief, and became a proponent of scientific modernization. Maximilian's other major position was as viceroy of the Kingdom of Lombardy-Venetia. In that post, his liberal political views proved too radical for his brother, Emperor Francis Joseph, so he and his wife, Princess Carlota of Belgium, retired at a relatively young age from public service. Maximilian was only twenty-seven years old, and his retirement was short-lived. Within a couple of years, delegations of Mexican monarchists and emperor Napoleon III of France were entreating him to consider an altogether different path.

Mexico suffered dramatic political swings from independence to 1857, as liberal and conservative politicians vied for national power. Liberals in Mexico advocated broader political representation, freedom of speech, and laissez-faire economic policies. Conservatives, by contrast, defended the interests of large landholders, a strong military, and the privileges of the Catholic Church. The boundaries between liberal and conservative policies, however, shifted to accommodate the needs of any given administration. Politics were so polarized that no Mexican government could control sufficient fiscal

Figure 8.2. Shown here in his admiralty jacket and with his distinctive center-parted beard, Maximilian began assuming roles of military and political importance from a young age. At twenty-two, he was appointed commander in chief of the Austrian navy. Just three years later he was made viceroy of the Kingdom of Lombardy-Venetia. When he arrived in Mexico as emperor in 1864, he was thirty-one years old.
Source: "Maximilian" (K. K. Hof-Photograph in Wien, circa 1857). Original in Prints and Photographs Division, Library of Congress, LC-USZ62-17159. Public Domain.

resources to fulfill long-term national goals. Mexico's severe political instability entered a new phase following 1855, when a liberal congress removed president-turned-dictator Antonio López de Santa Anna from office for the final time, in favor of less centralized government.

To achieve greater political freedom, liberals passed a variety of laws known collectively as the Reform (*la Reforma*), which aimed to do away with conservative policies that echoed colonial-era rule. Secularization was central to the reform because Mexico, unlike the United States, had not yet legislated the separation of church and state. Liberals hoped to diminish the power of the Catholic Church, the largest landholder in Mexico, by prohibiting corporations from owning private property. This 1856 legislation, called the Lerdo Law (*Ley Lerdo*), allowed the government to seize and sell church property. With this expropriation, the government aimed to raise revenue, stimulate the property market, and place more land in the hands of small property owners.

Regrettably, the law against corporate landownership also affected the communal lands of indigenous communities, putting them at risk of similar property seizures. Communal landholding was seen as a contradiction to liberal individualism and an obstruction to development of a free market. Liberal legal reforms upended centuries of land tenure policies that had protected Native Americans in Mexico. Looking forward, indigenous peoples' dispossession of their lands was one factor leading to the Mexican Revolution in the early twentieth century, fought under the banner of "Land and Liberty." Liberals could not have foreseen this particular legacy of the Reform, but church opposition to the Lerdo Law at the time threatened war as well.

The liberal government wrote a new constitution in 1857 that enshrined freedom of speech, equality before the law, and freedom of expression and also reaffirmed anticlerical legislation. Conservatives and churchmen ardently opposed it, with the support of a significant part of the overwhelmingly Catholic population. Their efforts to repeal the 1857 Constitution created a rift that erupted into a civil war known as the Reform War (*Guerra de Reforma*), which lasted from 1857 to 1861.

The United States kept close watch over its sister republic as it too drifted closer to civil war. President James Buchanan sympathized with the liberals, favoring constitutional order over conservative, religiously oriented, European-style rule. Liberalism's opposite, nineteenth-century conservatism, also advocated economic protectionism, which went against U.S. trade interests. A *New York Times* editorial from December 1860 illustrates this popular stand: "Our readers will bear witness with what perseverance we have adhered to the fortunes of the Liberal Party, confiding as we have always done in the honesty and sincerity of its chiefs."[2] This quotation expresses a majority U.S. opinion and explains why there was general rejoicing when liberals secured victory the following year.

President Benito Juárez, elected after the Reform War, faced a nation in a state of financial disaster and devastated by fratricidal warfare. The army and the civil servant corps were unpaid, and almost no currency was in circulation. The possibility of European invasion was an additional burden on government. To remedy this fiscal crisis, Juárez sought to convince U.S. investors to capitalize on the liberal government's victory, encouraging them with tax breaks. He granted a variety of concessions to U.S. companies, securing, for example, a mining concern that pledged US$100,000 in gold for a large swath of government lands in Baja California. The heartbreak of accepting U.S. California gold for Mexican land was likely not lost on those involved in the exchange. Juárez also had Mexican agents lobby U.S. investors in their own backyard, establishing clubs in New York and other major U.S. cities to disseminate information about Mexico's plight in order to secure donations for the liberal cause.

From Juárez's perspective, the United States needed to understand that Mexico was a kindred nation striving to embrace similar liberal policies. So, in early 1861, he sent a legate to Springfield, Illinois, to congratulate president-elect Abraham Lincoln on his victory. He also conveyed the Mexican administration's hope for commercial partnership between the two countries. Lincoln notably shared this ambition, as evidenced by his administration's signing two loan treaties with the Juárez government. This funding was meant to back the Juárez administration and its market-oriented liberalism, enabling Juárez to continue fighting conservative forces as well as to make foreign debt payments. The Lincoln administration partly justified this expense as a way to deter potential European governments from intruding into North American affairs, but the loans proved regrettably insufficient.

European invasion of Mexico was a serious concern to governments on both sides of the Rio Grande at mid-century. Europe held an enormous amount of Mexico's foreign debt, some dating back twenty-five years. In 1860, France, Prussia, Britain, and Spain all threatened to take military action if Mexico failed to meet its financial obligations. The liberal government's inability to repay foreign loans did nothing to reduce the lenders' insistence. Juárez well knew, in fact, that France, Spain, or Britain might at any moment resolve its debts by force of arms.

The presence of the United States was one of the few things preventing any of these nations from collecting their debts militarily. The Monroe Doctrine of 1823 had declared that the United States had a special responsibility to protect all new nations in the Americas from European interference in their national affairs. Despite this policy's imperialistic undertones, Juárez hoped that the United States would extend a sisterly arm to protect its southern neighbor during this period of crisis. Lincoln's initial loans were understood in this vein.

At this point the United States descended into its own civil war. In December 1860, South Carolina voted to secede from the Union, initiating the movement that created the Confederate States of America. The Lincoln administration may well have wished to do more to aid Mexico, but it now faced its own desperate struggle for survival.

The United States of America and the new Confederate States of America confronted enormous financial crises in the coming years, as the conflict consumed seemingly endless quantities of blood and treasure. To shore up their war reserves, the Union and the Confederacy looked overseas to secure financing with some success, but soon both governments were printing paper monies to overcome their respective bullion shortages. Passed within a year of the start of the war, the first Legal Tender Act empowered the U.S. Treasury to print bills that were not redeemable in specie and had to be accepted to settle debts. This was the first time that U.S. money was backed not by bullion reserves, at least in theory, but only by the force of law and the strength of the government. The reverse of this new currency was printed in green, leading to the name "greenback" for U.S. paper money. These notes rose and fell in value against gold as the Union experienced military victories and defeats, falling as low as 40 percent of the value of gold in the summer of 1864.

The Confederacy faced a similar crisis. It produced some coins early in the conflict after seizing the New Orleans branch of the U.S. Mint but never in significant volume. Like the Union, it was forced to issue paper notes called "greybacks" to meet the costs of war. The depreciation of these notes, combined with high inflation in the South, severely eroded their value. Though many in the North sympathized with Juárez and the republicans and a number of Confederates favored Maximilian's empire, neither side had the financial resources do more than try to win its own fight.

Gunboat Banking

The Reform War in Mexico ended under Juárez's leadership in January 1861. The costly fighting had stopped at last, but Mexico's finances had seldom been worse. When Juárez and the liberal forces took control of the capital, they found an empty treasury. The republic had survived the internal fractures brought on by conservative opposition to the reform movement, but the country badly needed money for day-to-day operations and to rebuild. Worse still, Mexico's inability to service its foreign debt remained a menace. As he could no longer turn to the U.S. government (a nation now divided, with each side reliant on greenbacks or greybacks), Juárez was forced into a decision that finally brought foreign invaders to Mexico's shores.

In July 1861, President Juárez had no alternative but to acknowledge the national debt while also declaring a two-year suspension of payments. Payments would resume once the Mexican economy had recovered. Juárez's suspension of payments was a far cry from a refutation of debts incurred by the previous governments, but his actions infuriated Mexico's European creditors. In October of that year, France, Spain, and Britain signed the Convention of London to engage in a joint naval occupation of the Mexican coast. French, Spanish, and English ships were to occupy the port of Veracruz, seize the customs house, and claim all duties until the debts were paid.

Recognizing that such an action could easily appear like an attempt at conquest, the treaty specifically stipulated that none of the three European powers would pursue anything other than what they were owed. In the words of the convention, the "contracting parties" would not seek "any acquisition of territory nor any special advantage" or "exercise in the internal affairs of Mexico any influences of a nature to prejudice the right of the Mexican nation to choose and to constitute freely the form of its government."[3] And yet the message was clear: European governments were quite willing to contemplate "coercive measures" in order to have their loans repaid. The inclusion of such a statement in an international convention illustrates the degree to which European expansion in Mexico seemed a very real possibility.

Spanish vessels arrived in Veracruz by the end of 1861, followed by those of Britain and France. Upon hearing that many locals feared the occupation marked the start of an invasion, the joint commanders of the expedition drew up a declaration reiterating the promise of the Convention of London to assuage them: "You have been deceived . . . by those who have dared to tell you that behind our just and reasonable demands there lurk any ideas of conquest."[4] Only the Spanish and English commanders actually believed in the document. Most Mexicans deemed it a thinly veiled cover for what certainly looked like an invasion, and rightly so. Those Spanish and English commanders soon caught on as well, realizing that their French allies had far more aggressive objectives in mind than those stipulated by the convention. France, not Spain or Britain, had indeed come to Mexico to exercise its own will over who should rule the nation. Spain and England promptly washed their hands of the affair and negotiated a settlement with the Juárez government. In April 1862, both nations withdrew their forces. With more than twenty-seven thousand soldiers in place, France remained.

Mexico, for French emperor Napoleon III, represented an opportunity to expand his political influence in Europe, as well as to augment his authority back home. Mexico, as the debtor nation, must be forced to pay its debts, but Napoleon had other plans as well. Specifically, he hoped to quiet opposition he faced from ardent Catholics, as well as liberals, back in France. There was also the problem of Austria, which Napoleon had recently pushed out of Lombardy. By overthrowing the liberal (read anticlerical) leadership of Mexico, he hoped to repair a frayed relationship with French Catholics. With luck, he might also placate French liberals (pro-free trade) with Mexican trade concessions and appease the Austrians by installing one of their own as head of Mexico. In addition, Napoleon had designs to open a crossing between the Gulf of Mexico and the Pacific through the Isthmus of Tehuantepec—a highly complicated, grand plan that he had mapped out before orchestrating the Convention of London.

The Mexican foreign debt crisis provided the perfect opportunity to secure Napoleon's aims. So France issued Mexico an ultimatum, demanding immediate payment of MX$27 million—an impossibly large figure and at least MX$12 million more than Mexico owed France. The additional monies allegedly covered nonspecific insults levied by Mexico against France. In reality, the difference was simply a buffer to ensure that Mexico could not pay and thus justify French military coercion.

The military action that followed laid the groundwork for Maximilian to become Mexico's last monarch. In April 1862, six thousand French soldiers marched inland from Veracruz to take the Mexican capital. Victory was assured, as articulated by French commander Brigadier General Charles Ferdinand Latrille in the casual racism of the time: "We are so superior to the Mexicans in race, organization, morality and devoted sentiments that I beg your Excellency to inform the Emperor that . . . I am already master of Mexico." Ten days later, Latrille's soldiers confronted a Mexican force at Puebla, which handed the astonished French a humiliating defeat on May 5—a day enshrined in Mexican culture as *Cinco de Mayo*.

It should have been an easy victory, but the French defeat at Puebla proved a profound embarrassment that delayed Napoleon's timetable by a full year. When the French returned in 1863 with thirty thousand men, they forced Juárez to evacuate Mexico City and occupied the capital. Napoleon's plan hinged on putting a European emperor in command of Mexico quickly, while the United States was too preoccupied to enforce the Monroe Doctrine. Two years after South Carolina's forces began shelling Fort Sumter, all of North America south of the Canadian border was at war.

The Empire

The Second Mexican Empire began as soon as the French took Mexico City, though it would be a full year before Maximilian arrived at the port of Veracruz in May 1864. In the meantime, French generals collaborated with Mexican monarchists to build a new imperial state. The chief French minister oversaw the appointment of 285 Mexican conservatives who were to rule on behalf of a European prince until his arrival. Within days, the provisional government declared that a Catholic monarch would hence govern Mexico. It remained only to secure the monarch himself. The European prince had, of course, long since been chosen; Napoleon III had approached Maximilian as early as 1861.

A Mexican delegation made the official approach in October 1863, tendering the Mexican throne to Maximilian at his seaside castle of Miramar. Though the prince had expected this offer, Maximilian said that he would only accept if Mexicans truly wanted him. So Napoleon's men quickly arranged a plebiscite in Mexico, polling only those known to support the cause of monarchy. Maximilian and Carlota thereafter agreed. In a ceremony the following April, Maximilian swore an oath accepting leadership of Mexico: "I Maximilian, Emperor of Mexico, swear to God by the Holy Evangelists, that I will try to promote, through all the means within my power, the welfare and prosperity of the nation, to defend its independence, and to preserve the whole of its territory."[5] Maximilian saw no contradiction in his swearing to defend the independence of Mexico though he himself was an Austrian who had gained entry into the country through the efforts of a French army. The incongruity did not escape many Mexicans.

Mexican liberals and conservatives engaged in open warfare about the turn of events. Conservatives rejoiced at the news that they had a European prince (the first Habsburg ruler to preside over Mexico since 1700, when Charles II of Spain died without an heir) to legitimize a return to monarchal rule. The provisional government prepared the way for the Second Mexican Empire with acts meant to redefine the Mexican state, including the issuance of medals bearing the profiles of Maximilian and Carlota. Conservatives failed, however, to orchestrate the response of the Mexican citizenry. Maximilian and Carlota arrived at Veracruz in May 1864 to a decidedly cool welcome. To avoid embarrassment, the local military commanders claimed that a recent epidemic had exhausted the people. Maximilian was likely unconvinced as the nation was clearly still at war.

Despite the liberal victory and Juárez's ascension to the presidency in 1861, conservatives in Mexico had never given up fighting for their cause. With the arrival of their new emperor, conservative forces allied with the French rallied to win a string of victories in 1864 and early 1865. Juárez had shifted his capital to the north, and liberal forces were holding out against the combined French and conservative Mexican army that defended the imperial government.

Meanwhile, Maximilian set himself the task of saving Mexico, undiscouraged by the fact that most Mexicans were not eager for an Austrian emperor to lead the nation. He naively believed that he could unify the disparate parts of the populace and heal the divisions that had riven the country since the Reform War, and really since independence. So, while Juárez struggled

Figure 8.3. This simple one-cent (centavo) coin die (engraved device in reverse) represents a fundamental shift in the reckoning of Mexican coins. Centavos were a departure from the centuries-old use of pieces-of-eight divided into eight *reales*. Pesos, a long-used term for pieces-of-eight, would henceforth be divided into one hundred centavos.

Source: "One-Cent Coin" (1864). Original in Casa de Moneda de México. Museo Numismatico Nacional. Photography by T. Seijas. Reproduction authorized by the Secretaría de Hacienda y Crédito Público, México.

to overthrow his empire, Maximilian sought to build unity in the country, in part by issuing new coinage.

A forward-looking Mexico should, to Maximilian's reasoning, have a modern system of currency. To that end, he decreed the denomination of Mexican dollars in decimals. The reader will remember that Thomas Jefferson had argued for the same shift in the United States some sixty years earlier. Mexico had retained the old Spanish system following independence, dividing its new currency (Mexican dollars) like pieces-of-eight, with fractional coins worth one, one-half, and one-quarter *real* (equivalent to 12 1/2, 6 1/4, and 3 1/8 U.S. cents), which made accounting difficult. The move to a decimal system (with one peso equal to one hundred centavos) was not entirely Maximilian's doing. President Ignacio Comonfort had tried and failed to institute a decimal coinage system back in 1857.

Maximilian's currency initiative also involved changing the appearance of Mexico's coins; symbolism, as always, was all-important. Mexican coins had borne the symbol of the liberty cap for forty-two years, and though circulation was limited, these small objects nonetheless represented the national government. Since the fall of the first emperor, Agustín Iturbide, the coins had carried a consciously chosen representation of republican liberty and, by the same token, rejected the symbolism of monarchical rule. Maximilian expressly sought to reverse that message. Decades of unstable republicanism had left Mexico impoverished and repeatedly beset by political upheaval and civil war. Maximilian had no intention of recreating Spanish colonialism and, by most measures, sought a liberal agenda, but his vision of a return to stability required a monarch.

Maximilian recast the peso in his own image, replacing the liberty cap with his profile (see figure 8.3). In an "empire" as nascent and fragile as Maximilian's, it was imperative to for the populace to see the emperor's face. The new coins were thus meant to forge a connection between Mexicans and their new ruler. The coin's reverse was also refashioned. The Mexican eagle, perched on a cactus, was recrowned, as it had last been under Iturbide. Reduced in size, the eagle was placed at the center of a Mexican imperial shield, upheld by griffons, and backed by two crossed swords. The coins were unambiguously imperial. IMPERIO MEXICANO (Empire of Mexico) replaced REPUBLICA MEXICANA (Republic of Mexico). In place of "Liberty in the Law," a new motto, "Equality in Justice," appeared on a small banner at the base of the imperial shield.

Despite the coin's fairly heavy-handed iconography, Maximilian apparently did see himself as the man who would modernize Mexico. But creating a powerful imperium, even in name only, required a great deal of expenditure.

Figure 8.4. Maximilian remade Mexican coinage to reflect monarchical ideals. He replaced the liberty cap with an image of himself, echoing the Spanish coinage of the colonial era, and reduced the Mexican eagle to a small centerpiece in the center of the Habsburg shield. These imperial coins were the first Mexican coins to bear the word "peso." Amid civil war, these coins aimed to declare the victory of conservative imperial power over liberal republicanism.
Source: "Maximilian 20 Pesos" (1866). Courtesy of the National Numismatic Collection, National Museum of American History. Public Domain

In 1865, with the backing of Napoleon III, Mexico floated a bond issue in France for 534 million francs. Far from lessening Mexico's foreign debt, this loan alone tripled it. A great deal of that money wound up servicing preexisting debt and paying for the French military occupation meant to solidify Maximilian's rule. Maximilian spent much of the rest on extravagances that an emperor might have seen as his due but could not be justified easily in a nation as poor as Mexico. His own annual remittance was MX$1.5 million, and Empress Carlota received MX$400,000. He also spent lavishly on restoring the Chapultepec Castle for his own occupation, then spent still more of the national budget on pageants held there (see figure 8.4). Many Mexicans deemed Maximilian's use of debt money to pay for his own exaltation unpardonable.

While Maximilian was burnishing his imperial image, the liberals led by Benito Juárez continued to fight. After the fall of Mexico City to the French and conservatives, Juárez had once again looked northward for sisterly assistance. He needed to prevent the U.S. government from recognizing the French position in Mexico and also to acquire military aid. The Lincoln administration, however, had publicly banned the export of arms in an effort

Figure 8.5. Chapultepec Castle was originally constructed during the colonial era. Following the war for independence, it fell into disuse until it became a military academy. In 1847 it was overrun by U.S. forces during the Mexican-American War. Maximilian spent lavishly, restoring the castle to serve as the seat of the royal court, where he could host galas and other state rituals. Perched on a hilltop on what was then the edge of Mexico City, it was an extravagant icon of the Second Mexican Empire.
Source: "Mexico, the Castle of Chapultepec," by William H. Jackson (Detroit Publishing Co., circa 1884–1900). Photocrom print. Original in Prints and Photographs Division, Library of Congress, LC-USZ62-138186. Public Domain.

keep weapons made in the U.S. North out of the hands of the Confederacy. That said, U.S. Secretary of War William Seward, concerned that the French government might recognize the Confederacy, was sympathetic to the appeals of Juárez's secret emissaries. Mexican representatives thus secured some support even as the Civil War was still ongoing.

Once war in the United States had ended, organizations sympathetic to the liberals in Mexico began to aid Juárez and his republican forces openly. The Mexican Emigration Company, founded by a former Union colonel, ran the following advertisement in major Northern newspapers in May 1865: "MEXICO, MAXIMILIAN AND MONROE DOCTRINE. All persons who desire joining a company soon starting 'to make a strike' for fame and fortune in the land of golden ores and luscious fruits, aided and protected by the patriotic President of that republic, will please address Benito J. Juarez, box 5,614 New York post office."[6] The hope was that Union veterans would see opportunity in the "land of golden ores" and take up arms for the republican government in Mexico. That same year, Mexican generals could be found in New York, Texas, and California, attempting to secure aid for the beleaguered Juárez government. Eventually, some three thousand Union veterans enlisted in the Mexican republican army, while two thousand

Confederates joined to fight alongside Maximilian. In both cases the numbers were too small to make a major difference in the outcome of the war against the French.

Mexican agents continued to secure support from the Union, which netted the Juárez government an ongoing supply of munitions. One such agent, a German-born munitions factory director in Indiana, Herman Sturm, alone secured US$2 million worth of munitions for the Juárez government between 1866 and 1867.[7] The equipment sent to republican forces from the United States included everything from rifles and medical kits to underwear. Juárez largely paid for these supplies with payment bonds as opposed to specie. The U.S. government and many of its citizens were willing to accept Mexican paper as a promise of later payment in genuine metal money. Mexico was, after all, the land of silver.

Despite covert aid from the United States and overt neighborly sympathy, republican armies in Mexico were unable to defeat Maximilian so long as he had the support of the French military. Time, however, favored Mexican nationalists. After the Union's victory, the U.S. government, fully mobilized for war, was once again in a position to enforce the Monroe Doctrine. The new U.S. president, Andrew Johnson, strongly opposed the French in Mexico, having said, as early as 1864, that after the Union won the Civil War, the next order of business would be to "attend to the affairs of Mexico." In the summer of 1865, Ulysses S. Grant ordered General Philip Sheridan into Texas along the Mexican border with as many as fifty thousand Union troops. The message was not subtle.

Napoleon III was not ready to engage in military conflict with the United States, so he soon announced a phased withdrawal of the French military from Mexico. The military tide immediately turned against Maximilian and in favor of Juárez and the liberals. Even after Napoleon abandoned the project, Maximilian attempted to persuade the United States to accept his position in Mexico—for example, by opening an office in New York to promote propaganda in the name of the imperial throne. If he thought that the United States would find common cause with a European emperor in the Americas, he was badly mistaken.

End of the Empire

As the citizens of the United States watched the war for Mexican control unfold, coin collectors looked on with something of a predatory eye. In early 1867, as republican forces were closing in on Maximilian, the following comments appeared in the *American Journal of Numismatics*: "If the emperor

Maximilian should unfortunately lose his head in the course of the present struggle in Mexico, he will at least have the satisfaction of knowing that he leaves an impression of it upon the coinage of the country; if such a catastrophe should not occur . . . he will doubtless take with him out of the country as many specimens of his mintage as possible; in either case, there is no doubt but that the money of Maximilian will hereafter become exceedingly rare, and much sought after by collectors."[8]

The editors of the numismatic journal foretold the future. Maximilian's decimalized peso coins did become rare. Just a month later, liberal forces captured the emperor in the city of Querétaro. Juárez ordered Maximilian's execution but delayed for a month as various quarters begged the president to commute the deposed emperor's sentence. Ultimately Juárez concluded that his authority as president did not permit him to overturn the legal punishment for Maximilian's treason. On June 19, soldiers led the now former emperor to the edge of town. There Maximilian and his two comrades climbed to the top the Hill of the Bells, where we found them at the start of this chapter.

No monarch would ever again sit at the head of the Mexican government or grace Mexico's coinage. The Juárez administration stopped minting the Maximilian coins in 1867 and had the nation's coinage redesigned (see figure 8.5). The eagle on the reverse of the coin was once again stripped of its

Figure 8.6. After the end of the Second Mexican Empire, Mexican coinage returned to earlier imagery that emphatically celebrated republican liberty. The liberty cap, scales of justice, and written law, depicted on this 1872 peso, all symbolized a nation that drew its strength from self-governing people bound by a constitution. One of Maximilian's innovations remained. Republican Mexico kept the word "peso" on its coins.
Source: "Mexican Silver Peso" (1872). Photography by Jake Frederick, from the authors' personal collection.

crown and shield and returned to an appearance more evocative of central Mexican mythology. The new coins also brought back the liberty cap design. This time, suspended from the liberty cap and sunbeams were the scales of justice; in front of these was a scroll inscribed with the word LEY (law). The coins of the new republic carried a distinct message. The power of Mexico resided not in the birthright of a royal leader but in the law. It was the law that provided equality to Mexican citizens, and that same law had required the death of Maximilian.

Conclusion

Only one visual artifact of the imperial reign remained on Mexico's coins: the word "peso." The common term for Mexican currency, unofficially used as far back as the colonial era, had at last been set onto the country's coinage. Mexico had its enduring currency, only ten years after U.S. dollars became the exclusive means of legal exchange in the United States. The Mexican peso, like the U.S. dollar, was an emphatically republican coin. Like its counterpart to the north, the new peso represented decades of struggle to establish a politically secure and economically viable state. During the 1860s Mexico and the United States had both survived the greatest threat to their continued existence.

Notes

1. Gene Smith, *Maximilian and Carlota: A Tale of Romance and Tragedy* (New York: Morrow, 1973), 279.

2. "The Latest Mexican Development," *New York Times*, December 28, 1860, 4.

3. Convention of London, Article II, cited in Frederic Bancroft, "The French in Mexico and the Monroe Doctrine," *Political Science Quarterly* 11 (1896): 31.

4. Cited in Percy F. Martin, *Maximilian in Mexico: The Story of the French Intervention (1861–1867)* (London: Constable and Co., 1914). 76.

5. Frederic Hall, *Life of Maximilian I, Late Emperor of Mexico, with a Sketch of the Empress Carlota* (New York: J. Miller, 1868), 93.

6. This advertisement ran in various U.S. newspapers. Quoted in Robert Ryal Miller, "Arms across the Border: United States Aid to Juárez during the French Intervention in Mexico," *Transactions of the American Philosophical Society* (New Series) 63, no. 6 (1973): 34.

7. Ibid., 53.

8. "Maximilian's Mint," *American Journal of Numismatics* 1, no. 12 (1867): 89.

Conclusion

In the twenty-first century, U.S. dollars and Mexican pesos are very different currencies. Originally equal to the Spanish piece-of-eight silver coin, they have drifted far from one another in value. Coins are no longer made of silver, and so for generations the value of dollars and cents, pesos and centavos, has rested entirely on the strength of the governments and economies that back them. The fortunes of the United States and Mexico have followed very different trajectories since the countries first designed their monies. In 2016 the peso fell to less than one-twentieth the value of a U.S. dollar.

Today the basic units of currency in Mexico and the United States are bills rather than coins. Though paper and coin money were once quite distinct, the intrinsic precious-metal value of coins no longer matches their face value, so they are now essentially what paper money has always been: a government promise. Paper bills and coins now have value because states ensure them. Their purpose remains the same; bills and coins facilitate commerce.

These objects also continue to impart messages about the countries that have created them. Centuries after independence, the ideas behind those messages remain largely the same: Mexico and the United States are sovereign nations with constitutional, democratic governments. Back in 1792, Congressman John Page successfully argued that new U.S. coins should carry imagery "emblematic of liberty" rather than the face of a king or even a president. The Mexican Congress came to a similar conclusion. Yet today both countries depict historical figures on their money, so opinions have obviously changed about the wisdom of representing people on currency. We can imagine Page's ghost admonishing that no leader or citizen deserves such a status, but something about the face of George Washington or Benito Juárez today inspires patriotism and trust (see figures C.1 and C.2).

The histories of the United States and Mexico begin with money. The Continental dollars printed during the war for independence reflected the colonies' aspirations. The insurgents believed they could build a nation with the same authority and reliability as Spain, so they claimed that holders could one day redeem every note in Spanish silver coin (which proved impossible). Those Continentals simultaneously served as tools of propaganda, reminding their possessors that by staying united, they could win their independence from Britain.

After independence, Congress maintained the desire to equate U.S. coins with those of Spain. Revolutionary ideals aside, the United States aspired to attain the reliability of an established European economy. So it set the value of its new dollars as equal to Spanish pieces-of-eight. These coins had long since circulated in the colonies by way of Mexico, which had minted them since the sixteenth century. At the same time, U.S. leaders innovated by counting coins in an entirely new way, doing away with the complicated fractions of Spain and England and instead dividing the U.S. dollar into one hundred subunits, or cents.

The vaults of Stephen Girard, the United States' first millionaire, were filled not with piles of U.S. dollars but with pieces-of-eight. He was a citizen

Figure C.1. Unlike many world currencies, the U.S. one-dollar bill is very traditional. It includes little imagery and just two colors, green and black. A portrait of George Washington appears in the center, and the note is bordered with detailed etching, including olive branches. All U.S. bills are the same size.
Source: "One-Dollar Bill, Series 2013." Photography by J. Frederick. This reproduction meets the U.S. Bureau of Engraving requirements. Title 18, United States Code, Section 504.

of a nation full of promise, but one that still lacked the bullion necessary to make specie. The United States remained dependent on foreign currency, and investors thought in terms of Spanish rather than American dollars. As testament, the founders of the New York Stock Exchange in 1792 opted to record the movement of stock prices in fractions based on the Spanish coin (a system that remained in place until 2001). Banking in the early republic was also chaotic, as evidenced by the short twenty-year lifespan of the first Bank of the United States (which became Girard's own bank) and the subsequent need to open the Second Bank of the United States. Girard's experiences illustrate how difficult it was to create a stable economy in the young republic. For all citizens, having a silver dollar coin embossed with the words "UNITED STATES OF AMERICA" remained a national ambition.

After independence, Mexico faced some of the same decisions as the United States with regard to money and nation building. Its story offers another model of how a new republic adapted a colonial currency to its own needs. José Ignacio Esteva served as a central figure in the country's turbulent years, first on behalf of the First Mexican Empire and then for the United States of Mexico. Esteva well understood the need for an organized system of reliable currency that celebrated the ideals of a constitutional republic. As heir to history's most trusted currency, the Spanish piece-of-eight, the Mexican nation retained the Spanish dollar as the basis of its money and sought to maintain its place as a producer of reliable coins. That the coin was Mexican, not Spanish, had to be clear, however. The Mexican Congress, like that of the United States, chose a symbol of liberty, designing a new coin, for a new nation, governed on a new model.

The story of Sam Houston, a founder and leader of North America's third republic, illustrates the difficulty of financing a new nation and creating a reliable currency. In the face of a near-total lack of bullion, the Republic of Texas issued series after series of paper bills. Statesmen hoped that the potential of this newly independent land would serve as sufficient collateral to earn citizens' trust in its national currency. But, as we saw in both the United States and Mexico, it takes more than a decade to build a tradition of reliability that gives a people faith in their government. The paper money of Texas fell in value as fast as it was printed. The Texas economy at last began to rally only as it became clear that the short-lived nation would join the United States.

The U.S. annexation of Texas realized one of Mexico's long-held fears: invasion by a foreign power. The American Southwest would be next. Various parties proposed purchase over conquest, but for Mexicans, including President Antonio López de Santa Anna, no price was high enough to compensate for the loss of this territory. The Mexican government rejected U.S. offers to purchase the region that became New Mexico, Arizona, and California, a refusal that contravened the belief in the United States' destiny to span the continent. The sister republics had reached an impasse, with the ambition of one pitted against the sovereignty of the other. Severe military setbacks and U.S. control of the capital city forced Mexico to accept MX$15 million for the northern half of the country. The value of what Mexico lost is beyond calculation.

As John Russell Bartlett traversed the new boundary between the United States and Mexico, people on the frontier were unconvinced that they could trust his money. Mexico had been independent for thirty-some years, and the United States had just acquired the Mexican Cession; yet the citizens of both countries remained skeptical about the value of pesos and dollars. The residents of a town in Sonora, for example, refused to accept Bartlett's gold and silver coins, whether Mexican or American. They preferred local copper tokens. These kinds of everyday exchanges show that neither country had yet earned citizens' trust when it came to money. Shifting boundaries no doubt contributed to the general air of economic instability in the borderlands.

Robert Maskell Patterson's experience as director of the U.S. Mint reveals the complexity of stabilizing a national economy. Even vast quantities of gold and a sufficient supply of national currency are not enough to ensure prosperity. During his tenure, banks were too quick to make speculative loans without the reserves to back them up. The resulting Panic of 1837 demonstrated that the country needed greater banking regulation and more real money in the form of bullion. After the discovery of gold in California, Patterson lobbied for creation of a new branch of the mint to help funnel that gold into the economy; it opened in 1854. In 1857, sixty-five years after Congress enacted a bill to make the United States' first mint, the country finally had enough of its own coins in circulation to forswear the monies of other countries. That gold, however, once again prompted reckless speculation that drove yet another financial crisis. It seemed that even vast quantities of newly minted gold could not shield the economy from upheaval.

Emperor Maximilian's creation of the modern peso during the French Intervention in Mexico reminds us that specie is a tool of political propaganda. Maximilian modernized Mexican currency through decimalization, and when he put his own face on the Mexican peso, he saw himself as a modern liberal monarch. But he failed to grasp that the time was long past when Mexico would accept outside rule. Having become a republic soon after independence, it was unwilling to return to monarchy. When Juárez reestablished the republic with the defeat of Maximilian, the message encoded in Mexican money changed once again. Old symbols of liberty, combined with new ones, emphatically declared that Mexico was a republic governed by law and justice and that those principles gave strength to the nation and worth to its coins. A century and a half later, the scales of justice and the Mexican Constitution, together symbolizing the rule of law, appear on the face of Mexico's most common and smallest-denomination paper note: the twenty-peso bill (see figure C.2). Mexico and the United States found common ground in their reaction to threats to republican governance in the face of European incursion on North American soil.

The sister republics in the 1860s were hardly at the end of their journeys to becoming enduring political entities in command of their own economies. In the fifty years following the Civil War, the United States faced a period of enormous trial and evolution. For eleven years Union soldiers occupied the states of the former confederacy as the country tried to reassemble the Union. Reconstruction gave way to an era of southern retrenchment, constant war by the federal government against Native American populations, and ongoing territorial expansion at Spain's expense. Between 1873 and 1900, the

Figure C.2. The twenty-peso bill is the smallest note in circulation in Mexico. It depicts Benito Juárez, one of the nation's great republican leaders. The bill also includes icons drawn from the peso coins he introduced in the 1870s: the scales of justice and the Mexican constitution symbolize the supreme value placed on the rule of law. Mexican bills are made from polymers for durability and increase in size with their face value.
Source: "Billete de 20 pesos, tipo F." Photography by T. Seijas. This image meets the requirements of the Ley Monetaria de los Estados Unidos Mexicanos. Reproduction authorized by the Secretaría de Hacienda y Crédito Público, México.

United States moved in stages from a bimetallic standard (established in 1792) to a gold standard. Gold prices at this time were less volatile than those of silver, which fell dramatically relative to gold in the 1870s. Having struggled for much of the century to accumulate enough silver to meet its needs, the United States ended the century basing its money on gold.

The decades following the French Intervention were no less eventful for Mexico. Just ten years after the execution of Maximilian, Porfirio Díaz was elected president of Mexico for the first time. Over the next thirty-five years, Díaz aggressively sought to modernize the country by attracting foreign investment, encouraging immigration, and ensuring the stability of the Mexican government by whatever means necessary (including establishing a dictatorship). He saw British and U.S. citizens invest in rail, mining, shipping, and other industries across the nation. He placed Mexico on a gold standard in 1905, emulating the actions of other "modern" nations such as Germany, France, and England. By the early twentieth century, Díaz's policies had transformed Mexico into an attractive investment locale for international companies. This achievement, however, depended on the ruthless exploitation of the majority of the Mexican population. By 1910, the ever-widening gap between the rich and the poor culminated in the Mexican Revolution—a civil war that many say marked the creation of modern Mexico. The war unfolded on a greater scale than the U.S. Civil War, claiming approximately 1.3 million Mexican lives before it was over. One of the great social revolutions of the twentieth century, it saw the creation of the Constitution of 1917, which still governs the nation today and appears next to the face of Benito Juárez on the twenty-peso bill.

The preceding eight chapters have discussed the role of money, most often coins, in the shared experiences of the early United States and Mexico. The histories of these two nations, of course, differ vastly. Their economies have gone in very different directions since the Mexican-American War, which remains a source of considerable tension to this day. The two countries still have a challenging relationship, yet share a common heritage. These two North American nations secured their independence from European dominion through warfare and faced similar challenges in their early years—similarities that are often forgotten.

Nathan C. Brooks coined the term "sister republics" following the Mexican-American War in an attempt to justify the U.S. incursion into Mexico. While that usage may seem a bit insincere, he created the term on the understanding that the United States and Mexico had a kinship based on shared political ideals and a common colonial heritage. This book has tried to acknowledge some of these commonalities, not by claiming that Mexican and

U.S. political and cultural traditions are more similar than they seem, but by exploring the similar historical processes, questions of national identity, and economic trials the two nations confronted.

Reach into your pocket and pull out a coin. Whether you hold a lightweight dime, or a single peso, or the heftier ten-peso or one-dollar coin, you are engaging in a process as old as the nation in which you stand—and older still. You trust that a seller will accept these coins when you make a purchase. There is no risk that in its country of issue, a merchant, or clerk, or bank, or private individual will say that the coin is untrustworthy. Its feel, the message it conveys, and the fact that it will work, without fail, every time are the results of long effort by Mexico and the United States to build their currencies and their nations.

Acknowledgments

This project began as a conversation at the John Carter Brown Library (JCB) at Brown University. Fellowship support from the JCB allowed us to pursue independent research and also to conceive of a book neither of us had envisioned before. We are indebted to the JCB staff, especially director and librarian Neil Safier, Kimberly Nusco, Susan Newbury, and Ken Ward, for their encouragement and feedback on the original book proposal. Thank you as well to Richard J. Boles.

We are grateful for the feedback of anonymous peer reviews and also to Kris Lane and James P. Ambuske, whose authoritative suggestions improved this book considerably. All errors are our own.

For their help in securing images for this book, we would like to thank Emma Darbyshire from the Fitzwilliam Museum, University of Cambridge; Andrea Felder at the New York Public Library; Aryn Glazier of the Dolph Briscoe Center for American History, University of Texas, Austin; Halley Grogan of the Texas State Archives; Peter E. Hanff and José A. Barragán-Álvarez of the Bancroft Library at the University of California, Berkeley; Terre Heydari and Katie Dziminski at Southern Methodist University Libraries; Mayra Mendoza Avilés and Gabriela Mota from the Fototeca Nacional, Instituto Nacional de Antropología e Historia; John Minichiello at the JCB; Eric C. Novotny from the Pennsylvania State University Libraries; Leslie Tobias Olsen; Melissa Parris and Laura Fogerty at the Muscarelle Museum of Art of the College of William & Mary; Philip R. Rutherford and Philip T. Rutherford; Hector Manuel Salazar Newman from the Dirección General

Adjunta de Banca y Valores, Secretaría de Hacienda y Crédito Público; Alan M. Stahl of Princeton University Library; Mary Grace Wahl at the American Philosophical Society Museum; W. Crutchfield Williams II; Lawrence University alumni Jean Lampert Woy '65 and Richard Woy '64; and Penn State's Forster Fund.

Tatiana Seijas is thankful for having had as her mentor Andrew R. L. Cayton, who encouraged her continental perspective; he is dearly missed. Gracias siempre a Pilar A. Parra y Max J. Pfeffer.

Jake Frederick would like to thank Kate Moody, David McGlynn, Dominica Chang, Michael Tuttle and Lori Rose.

Glossary

Assayer	A technician who determines the purity of precious metals; assayers employed by the U.S. and Mexican mints assured that coins contained the legally required ratio of gold or silver.
Base metal	Inexpensive metal, such as copper, used in coins to add durability.
Bimetallism	A monetary standard based on a fixed value of both silver and gold.
Bond	An interest-bearing loan, typically for a fixed period; bond issuers (borrowers) are corporate entities, including companies, municipalities, and state or national governments.
Bullion	Gold or silver not minted into coins.
Bushel	A volume measurement equivalent to eight gallons, used for grains and other commodities with different standard weights.
Cob	Crudely made hand-cut coins.
Continental dollar	Paper currency printed during the U.S. Revolutionary War, meant to be redeemable in Spanish dollars.
Consultation	The name of the provisional government of Texas during its war of independence.

Cost	Measurement of any one thing that takes into account the resources (e.g., time, labor, materials) used to make it, in addition to the opportunity cost of having made this one thing rather than using those same resources to make something else; not the same as price.
Currency	System of money that can include coins and paper notes.
Debasement	Lowering the value of coinage by substituting base metal for specie.
Demonetization	Removal of the monetary value of a precious metal; to deprive gold/silver coins of their status as money; the United States demonetized silver coins in 1873, and Mexico did so in 1945.
Empresario	Spanish for "impresario"; an agent, such as Stephen Austin, who contracted with the Mexican government to settle families in the Texas region.
Fanega	A Spanish measurement of volume or capacity equivalent to nearly three bushels or some fifty-six liters; the corresponding weight measurement depended on the content (e.g., one *fanega* of maize weighed approximately sixty-five kilograms).
Fiat money	A currency that has legal value but no inherent value, such as paper money.
Fractional currency	Currency in denominations less than the national standard currency (e.g., any denomination less than one dollar or one peso).
Fugio dollar	A revolutionary coin proposed in 1776; it never went into circulation, but the design appeared on Continentals and on the first U.S. one-cent coin.
Gold standard	A system in which a currency's value is based on a fixed amount of gold.
Labor	A Spanish unit of measure equivalent to 177 acres
Ley Lerdo	An 1856 Mexican land reform named for Treasury Secretary Miguel Lerdo de Tejada that targeted church property for public auction and fiscal gain.
Manifest Destiny	A term coined in 1845 in the popular U.S. press to describe the idea that the country was destined to spread "American" values across the continent.

Mexican Cession	Territory ceded by Mexico to the United States at the conclusion of the Mexican-American War.
Milled dollar	"Spanish milled dollar"; a piece-of-eight coin with grooves or "milling" around the outer edge to prevent silver from being shaved from the edge of the coin.
Monroe Doctrine	U.S. foreign policy put forth by President James Monroe in 1823 stating that the United States would resist any European nation that sought to interfere in the internal governance of any independent country in North or South America.
Obverse	The face of a coin or bill (as opposed to the reverse).
Piece-of-eight	A Spanish coin equal in value to eight *reales*.
Pileus	A Roman cap used to symbolize manumission, often conflated with the Greek Phrygian cap.
Price	The amount of money paid for any one thing; not the same as cost.
Real	Spanish, later Mexican, unit of currency equivalent to one-eighth of a piece-of-eight (or peso) or thirty-two *maravedís*.
Redback	Paper currency issued by the Republic of Texas in 1839 and 1840.
Republic	A state in which power resides with the electorate.
Scrip	A paper certificate entitling the bearer to payment.
Shaver	Someone who secretly "shaves" or "clips" small amounts of silver or gold from the edges of coins; in the early republic, "shaver" also described someone who bought promissory notes at less than face value.
Silver standard	A system in which a currency's value is based on a fixed amount of silver.
Sitio	A Spanish unit of measure roughly equivalent to 4,448 acres.
Specie	Coined money.
Tender (legal)	A medium, such as coins or paper notes, that by law must be accepted to discharge debts.
Warrant	A certificate of payment made out to a particular individual, normally nonnegotiable.

Bibliography

Bibliographical Notes

This section lists the primary and secondary sources employed in writing each chapter, as well as some additional works for further reading. A number of comprehensive studies and catalogues have considered the rich and extensive history of the U.S. dollar. A few classic studies are Evans 1885, Hepburn 1903, Nussbaum 1957, Schwarz 1980, and Yeoman 2007. For the history of coinage in Mexico, see Pradeau 1938, Romero de Terreros 1952, Vogt and Utberg 1976, Vogt 1978, and Bátiz Vázquez and Covarrubias 1998. For information on unusual forms of currency, see Einzig 1966.

Introduction

The production of bullion in colonial Latin America (including Mexico until 1820) is analyzed in TePaske and Brown 2010; see also Rodríguez 1986 and Rankine 1992. For the piece-of-eight in Asia, see Giráldez 2015.

Chapter One

The history of the Continental dollar is examined in Calomiris 1988. For a history of the U.S. Mint, see Lange and Mead 2006. For the decimilation debate, see Hellman 1931 and Garson 2001. Two main works detailing eighteenth-century symbols of liberty are Korshak 1987 and Winterer 2005. For the connection between the iconography of the first coin money in the United States and national identity, see Ambuske 2006.

Chapter Two

Several biographies detail the life of Stephen Girard, the United States' first millionaire; the authors recommend Simpson 1832, Wildes 1943, and Wilson 1995. For Girard's early business dealings and his eventual purchase of the first Bank of the United States, see Adams 1972 and Doerflinger 2015. For a discussion of several other prominent figures in the economic history of the Early Republic, see Wright and Cowen 2006. For the War of 1812, see Stagg 2012. Excellent examinations of banking, credit markets, and financial crises during this period include Rothbard 1962, Bodenhorn 2000, and Kamensky 2008. On the Second Bank of the United States, see Nelson 2012. For a hemispheric analysis of the Age of Revolutions, see Fitz 2016.

Chapter Three

José Ignacio Esteva was a prolific writer of political commentary, as well as legislation; for some of his printed work, see Esteva 1824a, 1824b; Mexico 1825–1827; Esteva 1827a, 1827b; and Dublán and Lozano 1876. Esteva's main biography is Meade 1953. For an analysis of Esteva's economic policy, see Jáuregui 2002. For Mexican government sources of revenue, see McCaleb 1921, Coatsworth and Williamson 2004, and Aboites and Jáuregui 2005. The history of Mexico's debt is outlined in Téllez Mosqueda 2014; see also Baur 1963 and Zaragoza 1996. For comparison, the financial costs of the American War of Independence are examined in Baack 2001; for U.S. government sources of revenue, see Wallis 2000. For Mexico's ongoing struggle with Spain, see Sims 1990.

Chapter Four

Sam Houston has been the subject of biographies since before his death in 1863. Informative references about his life and work can be found in Lester 1855, Crane 1884, and J. H. Williams 1993. For a less laudatory perspective, see Meed 2001. For an in-depth and well-illustrated study of Texas currency, see Bevill 2009. Earlier works on the money of Texas include Gouge 1852, Miller 1949, and Heusinger 1953. For U.S. settlement in Texas during the 1820s and 1830s, see Henderson 1928a, 1928b; Cayton 2004; and Anderson and Cayton 2005.

Chapter Five

The best biography of Antonio López de Santa Anna is Fowler 2007; see also Scheina 2002 and Fowler 2015. For this famed president's autobiography and other materials, see García 1991. A fine examination of the history of the Mexican Cession territories before the war is Weber 1982. For the Mexican-American War and its leadup, see Vázquez 1997, Howe 2007, DeLay 2008, Greenberg 2012, and Watson 2013. An excellent study of U.S. imperialism, including the war, is Anderson and Cayton 2005. The figures and analysis on the fate of the Mexican Cession money are from Salvucci 2009; see also Griswold del Castillo 1990. For the correspondence between the parties and the full agreement with English holders of Mexican government bonds, see Robertson 1850. For figures on Mexico's debt, see Lill 1919. For the Gadsden Treaty logistics, see Rippy 1923. For an excellent analysis of imperial expansion more broadly, see Doolen 2014. For Texas's intersection with Native American history, see Hämäläinen 2008 and DeLay 2008.

Chapter Six
John R. Bartlett was a prodigious writer and painter. His work, mainly held at the John Carter Brown Library at Brown University, is a great resource, as are Bartlett 1854 and Sweeney 1996. For the broader U.S.-Mexican boundary line project and its effects, see Griswold del Castillo 1990, Rebert 2001, Greenberg 2009, St. John 2011, and Baumgartner 2015. U.S. government records on this topic include Congress 1848 and Emory 1857. For the history of commercial transactions between Mexico and the United States prior to the Mexican-American War, see Isenberg 2001. For an insightful dual history of Ciudad Juárez and El Paso, see Martínez 1978. The history of border instability in the context of transborder raids and indigenous resistance can be found in DeLay 2008 and Blyth 2012. For a history of the Chino mines at Santa Rita, see Walker 1979 and Huggard and Humble 2012. The challenges of using copper coinage in Mexico are discussed in Covarrubias 2000.

Chapter Seven
Though Robert Maskell Patterson excelled as mint director, he was primarily a scientist, and his papers, now located at the American Philosophical Society, express his intellectual rather than administrative interests. His family history can be found in Du Bois 1847. For an analysis of the consequences of President Andrew Jackson's opposition to the Second Bank of the United States, see Gordon 2004 and Knodell 2006. For an analysis of the domestic and international factors that resulted in the Panic of 1837 and its consequences, see Rousseau 2002 and A. Roberts 2012. For an examination of British capital and the financing of western expansion, see Cronon 1991. The histories of the eastern mines can be found in Knapp 1975, Birdsall 1988, and D. Williams 1993. The California Gold Rush has received a lot of popular and scholarly attention. Some notable titles include Holliday and Swain 1981, Rohrbough 1997, B. Roberts 2000, and Owens 2002. For the SS *Central America* story, see Kinder 1998.

Chapter Eight
For the life of Emperor Maximilian I, see Hall 1868 and McAllen 2014. McAllen also examines Maximilian's modernization of Mexican currency; for more information, see Doty 1992. For Maximilian's efforts to gain Mexican and U.S. support, see Duncan 1996. On U.S. interests in Mexico and enforcement of the Monroe Doctrine, see Topik 2000 and Heiss 2002. The Benito Juárez administration's mission to secure aide from the Union is examined in R. Miller 1973. For Juárez's perspective,

see Juárez 2006. For a review of the Reform War and Napoleon III's objectives in Mexico, see Vanderwood 2000.

Conclusion

For the shift to the gold standard in the United States and Mexico, see Pletcher 1958, Myers 1970, Friedman and Schwartz 1993, and Schell 1996, 2001.

Bibliography

Aboites, Luis, and Luis Jáuregui. 2005. *Penuria sin fin: historia de los impuestos en México siglos XVIII–XX*. México: Instituto Mora.

Adams, Donald. 1972. "The Bank of Stephen Girard, 1812–1831." *Journal of Economic History* 32 (4):841–68.

Ambuske, James Patrick. 2006. "Minting America: Coinage and the Contestation of American Identity, 1775–1800." MA thesis, History, Miami University.

Anderson, Fred, and Andrew R. L. Cayton. 2005. *The Dominion of War: Empire and Liberty in North America, 1500–2000*. New York: Viking.

Baack, Ben. 2001. "Forging a Nation State: The Continental Congress and the Financing of the War of American Independence." *Economic History Review* 54 (4):639–56.

Bartlett, John Russell. 1854. *Personal Narrative of Explorations and Incidents in Texas, New Mexico, California, Sonora, and Chihuahua*. 2 vols. New York: D. Appleton & Company.

Bátiz Vázquez, José Antonio, and José Enrique Covarrubias, eds. 1998. *La moneda en México, 1750–1920*. México: Instituto Mora; UNAM.

Baumgartner, Alice L. 2015. "The Line of Positive Safety: Borders and Boundaries in the Rio Grande Valley, 1848–1880." *Journal of American History* 101 (4).

Baur, John E. 1963. "The Evolution of a Mexican Foreign Trade Policy, 1821–1828." *Americas* 19 (3):225–61.

Bevill, James. 2009. *The Paper Republic: The Struggle for Money, Credit and Independence in the Republic of Texas*. Houston, TX: Bright Sky Press.

Birdsall, C. M. 1988. *The United States Branch Mint at Charlotte, North Carolina: Its History and Coinage*. Easley, SC: Southern Historical Press.

Blyth, Lance R. 2012. *Chiricahua and Janos: Communities of Violence in the Southwestern Borderlands, 1680–1880*. Lincoln: University of Nebraska Press.

Bodenhorn, Howard. 2000. *A History of Banking in Antebellum America*. Cambridge: Cambridge University Press.

Calomiris, Charles W. 1988. "Institutional Failure, Monetary Scarcity, and the Depreciation of the Continental." *Journal of Economic History* 48 (1):47–68.

Cayton, Andrew R. L. 2004. "Continental Politics: Liberalism, Nationalism, and the Appeal of Texas in the 1820s." In *Beyond the Founders: New Approaches to the Political History of the Early American Republic*, edited by Jeffrey L. Pasley, Andrew W.

Robertson, and David Waldstreicher, 303–27. Chapel Hill: University of North Carolina Press.

Coatsworth, John H., and Jeffrey G. Williamson. 2004. "Always Protectionist? Latin American Tariffs from Independence to Great Depression." *Journal of Latin American Studies* 36 (2):205–32.

Congress, United States. 1848. *Treaty of Peace, Friendship, Limits, and Settlement between the United States of America and the United Mexican States Concluded at Guadalupe Hidalgo*, edited by Records of the U.S. Senate. Washington, DC.

Covarrubias, José Enrique. 2000. *La moneda de cobre en México, 1760–1842: un problema administrativo*. México: UNAM.

Crane, William Carey. 1884. *Life and select literary remains of Sam Houston of Texas*. Philadelphia: J. B. Lippincott Company.

Cronon, William. 1991. *Nature's Metropolis: Chicago and the Great West*. New York: W. W. Norton.

DeLay, Brian. 2008. *War of a Thousand Deserts: Indian Raids and the U.S.-Mexican War*. Lamar Series in Western History. New Haven, CT: Yale University Press.

Doerflinger, Thomas M. 2015. "Capital Generation in the New Nation: How Stephen Girard Made His First $735,872." *William and Mary Quarterly* 72 (4):623–58.

Doolen, Andy. 2014. *Territories of Empire: U.S. Writing from the Louisiana Purchase to Mexican Independence*. Oxford: Oxford University Press.

Doty, Richard G. 1992. "*Juaristas, Imperialistas*, and *Centavos*: Decimalization and Civil War in Mexico, 1857–1870." *American Journal of Numismatics* 3/4:135–46.

Du Bois, William Ewing. 1847. *A Record of the Families of Robert Patterson (the Elder), Emigrant from Ireland to America 1774*. Philadelphia: Press of J. C. Clark.

Dublán, Manuel, and José María Lozano, eds. 1876. *Legislación mexicana o colección complete de las disposiciones desde la independencia de la república*. Vol. 1. México: Imprenta del Comercio, a cargo de Dublan y Lozano, Hijos.

Duncan, Robert H. 1996. "Political Legitimation and Maximilian's Second Empire in Mexico, 1864–1867." *Mexican Studies/Estudios Mexicanos* 12 (1):27–66.

Einzig, Paul. 1966. *Primitive Money in Its Ethnological, Historical, and Economic Aspects*. 2nd ed. Oxford, NY: Pergamon Press.

Emory, William H. 1857. *Report on the United States and Mexican Boundary Survey Made under the Direction of the Secretary of the Interior*. Washington, DC: 34th U.S. Congress.

Esteva, José Ignacio. 1824a. *Circular impresa. Indica que el Congreso decretó que el Jornalero que en el servicio de la casa de Moneda y apartado de esta ciudad cuenta 20 años de buenos y acreditados servicios legalmente comprobados, será acreedor, si está imposibilitado, a la tercera parte del jornal que percibía*. México: Centro de Estudios de Historia de México CARSO.

Esteva, José Ignacio. 1824b. *Circular impresa. Informa que el Congreso decretó que el cobre en planchas extraído de las minas de la República, no pagará alcabala en la aduana de la ciudad de México, ni en los territorios de la Federación*, edited by Secretaria de Hacienda. México: Centro de Estudios de Historia de México CARSO.

Esteva, José Ignacio. 1827a. *Apuntaciones que el ciudadano José Ignacio Esteva al separarse del despacho del Ministerio de Hacienda entrega a su succesor el ecsmo señor D. Tomás Salgado*. México: Imp. del Aguila, 1827.
Esteva, José Ignacio. 1827b. *Rasgo analítico*. México: Imprenta del Aguila.
Evans, G. G. 1885. *Illustrated History of the United States Mint with a Complete Description of American Coinage*. Philadelphia: G. G. Evans.
Fitz, Caitlin. 2016. *Our Sister Republics: The United States in an Age of American Revolutions*. New York, W. W. Norton.
Fowler, Will. 2007. *Santa Anna of Mexico*. Lincoln: University of Nebraska Press.
Fowler, Will. 2015. "Santa Anna and His Legacy." *Oxford Research Encyclopedias: Latin American History*. http://latinamericanhistory.oxfordre.com/view/10.1093/acrefore/9780199366439.001.0001/acrefore-9780199366439-e-18.
Friedman, Milton, and Anna J. Schwartz. 1993. *A Monetary History of the United States, 1867–1960*. Princeton, NJ: Princeton University Press.
García, Genaro, ed. 1991. *Documentos inéditos o muy raros para la historia de México*. 3rd ed. Vol. 59. México: Porrúa.
Garson, Robert. 2001. "Counting Money: The U.S. Dollar and American Nationhood, 1781–1820." *Journal of American Studies* 35 (1):21–46.
Giráldez, Arturo. 2015. *The Age of Trade: Manila Galleons and the Dawn of the Global Economy*. Exploring World History. Lanham, MD: Rowman & Littlefield.
Gordon, John Steele. 2004. *An Empire of Wealth: The Epic History of American Economic Power*. New York: HarperCollins.
Gouge, William M. 1852. *The Fiscal History of Texas. Embracing an Account of Its Revenues, Debts, and Currency, from the Commencement of the Revolution in 1834 to 1851–52. With Remarks on American Debts*. Philadelphia: Lippincott, Grambo, and Co.
Greenberg, Amy S. 2009. "Domesticating the Border Manifest Destiny and the 'Comforts of Life'in the US-Mexico Boundary Commission and Gadsden Purchase, 1848–1854." In *Land of Necessity: Consumer Culture in the United States–Mexico Borderlands*, edited by Alexis McCrossen, 83–112. Durham, NC: Duke University Press.
Greenberg, Amy S. 2012. *A Wicked War: Polk, Clay, Lincoln, and the 1846 U.S. Invasion of Mexico*. New York: Alfred A. Knopf.
Griswold del Castillo, Richard. 1990. *The Treaty of Guadalupe Hidalgo: A Legacy of Conflict*. Norman: University of Oklahoma Press.
Hall, Frederic. 1868. *Life of Maximilian I, Late Emperor of Mexico, with a Sketch of the Empress Carlota*. New York: J. Miller.
Hämäläinen, Pekka. 2008. *The Comanche Empire*. New Haven, CT: Yale University Press.
Heiss, Mary Ann. 2002. "The Evolution of the Imperial Idea and US National Identity." *Diplomatic History* 26 (4):511–40.
Hellman, Doris C. 1931. "Jefferson's Efforts towards the Decimalization of United States Weights and Measures." *Isis* 16 (2):266–314.

Henderson, Mary Virginia. 1928a. "Minor Empresario Contracts for the Colonization of Texas, 1825–1834, part I." *Southwestern Historical Quarterly* 31 (4):295–324.
Henderson, Mary Virginia. 1928b. "Minor Empresario Contracts for the Colonization of Texas, 1825–1834, part II." *Southwestern Historical Quarterly* 32 (1):1–28.
Hepburn, A. Barton. 1903. *History of Coinage and Currency in the United States and the Perennial Contest for Sound Money*. New York: Macmillan.
Heusinger, Edward W. 1953. "The Monetary History of the Republic of Texas." *Southwestern Historical Quarterly* 57 (1):82–90.
Holliday, J. S., and William Swain. 1981. *The World Rushed In: The California Gold Rush Experience*. New York: Simon & Schuster.
Howe, Daniel Walker. 2007. *What Hath God Wrought: The Transformation of America, 1815–1848*. New York: Oxford University Press.
Huggard, Christopher J., and Terrence M. Humble. 2012. *Santa Rita del Cobre: A Copper Mining Community in New Mexico, Mining the American West*. Boulder: University Press of Colorado.
Isenberg, Andrew C. 2001. "The Market Revolution in the Borderlands: George Champlin Sibley in Missouri and New Mexico, 1808–1826." *Journal of the Early Republic* 21 (3):445–65.
Jáuregui, Luis. 2002. "Control administrativo y crédito exterior bajo la administración de José Ignacio Esteva." In *Los secretarios de hacienda y sus proyectos: 1821–1933*, edited by Leonor Ludlow, 55–86. México: UNAM.
Juárez, Benito. 2006. *Apuntes para mis hijos*. México: Fondo de Cultura Económica.
Kamensky, Jane. 2008. *The Exchange Artist: A Tale of High-Flying Speculation and America's First Banking Collapse*. New York: Viking.
Kinder, Gary. 1998. *Ship of Gold in the Deep Blue Sea: The History and Discovery of the World's Richest Shipwreck*. 1st ed. New York: Atlantic Monthly Press.
Knapp, Richard F. 1975. "Golden Promise in the Piedmont: The Story of John Reed's Mine." *North Carolina Historical Review* 52 (1):1–19.
Knodell, Jane. 2006. "Rethinking the Jacksonian Economy: The Impact of the 1832 Bank Veto on Commercial Banking." *Journal of Economic History* 66 (3):541–74.
Korshak, Yvonne. 1987. "The Liberty Cap as a Revolutionary Symbol in America and France." *Smithsonian Studies in American Art* 1 (2):52–69.
Lange, David W., and Mary Jo Mead. 2006. *History of the United States Mint and Its Coinage*. Atlanta, GA: Whitman Pub.
Lester, C. Edwards. 1855. *The Life of Sam Houston: The Only Authentic Memoir of Him Ever Published*. New York: J. C. Derby.
Lill, Thomas Russell. 1919. *National Debt of Mexico: History and Present Status*. New York: Searle, Nicholson, and Lill.
Martínez, Oscar J. 1978. *Border Boom Town: Ciudad Juárez since 1848*. Austin: University of Texas Press.
McAllen, Mary M. 2014. *Maximilian and Carlota: Europe's Last Empire in Mexico*. San Antonio, TX: Trinity University Press.
McCaleb, Walter F. 1921. *The Public Finances of Mexico*. New York: Harper & Bros.

Meade, Joaquín. 1953. "Biografías veracruzanas. José Ignacio Esteva." *Memorias de la Academia Mexicana de la Historia* 12 (1–4):1–338.

Meed, Douglas V. 2001. *The Fighting Texas Navy, 1832–1843*. Plano: Republic of Texas Press.

Mexico. 1825–1827. *Guía de hacienda de la República Mexicana. Parte legislativa*. México: Imprenta del Supremo Gobierno de los Estados Unidos, en Palacio.

Miller, E. T. 1949. "The Money of the Republic of Texas." *Southwestern Historical Quarterly* 52 (3):294–300.

Miller, Robert Ryal. 1973. "Arms across the Border: United States Aid to Juárez during the French Intervention in Mexico." *Transactions of the American Philosophical Society* (New Series) 63 (6).

Myers, Margaret G. 1970. *A Financial History of the United States*. New York: Columbia University Press.

Nelson, Scott R. 2012. *A Nation of Deadbeats: An Uncommon History of America's Financial Disasters*. New York: Alfred A. Knopf.

Nussbaum, Arthur. 1957. *A History of the Dollar*. New York: Columbia University Press.

Owens, Kenneth N., ed. 2002. *Riches for All: The California Gold Rush and the World*. Lincoln: University of Nebraska Press.

Pletcher, D. 1958. "The Fall of Silver in Mexico, 1870–1910, and Its Effect on American Investments." *Journal of Economic History* 18 (1):33–55.

Pradeau, Alberto Francisco. 1938. *Numismatic History of Mexico from the Pre-Columbian Epoch to 1823*. Los Angeles, CA: Western Printing Company.

Rankine, Margaret E. 1992. "The Mexican Mining Industry in the Nineteenth Century with Special Reference to Guanajuato." *Bulletin of Latin American Research* 11 (1):29–48.

Rebert, Paula. 2001. *La Gran Línea: Mapping the United States–Mexico Boundary, 1849–1857*. Austin: University of Texas Press.

Rippy, J. Fred. 1923. "The Negotiation of the Gadsden Treaty." *Southwestern Historical Quarterly* 27 (1):1–26.

Roberts, Alasdair. 2012. *America's First Great Depression: Economic Crisis and Political Disorder after the Panic of 1837*. Ithaca, NY: Cornell University Press.

Roberts, Brian. 2000. *American Alchemy: The California Gold Rush and Middle-Class Culture*. Chapel Hill: University of North Carolina Press.

Robertson, William P. 1850. *The Foreign Debt of Mexico, Being the Report of a Special Mission to That State, Undertaken on Behalf of the Bondholders*. London: Smith, Elder, & Co. http://hdl.handle.net/2027/hvd.32044080423775 (accessed July 31, 2016).

Rodríguez, Jaime. 1986. "La crisis de México en el siglo XIX." In *Estudios de historia moderna y contemporánea de México*, edited by Álvaro Matute. México: Universidad Nacional Autónoma de México, Instituto de Investigaciones Históricas.

Rohrbough, Malcolm J. 1997. *Days of Gold: The California Gold Rush and the American Nation*. Berkeley: University of California Press.

Romero de Terreros, Manuel. 1952. *La moneda mexicana: bosquejo histórico-numismático*. México: Banco de México.
Rothbard, Murray Newton. 1962. *The Panic of 1819: Reactions and Policies*. New York: Columbia University Press.
Rousseau, Peter L. 2002. "Jacksonian Monetary Policy, Specie Flows, and the Panic of 1837." *Journal of Economic History* 62 (2):457–88.
Salvucci, Richard J. 2009. "Santa Anna Never Had an iPhone: Some Thoughts on the Price of Peace and the Financial Misfortunes of the Treaty of Guadalupe Hidalgo in 1848." *Journal of the Historical Society* 9 (1):67–86.
Scheina, Robert L. 2002. *Santa Anna: A Curse upon Mexico*. Washington, DC: Brassey's, Inc.
Schell, W. 1996. "Money as Commodity: Mexico's Conversion to the Gold Standard, 1905." *Mexican Studies/Estudios Mexicanos* 12 (1):67–89.
Schell, W. 2001. "Silver Symbiosis: Reorienting Mexican Economic History." *Hispanic American Historical Review* 81 (1):89–133.
Schwarz, Ted. 1980. *A History of United States Coinage*. San Diego, CA: A. S. Barnes.
Simpson, Stephen. 1832. *Biography of Stephen Girard, with His Will Affixed Comprising an Account of His Private Life, Habits, Genius, and Manners: Together with a Detailed History of His Banking and Financial Operations for the Last Twenty Years: Accompanied with Philosophical and Moral Reflections, upon the Man, the Merchant, the Patriot, and the Philanthropist*. Philadelphia: T. L. Bonsal.
Sims, Harold Dana. 1990. *The Expulsion of Mexico's Spaniards, 1821–1836*. Pitt Latin American Series. Pittsburgh: University of Pittsburgh Press.
St. John, Rachel C. 2011. *Line in the Sand: A History of the Western U.S.-Mexico Border*. America in the World. Princeton, NJ: Princeton University Press.
Stagg, J. C. A. 2012. *The War of 1812: Conflict for a Continent*. New York: Cambridge University Press.
Sweeney, J. Gray, ed. 1996. *Drawing the Borderline: Artist-Explorers of the U.S.-Mexico Boundary Survey*. Albuquerque, NM: Albuquerque Museum.
Téllez Mosqueda, Juan Carlos. 2014. "Brief Review of Mexico's Foreign Debt, 1824–2010." In *Economic Development and Global Crisis: The Latin American Economy in Historical Perspective*, edited by José Luís Cardoso, Maria Cristina Marcuzzo, and María Eugenia Romero, 205–38. London: Routledge, Taylor & Francis Group.
TePaske, John Jay, and Kendall W. Brown. 2010. *A New World of Gold and Silver*. Leiden: Brill.
Topik, Steven C. 2000. "When Mexico Had the Blues: A Transatlantic Tale of Bonds, Bankers, and Nationalists, 1862–1910." *American Historical Review* 105 (3):714–38.
Vanderwood, Paul. 2000. "Betterment for Whom? The Reform Period: 1855–1875." In *The Oxford History of Mexico*, edited by Michael C. Meyer and William H. Beezley, 349–372. New York: Oxford University Press.
Vázquez, Josefina Zoraida, ed. 1997. *México al tiempo de su guerra con Estados Unidos, 1846–1848*. 1st ed. México: El Colegio de México.

Vogt, George W. 1978. *Standard Catalog of Mexican Coins, Paper Money, and Medals*. Iola, WI: Krause Publications.

Vogt, George W., and Neil S. Utberg. 1976. *The Coins of the Republic of Mexico, 1823–1905, and the Empire of Maximilian, 1864–1867*. Houston, TX: Colonial Coins.

Walker, Billy D. 1979. "Copper Genesis: The Early Years of Santa Rita del Cobre." *New Mexico Historical Review* 54 (1).

Wallis, John J. 2000. "American Government Finance in the Long Run: 1790 to 1990." *Journal of Economic Perspectives* 14 (1):61–82.

Watson, Samuel J. 2013. *Peacekeepers and Conquerors: The Army Officer Corps on the American Frontier, 1821–1846*. Lawrence: University Press of Kansas.

Weber, David J. 1982. *The Mexican Frontier, 1821–1846: The American Southwest under Mexico*. Albuquerque: University of New Mexico Press.

Wildes, Harry Emerson. 1943. *Lonely Midas: The Story of Stephen Girard*. New York: Farrar & Rinehart.

Williams, David. 1993. *The Georgia Gold Rush: Twenty-Niners, Cherokees, and Gold Fever*. Columbia: University of South Carolina Press.

Williams, John Hoyt. 1993. *Sam Houston: A Biography of the Father of Texas*. New York: Simon & Schuster.

Wilson, George. 1995. *Stephen Girard: America's First Tycoon*. Conshohocken, PA: Combined Books.

Winterer, Caroline. 2005. "From Royal to Republican: The Classical Image in Early America." *Journal of American History* 91 (4):1264–90.

Wright, Robert E., and David J. Cowen. 2006. *Financial Founding Fathers: The Men Who Made America Rich*. Chicago: University of Chicago Press.

Yeoman, R. S. 2007. *A Guide Book of United States Coins*. Racine, WI: Whitman Pub.

Zaragoza, José. 1996. *Historia de la deuda externa de México 1823–1861*. Colección Historia Económica y Social. México: Universidad Nacional Autónoma de México, Instituto de Investigaciones Económicas, Editorial Cambio XXI, S.A. de C.V. http://ru.iiec.unam.mx/id/eprint/1445 (accessed July 31, 2016).

Index

Age of Revolutions, 25, 27, 32
The Alamo, 66
Alaska, 95
American Philosophical Society, 125
Analytical Expression (Esteva), 60
Apaches, 114
Apartado General de la Nación (Mexican Mint), 91
Astor, John Jacob, 40
Austin, Stephen, 68
Austria, 135

Badger, Edmund, 98
bankers: characterization of, 39; in Early Republic, 28; Girard as, 35–39, 43; trust and, 29
Bank of England, 131
Bank of Maryland, 23
Bank of Stephen Girard, 30, 31, 38
Bank of the United States, 25; closure of, 39; Hamilton proposal for, 36; opposition to, 37, 38
banks, 130; government and, 36; as informal network, 111; as private, 27; state charter of, 30

Barbary states, *32*, 41–42
barter, 44, 67, 75
Bartlett, John R., 5, *108*; as commissioner, 103; as ethnologist, 120n3; *Personal Narrative* by, 106–7, 108–9, 120n1; as Protestant, 114
Battle of New Orleans, 41
Birdsall, L.A., 130
Bolton, Herbert Eugene, 6
borders: conflict at, 89; map of, *74*; before Mexican-American War, 84–85; as problematic, 6; Rio Grande as, 88, 100
Brooks, Nathan C.: term sister republics by, 156
Buchanan, James, 138

California: acquisition of, 86; Baja in, 139; gold in, 128–33, 154; prospectors to, 119; San Francisco in, 117–19; travelers to, 112; U.S. economy and, 133
"California Gold, a Song for the Occasion," 129

California Gold Rush, 109; onions and, 119
Canada: invasion of, 40
Catholic Church, 91; influence of, 114; monarchs and, 143; offerings to, 116; opposition from, 142; power of, 138; traditions of, 115
Centralists: in Mexico, 55, 56
Chapultepec Castle, 146, *147*
charity, 115
Cheves, Langdon, 43
China: goods from, 33; trade with, 44
Cinco de Mayo, 142
coins, 19, *127*; collectors of, 148–49; colonists use of, 15; copper and, 103–21; dependence on, 30; design of, *22, 25*, 151; eagle on, *22, 24, 53, 54, 56, 104*; of Early Republic, 11; eight-real as, *52, 54*; fugio dollar as, *12*, 12–13; gold, *130*; metal in, 126; of Mexico, *144, 146*; minting of, 129; as monetary nationalism, 57; pieces-of-eight as, 1, *3, 4*, 13, *19*, 48; of specie, 97; substitutes for, 67
colonies: economy and, 51; of Spain, 117; symbolism and, *12, 13*
colonists, 66; in British America, 2; coins used by, 15
Comonfort, Ignacio, 145
Condé, Pedro Garcia, 105
Confederate States of America, 140
Constitution of 1917, 156
The Consultation, 71
Continental Congress, 11, 12, 13, 14
Convention of London, 141, 150n3
copper: coins of, 103–21; mining of, 109
credit: bank notes as, 130; commerce and, 67; economy and, 132; as resource, 45; beyond specie, 39, 131
currency: as authorized, 118; circulation of, 139; decimal system as base for, 15–17, 25, 154; devaluation of, 14, 17; *empresarios* use of, 80n2; as fiduciary, 36; as foreign, 15–16, 23, 132, 153; insurgents and, 51; Lady Liberty on, *24, 127*; minting of, 16–20, 23; of nations, 20, 57, 149; as objects, 17; ordering of, 78; people on, 152; pieces-of-eight, 1, *3, 4*, 13, *19*, 48, 152; production of, 23, 44, 54, 120, 128; shortage of, 3, 67; soap as, 118; of Spanish Empire, 6n1, 18; standards for, 2, 124, 156; symbols on, 3–4, *12*, 18, *76*; as valid, 23; value of, 19, *24*, 151; Washington on, 19

Davis, Jefferson, 26n8
Davis, John, 98
debt: as crushing, 73; as foreign, 61, 83, 97, 141, 142; war and, 49, 54, 71, 74
decimal system, 5; currency based on, 15–17, 25, 154; Mexican dollars based on, 145
de la Peña y Peña, Manuel, 94
de Santa Anna, Antonio López, 5, *82*, 87; as dictator, 100; Houston capture of, 72; Mexican Congress and, 90; Mexico defense and, 86–100; Plan Cuernavaca by, 71; Polk and, 81, 88, 92, 101; presidential order by, *91*; as Savior of the Fatherland, 87
DeWitt, Green, 69, 69
Díaz, Porfirio, 156
dimes: as silver, *127*
dollars: ghost of, 27–45; as silver, 17, *24*
Dupré, Augustin, 20, 21

eagle: on coins, *22, 24, 53, 54, 56, 104*; Mexico and, *116*, 145
Early Republic, 27; bankers in, *28*; coins of, 11
Eckert, Nicholas George, 129
economy, 60, 104; as barter, 75; boom in, 130; California and, 133; as colonial, 51; credit and, 132; as

debilitated, 40; as established, 152; as frontier, 103; as local, 111; of Mexico, 47, 58; policy and, 31; rebuilding of, 42; sectors of, 4, 35, 43; stabilization of, 97; stimulation of, 69; as successful, 39
Edwards, Haden, 70
El Paso Commissioner Quarters, *110*
Emory, William H., 105
empresarios (settlement agents or recruiters), 68; currencies of, 80n2; DeWitt as, 69
Estados Unidos Mexicanos (United Mexican States), 55, 67
Esteva, José Ignacio, 5, 48, 62n1; *Analytical Expression* by, 60; life and death of, 49, 61; as pragmatist, 59; as secretary of Treasury, 47, 58; on Treasury Commission, 57
exports. *See* imports and exports

Farías, Valentín Gómez, 91
Federalists, 37; in Mexico, 55; model for, 59
First Federal Republic, 56
First Mexican Empire, 48
forgery, 104
France: allies of, 144; invasion of Mexico, 136
Franklin, Benjamin: Liberty Medal commission by, *21*; myths and, 22
Fredonia, Texas, 70
Freemasonry, 58, 62n7
Frémont, John Charles, 105
French Intervention in Mexico, 135, 156

Gadsden, James, 99
Gadsden Purchase, 95, 96, 99, 105
gambling, 116
Girard College, 123
Girard, Stephen, 5, *29*; address to Congress, 34, 45n1; as banker, 35–39, 43; as first U.S. millionaire, 30, 152; as protagonist, 27; will of, 123
Gobrecht, Christian, *127*
gold: in California, 128–33, 154; as coins, *130*; price of, 156; and recklessness, 123–34
Goldschmitt and Company, 57
government: bank regulation and, 36–37; as conservative, 48; corruption and, 58; expenditures by, 77; as fractured, 87; interpretation of, 15; of Mexico, 113; minting and, 61; against Native Americans, 155; nature of, 136; as republican, 49; of U.S., 14
Great Britain, 14; intervention by, 97; relations with, 38
greenback, 140
Guerra de Reforma (Reform War), 138, 140
Guerrero, Vicente, 70

Haitian Revolution, 33
Hamilton, Alexander, 17; proposal by, 36; as secretary of the Treasury, 30
Hidalgo y Costilla, Miguel, 50
history: of money, 6; of Spanish Empire, 117; of U.S. and Mexico, 2, 152, 157
Houston, Sam, 5, 64; and fight for Texas, 70–73; paycheck of, 79; as president of Texas, 63, 76, 78; role of, 80; Santa Anna capture by, 72; story of, 153; in Tennessee, 65
human capital, 76

ideals: as allegorical, 76; for founding, 4; national, 18; politics and, 37
imports. *See* imports and exports
imports and exports, 60, 75
independence: for Mexico, 47–62; as political achievement, 44; Texas and, 65–69, 72; of U.S., 11; war for, 65

178 ~ Index

Intervención Estadounidense (United States Intervention). *See* Mexican-American War
Isthmus of Tehuantepec, 142
Iturbide, Agustín, 49; coins issued by, 54; leadership of, 53; reign of, 57, 59

Jackson, Andrew, 41, 72, 127
Jefferson, Thomas: measuring systems and, 15–16; as Virginia secretary of state, 37
Johnson, Andrew, 148
Joseph, Ferdinand Maximilian, *137*; birth of, 136; on coins, *146*; as Emperor, 135, 143; execution of, *136*; peso recast by, 145; Princess Carlota wife of, 137, 150n1, 150n5
Juárez, Benito, 141, 147; ascension of, 144; election of, 139; liberals led by, 146; Lincoln and, 139; on twenty-peso bill, *155*

Kino, Eusebio, 121n10

labor, 113
Lady Liberty, 24, 78, *127*
La Jeune Bebe (boat), 31
Lamar, Mirabeau, 77; fiscal policy of, 79; as president of Texas, 76
land: acquisition of, 88; payment in, 68, 72, 80n4; price of, 95
Landberg, Emilio, 111
Lardo Law (*Ley Lardo*), 138
Latrille, Charles Ferdinand, 142
laws, 34, 80n1; on immigration, 68; *Ley Lardo* as, 138; money and, 125
Legal Tender Act, 140
Lewis and Clark expedition, 132
liberty: cap of, 57, 128, 145, 149; emblems of, 9–26; medal of, 21; pictures of, 20–22
Liberty Medal, *21*
Lincoln, Abraham, 139

Livermore, Samuel, 9, 20
loans, 75, 139
loyalists, 53

Macedonian (Great Britain), *41*
Mackenzie, Alexander Slidell, 81
Magdalena de Kino, 114–16
Manifest Destiny, 83, 120
Manila Galleon, 118, 119
maps, 8; of Mexico, *84–85*, *106–7*; of New Spain, *66*; of Texas borders, *74*; of U.S., *96*, *106–7*
Maximilian I. *See* Joseph, Ferdinand Maximilian
Mejía, Tomás, 135
metal, 126, 133n3–133n4
Mexican-American War, 5, 80; borders prior to, 84–85; territory after, 81, 83, 94; years after, 103, 112
Mexican Cession, 94, 95, 96, 154
Mexican Congress, 56, 61, 151; Santa Anna and, 90; war declaration by, 89
Mexican Emigration Company, 147
Mexican Mint (*Apartado General de la Nación*), 91
Mexico: Acapulco in, 118, *118*; buying of, 81–101; Centralists in, 55, 56; Chapultepec Castle in, 146, *147*; *Cinco de Mayo* in, 142; coins of, *144*, *146*; Constitution of, 155, 156; eagle and, *116*, 145; economy of, 47, 58; Emperor Maximilian I of, 135; European occupation of, 141; Federalists in, 55; foreign debt for, 141, 142; France invasion of, 136; Gadsden Purchase signing by, 99; history of, 2, 152, 157; immigration laws in, 68; imports and exports of, 60; independence for, 47–62; Juárez as president of, 139; Magdalena de Kino, Sonora, 114–16; maps of, *84–85*, *106–7*; markets in, 109; Mexico City, 93, 115; minting in, 25, 47–62; mythology

of, 53, 150; power of, 150; royalists in, 50, 52; Santa Anna defense of, 86–100; silver from, 45, 61, 115, 148; Spain and, 87; Texas and, 70; U. S., 48, 63, 93; U.S. parallels to, 48
Mexico Boundary Commission, 105
military, 60, 89; coup by, 99; funding of, 74; insignia of, 82; posts of, 110; resources for, 92
mining, 51; of copper, 109; minting and, 126; of silver, 1; tools for, 119
Mint and Coinage Act of 1792, 17–22
minting: of coins, 129; of currency, 16–20, 23; governments and, 61; in Mexico, 25, 47–62; mining and, 126; as provisional, 51, 52
Miramón, Miguel, 135
monarchies: Catholic Church and, 143; last of, 142; practices of, 9; support for, 143
money, 1, 104, 140; in context, 11; counting systems for, 14–16; history of, 6; laws and, 125; nationhood and, 73–80; paper notes as, 13, *13*, 55, 56, 63, 69, 76, 77; printing of, 38; redback notes as, 77, 78; regulation of, 131; value of, 151; in wartime, 11–12, 50–52
Monroe Doctrine, 148
Monterrey, 90
Morelos, José María, 51, 121n8
Morris, Richard, 16

Napoleonic Wars, 33
Napoleon III of France, 137, 142
nations: building of, 9; currency of, 20, 57, 149; ideals of, 18; money for, 73–80; recognition by, 77, 78, 147; revenue for, 59; as sister republics, 6, 154, 155, 156; as sovereign, 151
Native Americans: Apaches, 114; British and, 40, 42; consideration for, 65; government against, 155; raids by, 98, 99; regional control by, 112; removal of, 78; in Texas, 68
New Mexico: copper mining in, 109; occupation of, 89; Santa Rita del Cobre in, 112–17
New Spain, 100; map of, 66; trade in, 49; Viceroyalty of, 3, 66
New York Stock Exchange, 153
Nueces River, *74*; as boundary, 89

Ohio Life Insurance and Trust Company, 132
opium, 34

Page, John, 5, 9, *10*, 11; speech of, 25n1; as Virginia Congressman, 19
Panic of 1819, 43, 68
Panic of 1837, 130, 133, 154
paper notes: as credit, 130–31; greenback as, 140; as money, 13, *13*, 55, 56, 63, 69, *76*, 77
Parish, David, 40
patriotism, 65
Patterson, Robert Maskell, 5, *124*; as U.S. Mint director, 123, 125, 154
Personal Narrative (Bartlett), *106–7*, 108–9, 120n1
peso, *149*; official use of, 150; recast of, 145; as silver, *116*
Philadelphia: yellow fever outbreak in, 34–35
pieces-of-eight: as Mexican dollars, 48, 152; silver coins as, 1, *3*, *4*, 13, *19*, 48
Pike, Zebulon Montgomery, 112, 120n7
pileus, 26n7
Pillars of Hercules, 3, 19
Poinsett, Joel Roberts, 58
policy, 31, 45
Polk, James K., *124*; Santa Anna and, 81, 88, 92, 101; as U.S. President, 86; war declaration by, 89
power: Catholic Church and, 138; of Europeans, 83; of Mexico, 150;

of Spanish Empire, 18; of United States, 129
Princess Carlota of Belgium: as Empress, 146; Maximilian I and, 137, 150n1, 150n5
Protestants: Bartlett as, 114; perspective of, 116; work ethic of, 115
provisions, 109–12

railroads, 99, 117, 121n11
Randall, Thomas, 31
Real Casa de Moneda de México (Royal Mint), 2
redback notes, 77, 78
Reed Gold Mine, 126
Reed, John, 126
Reform War (*Guerra de Reforma*), 138, 140
republics: defending of, 135–50; government as, 49; nations as sister, 6, 154, 155, 156; Texas as, 63–80, 83
revenue, 79
Rio Grande, 74; as border, 88, 100; trading along, 111
Robertson, William, 97
royalists, 50, 52
Royal Mint (*Real Casa de Moneda de México*), 2
Russia, 95

Scott, Winfield, 92
Second Bank of United States, 43
Second Mexican Empire, 143–50, *147*, *149*
settlement agents or recruiters (*empresarios*), 68
Seward, William, 147
Sheridan, Philip, 148
shipping, 31
silver: as bullion, 33; as dimes, *127*; as dollars, 17, 24; importance of, 42; Mexico and, 45, 61, 115, 148; mining of, 1; as pesos, *116*; as pieces-of-eight, 1, *3*, *4*, 13, *19*, 48
slavery, 3–4; abolition of, 70; state conflict and, 21; U.S. North-South divisions and, 86
Smith, Caleb, 92
soap, 118
Soulé, Pierre, 98
sovereignty: challenges to, 69; extension of, 111; national, 151; as territorial, 98
Spain: Charles II, 143; Charles IV of, 27, *30*; colonies of, 117; Ferdinand VIII of, 121n8; loyalists from, 53; Manila Galleon fleet of, 118, 119; Mexico and, 87
Spanish Empire, 1, 6n1; history of, 117; power of, 18
specie, *28*, *79*; coins made of, 97; credit beyond, 39, 131; on deposit, 36; as scarce, 29
Specie Circular, 127
SS *Central America, 131*
Sturm, Herman, 148
Sutter's Mill, 128
symbols: colonies and, *12*, *13*; on currency, 3–4, *12*, 18, *76*; eagle as, *22*, *24*, *53*, *54*, *56*, *104*; of manumission, 20

Taylor, Zachary, 90, 92
Texas: the Alamo in, 66; annexation by U.S., 72, 73, 79, 86, 153; economy of, 75; Houston as president of, 63, 76, 78; imports and exports of, 75; independence for, 65–69, 72; Indianola port in, 113; Lamar as president of, 76; maps of, *74*; Mexico and, 70; Native Americans in, 68; as new state, 71; paper bills issued by, 153; Rio Grande border of, 88, 100; as third republic, 63–80, 83; value of, 80

Texas Railroad, Navigation, and Banking Company, 75
trade: with China, 44; as global, 34; human capital and, 76; as maritime, 31; networks for, 32; in New Spain, 49; regulation of, 33; Rio Grande and, 111; as transatlantic, 40
transportation, 113
treaties, 120n2; loans and, 139; Treaty of Guadalupe Hidalgo, 81, 94, 98
Treaty of Amity, Navigation, and Commerce, 59
Treaty of Guadalupe Hidalgo, 81, 94, 98
Trist, Nicholas, 94

United Mexican States (*Estados Unidos Mexicanos*), 55, 67
United States: Alaska purchase by, 95; Barbary states and, 41–42; California in, 133; civil war in, 140; Constitution of, 37; expansion of, 108, 117, 129; expatriates from, 83; government of, 14; history of, 2, 152, 157; map of, 96, *106–7*; Mexico and, 48, 63, 93; Michigan in, 121n9; power of, 129; Texas annexation by, 72, *73*, 79, 86, 153; trial and evolution of, 155

United States Intervention (*Intervención Estadounidense*). *See* Mexican-American War
United States-Mexican Boundary Survey, 103
University of Pennsylvania, 125
U.S. *See* United States
U.S. Army Quartermasters Office, 110
U.S. Mint, 114; branches of, 123, 126, 130, 154; coin production and, 23, 128, 134n7; Patterson as director of, 123, 125, 154; in Philadelphia, 35
USS Philadelphia, 32

Victoria, Guadalupe, 49, 50, 58

war: borders before Mexican-American, 84–85; debt and, 49, 54, 71, 74; declaration of, 89; for independence, 65; money and, 11–12, 50–52; price of, 39–42, 67
War of 1812, 38, 44
Washington, George, 9; on bills, *152*; on coins, 19; declaration of neutrality by, 33

yellow fever, 34–35
Ylarregui, José Salazar, 105

www.ingramcontent.com/pod-product-compliance
Lightning Source LLC
Chambersburg PA
CBHW061833300426
44115CB00013B/2369